ON THE BORDER
OF A DREAM

**ONE MEXICAN BOY'S JOURNEY OF BECOMING
AN AMERICAN SURGEON**

By

Edgar H. Hernandez, MD, MS, FACS

Book®
Chix
Book Publishing

Published by BookChix Book Publishing
Phoenix, Arizona
www.bookchix.com

Design and composition by BookChix Book Publishing
Cover Design by Miguel Hernandez

First Edition

ISBN: 978-0-9989215-0-1

I have tried to recreate events, locales, and conversations from my memories of them. In order to maintain their anonymity in some instances I have changed the names of individuals and places. I may have changed some identifying characteristics and details, such as physical properties, occupations, and places of residence.

To my granddaughters—Elisa, Lucy, Sophia, Francie, Eva Rose, and Juliana

"Grandfather, what are you looking at?" asked Eva Rose.

"The moon," he replied.

"It's actually a crescent moon, Grandfather," the six-year-old commented and then asked again, "So, why do you look at it?"

"I'm thinking how once, a long time ago, when my own grandfather was staring at the moon, I asked him the same question. The reason I'm looking at it is because I'm thinking about tomorrow," he explained to his granddaughter.

She asked, "Why tomorrow?"

"There are many tomorrows. Every one will be different. I think tomorrow will be great—just wait and see."

"How do you know?" she questioned.

"Because the moon showed me—that's what your great-great-grandfather taught me—how the moon is our wise teacher," he answered.

FOREWORD

"Top Doctor" awards covered the walls in the waiting room. While these awards offered some reassurance, the room was still thick with tension. The people seated near me showed signs of anguish, apprehension, and distress. I know I surely did. I was desperate, scared, and anxious because I was under attack. Well, maybe I was under attack. I didn't know yet, but I wasn't taking any chances.

A few months earlier my sister called to say that she'd found a lump in her breast. She wanted me and our other sister to be tested for the BRCA gene, which she had tested positive for.

I was on vacation with Kevin, my fiancé, when I got news that I'd tested negative for BRCA—what a great way to celebrate the results!

However, my OBGYN warned me it wasn't a free pass and that I should remain diligent in getting annual screenings as well as doing monthly self-exams. A month later I had the annual mammogram and received those results by mail. I was in my car when I opened the letter informing me that the ultrasound detected a mass in my breast. I broke down crying. I was scared out of my mind. I called Kevin to share the news.

The secretary at my OBGYN's office recommended two breast specialists, and she gave me the two names. Then she went on to say, "If it were a member of my family, I'd go with Dr. Edgar Hernandez." Immediately after the call, I rushed to the computer to find information on both specialists. I learned that Dr. Hernandez was named "Top Doctor" in the Phoenix area year after year. The 5-star recommendations for him listed on the medical review pages were phenomenally positive too. Honestly, it was the secretary's words that had sealed my choice, "If it were a member of my family, I'd go with Dr. Edgar Hernandez." I called and scheduled an appointment.

And that's how I found myself, accompanied by Kevin, in the waiting room of Dr. Hernandez's office. Desperate, scared, anxious—like everyone else in that waiting room.

The nurse called my name, and we headed back to an examination room. A few minutes later, there was a knock on the door, and then in walked Dr. Hernandez. He was impeccably dressed in a sharp blue suit with a color-coordinated handkerchief in the suit pocket. He wore shiny wing-tip shoes. His nails looked manicured. His goatee was perfectly shaved. He spoke calmly and thoughtfully and had a slight Spanish accent. He made eye contact with both of us and touched my shoulder in an attempt to comfort me.

"I hate cancer. I've been spending my life trying to eradicate it," he told us. "You are going to be okay, Rebecca. I am here for you. Here is my personal cell phone number if you ever want to talk."

Kevin and I were immediately awestruck by the compassion, caring, expertise, and focus of this man. He not only knew how to deal with cancer; he knew how to connect with people and support them emotionally. We were no longer in the dark and alone with this mass and all the brutal possibilities it seemed to offer. Dr. Hernandez was there to take our hands and lead us out of the terror.

Based on the radiologists' findings, Dr. Hernandez recommended that he do a surgery to remove the mass from my breast. Once the mass was removed, then it could be biopsied.

And that's what we did.

Shortly after and with great anticipation we returned to Dr. Hernandez's office to receive the biopsy results.

Dr Hernandez looked directly at us and said "Today I have six patients that I have to review the results of their biopsies, yours is the only one I get to deliver good news to. Congratulations, the results are negative." Then he hugged me and hugged Kevin.

A month later, when I was checking in with Dr. Hernandez about the area where the tissue had been removed, he asked me, "Rebecca, what is it you do for a living?" I told him that I was an author coach and then explained what that meant.

"Well, I've got a story for you," he responded and then told me a condensed version of how he grew up in rural Mexico in the 1950s, dreamed of becoming a surgeon in the USA, and, overcame many obstacles with the help of some very fine people to achieve that dream.

Sitting on the exam table in my paper gown, I found myself immersed in Dr. Hernandez's life story. His vivid descriptions of serious difficulties, hard work, and humbling generosity moved me to tears.

"America needs your story—right now, people need your story. You must write a book," I told him.

So, he wrote this memoir.

★   ★   ★

We live in a world of great uncertainty today. In the United States, we have polarizing debates raging over a multitude of issues. Things are not black and white, they are grey and it's not for me to pass judgment on to you the reader.

And it is for this reason that we, human beings, need the life story of Edgar Hernandez.

This story is a testament to the goodness of humanity. It reminds us to encourage our children to dream big and to teach them that with persistent hard work, they can achieve those big dreams. This story reminds us of the importance of personal responsibility, family, education, and a good sense of humor. It reminds us that fundamentally people are good, loving, and caring.

Dr. Hernandez faced many obstacles in his life. So many times, the easiest thing for him would have been to simply stop and be satisfied where he was at, instead of focusing on all he still wanted to achieve. But he didn't stop—he persisted and figured out how to get around the obstacles, even if it took multiple attempts.

And you better believe that that's the kind of doctor you want to go to when you are faced with the possibility of cancer—someone very intelligent and very skilled, who doesn't give up. I and the many people whose lives he's saved are so thankful that he was determined to make it here to become a pioneering, world-class surgeon. His story is inspiring, compelling, and thought provoking.

Please take the life story of Edgar Hernandez, and reflect on it. Use it as a catalyst to become your best self—and to celebrate all that is good in your life and in humanity.

—Rebecca Ferente
Author Coach

PART ONE

PART ONE

1

"**D**octor Hernandez, his mother said he was bitten by a scorpion—it got him in the foot when he was playing in a sandbox," the nurse informed me.

All of the child's symptoms were consistent with a scorpion bite—nausea, profound vomiting, and now convulsions. The boy's eyes were rolling back into his head as his body was thrashing spastically.

The child was having a true seizure—though horrifically distressing to witness, it was also consistent with a scorpion bite and not unexpected.

We quickly placed an intravenous catheter into his arm. Equally as rapidly I ordered medications for him, intravenously, including oxygen. Fortunately, the child never stopped breathing and, once the seizures ceased, regained consciousness.

He was confused, dazed, and had started to cry. He complained of a pain in his right foot. He was slightly pale. I talked to the boy, giving him reassurance, and then finished my assessment. He was going to be fine.

Even still, I noticed that my own heart rate had increased, and I felt a bit dizzy and jolted. Before going out to speak to the boy's mother, I took a cold drink of water and tried to calm myself.

I explained to the boy's mother, "Ma'am, your child is fine, and soon he'll be able to go home. Scorpion bites are common, but still, it's good that you brought your boy in early because he had started to seize . . ."

Pausing to catch my own breath, I looked at the boy's mother, who'd been quite frightened. In Arizona, which is scorpion country, everyone knows that most scorpion bites are fine, but when it's a child that gets bitten, sometimes it can be fatal.

The mother gave a sigh of relief and started to hug me when—all at once—I broke down in tears.

Swiftly, she dropped the hug, took a step back, and demanded, "Doctor, what is it you aren't telling me? What's really going on with my son?"

In an attempt at regaining my composure I stepped back and took a seat.

The nurse turned to me and gently but firmly inquired, "Dr. Hernandez, are you okay?"

When I didn't immediately respond, she grabbed me by both shoulders, lifted my head up, looked me in the eye, and asked, "Dr. Hernandez, what is going on? You're worrying me, and I'm very concerned."

"I'm fine—I apologize for my sudden emotion. I'm as surprised as you are," I replied, looking at the nurse and then the mother.

I continued, addressing the anxious mother, "And I assure you, your son is doing really well. There is not a problem. It's just . . . seeing your boy—and his acute response to that bite—it brought me back to my childhood . . . when the same thing happened to me. Only I was in rural Mexico, and it happened when I was at the shore with my grandfather. It's one of my clearest memories and one that I've never told anyone about because it was so, so . . . scary. Seeing your boy zapped me back to that horrendous episode from own childhood—something I wasn't prepared for."

★   ★   ★

My grandfather and I were at a coconut plantation located on the shore of the Pacific Ocean near the town of Playa Azul.

I was pulling apart a partially opened coconut when I felt a stinging sensation in my hand. Then almost immediately I noticed a tightness in my chest. Confused and afraid, I screamed out, "Abuelito! Abuelito!"

I could feel my body trembling and at the same time becoming rigid. My lips and feet felt as if they were being besieged by ants. The burning sensation in my hand had traveled up and into my arm and was pulsing and growing by the second.

The world outside me seemed to spin and jump in a cruel kind of dance. I looked up at the clouds spiraling around me as if they wanted to pounce upon my face and beat me with their mass.

In my ears I heard the melancholic notes of a crying violin.

I managed to call again in a rushed but weak voice, "Abuelito! Abuelito! . . . Abuel—"

A distance from me I heard a man shout out, "Andres! Andres! ¡El niño!"

I spotted my grandfather rushing towards me, his beard slanting left as if the wind were brushing it to that side. His hat had fallen from his head and was hanging at his back from a string. I could see the machete on the side of his hip, flap-flapping as he raced. The look in his eye was one of anguish, as if witnessing an impending death.

He approached, getting closer and closer. Then I felt the strength of his arms, lifting my stiff, doll-like body.

I slurred out, " . . . escorpión . . ."

Next, I lost all ability to respond. I dropped into unconsciousness.

"Edgar, Edgar, mi hijo! Talk to me, talk to me, it's Abuelito. Can you hear me?" a voice beckoned me from my deep, heavy sleep.

It began to register—the voice of my beloved grandfather.

Next, I tasted saltwater on my lips and in my mouth, but I could not swallow. I noticed a stinging sensation in my hand and arm, but at the same time the area felt numb.

I half opened my eyes—two, maybe even three, grandfathers stood before me as my eyes bounced around.

Then I heard a loud crash—a tremendous ocean wave had thrown itself with great enthusiasm onto the beach.

"Edgar, Edgar, Edgar—wake up!"

With each of my hands, I dug into the wet sand that I found myself lying on. Looking up, I could make out my grandfather more clearly now.

"Look, Abuelito, look," I managed, pointing out to him that I had a fist full of sand in each of my hands.

My grandfather responded, "Thank you, Lord!"

He continued, "I prayed for your life, my Edgar. I prayed to

God, 'Why him and not me? Why him and not me?' "

He helped me up and then embraced me like never before. It was an embrace of strength and intense love.

I hugged him back, real tight, as if saying, "Hold me and don't ever let me go."

Meanwhile several men from the plantation had surrounded us. Their worried faces had changed to smiles of relief. They touched me on the head and the shoulders.

One of the men recommended to my grandfather, "Andres, you should bathe the boy in kerosene to kill the scorpion poison that entered his body. That's what we do in Playa Azul—that's what everyone does—if somebody gets bitten."

"*Gracias*, but I don't think it's a good idea. He's already gotten over the worst of it," my grandfather replied.

Another man confided to me, "You know something? Your grandfather is a brave man. There was only one thing he could think of when he grabbed you, and that was to take you to the ocean and place you in the water. You were sweating up a storm, and he wanted to get water on you to cool you down. He wanted to comfort you. You moved and thrashed in violent convulsions. You are lucky you were unconscious because I don't think any child could stand it—the way your body was rattling out of control. We couldn't stand seeing it. It was horrific. So many children, just as young and small as you, die from scorpion bites, but—*gracias a Dios*—you survived."

I knew this man was telling the truth because I'd seen it myself.

A few years earlier, I was walking hand in hand with my father. He was running an errand, and I was accompanying him when, all of a sudden, we came upon a gathering of people. They insisted that my father and I come in.

I saw a tiny wooden box, about three feet by 1.5 feet, sitting on a table. Men and women stood around it, sobbing. There was an old man dressed in the traditional *campesino* attire—white sackcloth drawstring pants and a shirt of the same material. A worn-out red handkerchief was tied around his neck—it was Santos Ortiz.

Santos Ortiz was the town hermit, bogeyman, and mystic all rolled into one. He hadn't really spoken in years. He did not work. He lived alone in a small hut of mud and sticks he'd built himself. He showed up at a different home each day, and the people of the home fed him.

What he did do was play the violin—and chant—at the funerals of children.

And that's what he was doing at this gathering.

"Ángel, ángelito *del cielo*, ángel *de los* ángeles, ángel *de Dios*, ángel *del cielo*, ángelito *inocente, miembro del cielo visitante a la Tierra que no olvidas que las alas te levantan al cielo*," Santos Ortiz rasped and warbled. He repeated this dirge four times, accompanying it with his crying violin.

He didn't play actual songs on the violin. Instead, Santos Ortiz made his violin weep dejected arrangements. His violin prayed, shouted, whispered, and purred beautiful, angry, begging, haunting, and dissonant disquietudes.

And this was my earliest memory—unexpectedly coming upon a child's funeral, a child who'd died from a scorpion bite, and witnessing Santos Ortiz, the town conjurer, invoking his violin to wail chords of despair as a family wept and wept for their dead little boy.

So, when this man told me how lucky I was that I'd survived the scorpion bite, a wave of chills flowed over my body. I recalled this memory of the child's funeral and Santos Ortiz so acutely that I thought I could feel the vibrations of that crying violin ringing in my ears.

Yes, I was very lucky that I'd survived and that my grandfather had been with me in this brief but desperate incident because it wasn't rare for scorpion bites to take the children in our area; in fact, scorpion bites were the number one cause of death for children where I was from.

My name is Edgar Hernandez, and I was born in La Mira in the state of Michoacán in Mexico. La Mira was a tropical town that has since joined with other nearby towns, like Playa Azul, to form the big seaport city Lázaro Cárdenas.

La Mira sat by the Pacific Ocean and had two large rivers framing its sides. These rivers emptied into the Pacific. The larger of the two rivers was the great Río Balsas, also known as the Atoyac, the largest river in Mexico and one of the largest rivers in the Americas. During the rainy season, the Río Balsas, as well as the second smaller river, Río Las Truchas, that ran parallel to it, could overflow, which flooded our town.

My grandfather told stories of having once swum in the areas that we normally walked through during past floods. Cattle, goats, chickens, horses, trees, homes, and even people got pummeled and dragged away in the swiftly moving floodwaters. Many lives were lost in the floods.

My mother regularly warned my sisters, my brother, and me to stay away from the Río Balsas since it was so dangerous, "*Mis hijos, tengan cuidado.* It may look welcoming on a hot day, but it can pull you in and drag you out to the ocean, never to reemerge again."

Once when I was with my grandfather we saw large oxen crossing the river. The cattle drivers found the narrowest, but still deep, segment of the river. There, the men directed the oxen into the water and stayed with them as the oxen swam across—by hanging from their tails!

My grandfather explained, "Those cattle drivers are excellent swimmers. The worst that can happen is if somehow they can't hold on. Then they let go and swim with the river until they reach the ocean. They land in the ocean and swim to the edge. They know how to move with the currents."

My grandfather, Andres Maldonado, knew the Río Balsas well because he came from a small village on its other side, opposite La Mira. He had three sons, who, like him, were farmers. He had three daughters, Magdalena, Dominga, and Maria. My mother, Magdalena, was his daughter. His sons moved to different areas in Mexico, and they had no children. So, my siblings and I were in the fortunate position to get much of his attention. I was even more fortunate since my sisters preferred spending time with our neighbors' children, five daughters, and my brother was just a few months old. This meant that I got my grandfather mostly to myself. He was the love of my life, my beloved Abuelito.

My grandfather was very smart. He could not read or write, but he knew everything about life. He was a spiritual philosopher. He knew all about the seasons. He could predict rain better than any weatherman with the finest training and gadgetry. He considered the universe and nature his biggest partners in life. He was a steady-minded man that rarely, if ever, panicked.

I remember my grandfather once talking to a man who had just entered town in a big delivery truck.

I asked my grandfather, "What did that man want? What was that all about?"

He responded, "That man asked if the roads to Santa Clara were okay for his large truck to travel on, and I told him that yes, he could get there, but he wouldn't be able to return from there for approximately two weeks."

He told me that the reason the man wouldn't be able to leave Santa Clara for a couple of weeks is that it would rain for approximately five days and the roads would become extremely muddy, so they would need an additional five days to dry. The man would not be able to drive out of Santa Clara because of the impassable roads. If he was planning on transporting produce out of Santa Clara, it would rot in his truck, and it would be a waste of his time.

He'd told the driver, "My recommendation is for you to wait at least three weeks before you go into Santa Clara. Then you can get out of there immediately with your produce and take it up into the city with no delays."

Not only did my grandfather answer his question, he took the time to explain the whole situation thoroughly, so the man would have the best chance of finding success. This was typical of my grandfather. He loved life and expressed appreciation for the health and the well-being of all around him. Everyone in our town loved him.

In La Mira everyone referred to my grandfather as "*el jefe*," and he truly was a chief. He was a chief of honesty, kindness, and sharing. He was a very loving gentleman in every sense of the word. He was given the designation "*el jefe*" as a form of respect. He was a man of wisdom, and he shared his knowledge, his understanding, and all the goodness of life with those around him.

As a lifelong farmer and appreciator of nature, my grandfather knew everything about seeds and crops. He knew the timing for planting and harvesting. He could look at seeds and identify the specific plants that would grow from them. He could talk for hours about sprouting seeds.

One time he confronted a vendor who'd come to La Mira to sell a variety of seeds to farmers. The man was making some grand claims about the seeds he was selling—falsely claiming that certain seeds would produce certain vegetables. However, my grandfather was keen to identify the falsehoods, so he showered the guy with lots of questions. The following day, the vendor was gone. He'd quickly disappeared and left town.

My grandfather taught me almost everything I knew. As a child, when I was with him, a daily occurrence, he taught me about everything that surrounded us. When I asked him a question, I had to be prepared for a lengthy discussion and lengthy explanation. And he had to be prepared for my many questions as well because I was known to be a ceaseless questioner with an ever-abundant store of curiosity.

My grandfather's small farm was located near Playa Azul, a town that was in walking distance from our home in La Mira. I remember going to his small farm with him when the watermelons were ripening. Though all the watermelons looked the same to me, he knew exactly which ones were ripe and the best time to harvest them. I can still see him out in the field thumping watermelons.

"Abuelito, what are you doing that for?" I questioned.

"Because it's going to tell me how sweet they are. When I hear a deep, hollow sound from inside, I know the watermelon is no good—it's too ripe. I try to never let that happen. I always cut them and remove them when they're perfect and the sound is good."

Then he chose a watermelon, cut it from the vine, and brought it to me.

With his machete, he cut the watermelon in half, and there it was—glistening and deep red in color. He cut a piece and handed it to me.

I took a bite—cool, crisp, sweet perfection.

"Abuelito, why do you plant your watermelons in between the rows of corn?" I asked.

He answered by explaining how the watermelon and corn acted like good friends together. The corn shaded the watermelon from the harsh sun, and the watermelon deposited nutrients into the soil that the corn liked. He saw it as a mutually beneficial relationship.

"And when one watermelon is ready, why don't you just cut and harvest them all?" I asked.

My grandfather explained that timing the harvest of each watermelon was a precision task. He hesitated cutting them too early and hesitated leaving them too long because they would lose their taste. If he cut too many and tried to transport them all to the market to sell, they would get bruised during the journey, and then people wouldn't buy them. He was a master at designating the moment of ripeness for each watermelon and the quantity of watermelons to sell in the market at a given time.

He explained, "We only sell portions of our crop because people will only buy them when they're nice and fresh. If the watermelons are sitting at the market for a day or two, no one buys them." He determined he could bring in fifty at a time, and all fifty would sell almost immediately.

When he was selling them and I happened to be there with my grandfather, he would look at me and wink, as if saying, "See what I mean?"

I never doubted what my grandfather said. He was a philosopher.

*　　*　　*

My grandfather awakened me early one morning, so we could set out on a special two-hour "trip of nature."

"Nature is our best friend, Edgar, and nature is always at work. I want you to see with your very eyes the special workings of nature. So let's get walking," he told me.

With my hand in his, we walked down a steep hill. I could feel the thick, sandpapery roughness of his hand and the strength of his grip. He had very muscular arms although he was a thin man. When he had his shirt off, you could see all the muscles in his chest and neck. He featured a long, straight nose, white hair, a white beard, and many wrinkles on his face. He had very leathered-looking skin, quite feathery, and, of course, a natural tan. He was a farmer, so he was exposed to the sun almost every day of his life. His generous smile complemented his kind nature. When anyone talked to him what was very apparent was that he always looked the person in the eye and smiled.

As was standard of all the men in our small town of subsistence farmers, my grandfather wore a white shirt and white pants that tied at the waist with a cord. The clothes were made out of the strong, rough white cotton material also used for making sacks that held grain, fruits, and vegetables. The kids in the town also wore clothes made of this sackcloth material, so it was what I was wearing too.

On his head my grandfather wore a straw hat with a string that tied around his neck. A machete strapped to his black belt hung at his left hip, parallel to his thigh—another feature of the men in our town.

I once asked my grandfather why he cleaned and sharpened his machete every single evening. He responded, "I use this machete in so many ways each day on my land. Today I used it to trim hedgerows, cut down bunches of bananas, and slice open watermelons. For our good health, it should always be clean. Just like our hands and dishes."

As we walked along the ocean shore in the still dark early morning, we talked about everything, including oysters, clams, sharks, and all types of fish. He warned me about being very careful about eating oysters because they can often cause illness if not fresh and clean. My grandfather described different types of fish—*huachinango, pargo, corvina*—and how every one of those fish tasted different. He said that from a single taste of its flesh usually he could determine exactly what type of fish it was.

He explained that ocean water offered special health benefits. He washed every day with salt water. The salty ocean water helped skin problems heal quickly. My grandfather had a cut that extended from his elbow to his wrist. It had healed beautifully with only a slight scar running along it. His ability to move the arm was absolutely perfect. He attributed the excellent healing to his application of salt-water baths.

My grandfather also talked about the benefits of the sun. He explained the concept of photosynthesis to me but didn't use that term because he didn't know it. He said the sun either allowed plants to grow or killed them. In the tropical area where we lived lots of sun was essential for crops to grow. He said that we owed our lives to the goodness of nature in the sun.

"Edgar, you know how to keep me young with your endless curiosity and persistent questioning," my grandfather often told me.

And it was true—I was a kid that asked many questions. "Why do we get old?" "Why do we have to die? "Why do we get sick?" Sometimes people around me would become irritated, but my grandfather said it was a true task of honesty to ask questions. My grandfather would answer pretty much all the questions I had for him. Sometimes he would not answer some questions either because he did not have the answer or because he just felt that he did not need to answer. He did admit too that sometimes I asked way too many questions.

We talked about papayas and papaya seeds. My grandfather thought that the papaya was one of the best fruits, saying, "People can live on papayas alone because they are rich with multiple substances for digestion. They've got great volumes of fluid in them and plenty of juices that are good for the body."

Then I asked, "What about coconut water? Why is it so good?"

He explained, "Because it has many substances in it that can keep you alive. You could probably live on coconut water all your life. The only problem that might occur is it might give you something like dysentery."

"What is dysentery?"

"It's a diarrhea—a real bad diarrhea like an infection in your insides."

There were lots of iguanas where we lived. They jumped from one tree to another. So, I asked, "Do people eat iguanas?"

He replied, "Yes. We can eat iguanas. They're very tasty. They're difficult to clean, but once you clean them out, you can eat them, and they taste just like chicken." He added, "Next time we're having something that tastes like chicken, you may be surprised. It could be iguanas that you're eating."

We were walking early enough to enjoy the moon. It was so bright that it made the ocean look like a glass surface. Abuelito told me that as the moon changed its shape, it created different activity on the ocean water. He said that the shape of the moon determined many things that we saw in our lives—when it would rain, when crops would die, when crops would grow.

He told me, "The moon moves with us and holds us in her arms." He explained how the attitudes of human beings changed due to the shape of the moon. "When the moon is in crescent, people are extremely unpredictable. We avoid discussing business of any sort when the moon is crescent. But, if we must talk business, we do so with extreme caution.

"Once there was a small crescent moon, and I had a business meeting the following day to sell some crafts. I canceled the meeting, postponing it for a week. A round, bright moon is the most preferable, but I'll accept a crescent moon, providing it's a large crescent—meaning the moon is closer to the full side. A small crescent, when the moon is very far from full, means the moon is feeling shy, so talking isn't good. When it's a bigger crescent, or a full, bright moon, it's willing to discuss and allow you to succeed in every tomorrow of life."

I was very puzzled about the things that he said about the moon, but it was a subject that my grandfather often talked about.

After about ninety minutes of walking, my grandfather announced, "Soon, you will see something you will always remember. And actually it is the moon that determined what you are about to see. Edgar, we both must be very quiet. Remember."

As we continued to walk, we moved slightly away from the shore of the ocean, inland a bit to an area with many coconut trees. The large palm leaves blocked the light from the moon, creating an almost complete darkness in the space underneath them. We kept walking.

Bird sounds filled the air. Some sounds were quite musical. Some were intense—screaming calls and aggressive chatter.

"Abuelito, the birds sound different from normal. Do you think we're in danger?" I inquired hurriedly.

My grandfather assured me, "The sounds you hear are simply all the birds waking up for a beautiful morning to come."

When we came to a hill of sand, we made our way to its top where we laid down to peer at the beach and ocean below.

My grandfather whispered, "Look over there. Look right by the waves, and let's not ask questions—simply observe."

At first, I saw only a couple of rocks and the waves moving over them.

My grandfather directed me, "Pay attention to those rocks. See what happens to them."

The large rocks were bathed by the waves of the ocean. The water ran right over them.

Suddenly, it hit me that the rocks were moving. Immediately, I knew that they were turtles. They were turtles coming out of the ocean—three large turtles.

I looked at my grandfather, and he smiled, saying, "The turtles will be at work real soon."

Slowly, slowly and very diligently the turtles exited the ocean and crawled up the beach. Just as slowly and carefully, they began digging individual holes. In their holes, they laid their eggs and took great care to bury their eggs and refill the holes with sand. This was a long undertaking. I think it took longer than our walk. The turtles' return to the ocean was also a spectacular and lengthy process. It was a very smooth walk into the ocean. All you could see were the ripples of water from the waves going right over the humps of the turtles themselves. Gradually, they disappeared, almost as if someone had taken a great eraser and erased them right in front of us.

Once the turtles disappeared, I inquired, "How is it that you knew that we would be seeing this wonderful event?"

"Because I saw it when I was a child, and I have seen it many times. You see, your grandfather walks through here almost every morning to work on the farm. It's just a beautiful walk that I never get tired of—and I get energy from the moon and from the salt water. In all the walks that I've made going to the farm, I see these turtles occasionally. Yesterday I determined that this was the morning that they'd emerge from the ocean."

I continued, asking, "How did you know in particular that they would be here today?"

"The moon. The moon and its shape told me that the turtles were ready to lay their eggs."

As we walked back, we ran into two men carrying baskets on their back. As they passed us, they greeted us, saying, "¡*Buenos días*!"

My grandfather tipped his hat to them, and we continued on.

A few minutes later, he confessed, "Edgar, I didn't want to tell you this, but I will say it. Those two men who passed us also knew the turtles would be laying eggs this morning, and they are going to gather the eggs to sell in the market today. If we go to the market, we can have them for breakfast."

In the market they would drop turtle eggs into hot water for just a minute or so and then pull them out. The eggs would look like soft golf balls. Then they'd put a hole in each egg, drip in a little lemon juice and some hot sauce. To eat it, you would squeeze it into your mouth and then toss away the squashed-down eggshell. You could even make scrambled turtle eggs.

Later, on our return walk, I asked my grandfather to tell me about his father and grandfather.

"Edgar, we'll need a year and a half for me to tell you everything about my father and grandfather."

I responded, "Okay, by the time you finish, I'll be nine-and-one-half years old."

He laughed.

"My father was a pure-blooded Indian, and my mother was light-skinned with light eyes," he began.

He told me his father was a man of small stature, very strong and handsome. His grandfather was tall with a lengthy nose and a white beard. People told my grandfather that he could have been his own grandfather's twin.

According to my grandfather, his parents and grandparents were quite spiritual, and they seemed to base almost everything on their faith in mystical nature. They relied on the environment and nature and all the stars in the universe. They felt that all of those things up in the universe would lead us to fruitful and wonderful lives.

He added, "Also, to very safe lives. Look at me—I see the natural world as our spirit guide, directing us how to live safely and how to live well. And that's what's happened to me. I'm full of life—and I'm here with you, the love of my life." I determined that's why grandfather talked so much about the shape of the moon because to him it determined the optimal future of our lives.

He said both his father and grandfather were quite fluent in a native Indian tongue, one that he had only a small familiarity with.

I'd seen him one time talking to a very old Indian lady, a long time ago, probably one of my most early memories. To me, it seemed she spoke kind of funny, and I heard him speak in that different, funny way with her.

He said he once knew how to speak this other language but had since forgotten most of the words. He said, however, if someone talked to him in that language it would come back to him.

Before we reached home, my grandfather turned to me and said, "Edgar, you're meant for something real big in life. I know that. And it's not becoming a farmer like me."

2

Two days prior to my starting the clinical rotation element of medical school, I went to have a teeth cleaning. As I sat in the chair at the dentist's, I found myself examining the instruments. I touched them, noting their incredible smoothness and strength. I saw drills, tools for cleaning teeth, and tools for sanding—all with the words "Made in Germany" stamped on them.

Two days later when I started my clinical rotations and spent time in the operating room, I saw and learned about many instruments, machines, generators, and pieces of equipment there. The finer tools for surgery—needle drivers, needle holders, hemostats, scissors, shears, knives, scalpels, forceps—were heavy, high-quality metallic pieces, very strong and precise; I noticed that many of these were stamped "Made in Germany."

"Made in Germany"—first as a young surgeon and now, with more than thirty years under my belt, I see these words stamped on the surgical instruments I use. They are words that conjure in me feelings of tremendous nostalgia and real happiness. They remind me of where I grew up in Michoacán because there we had mines from which a German company excavated metals that were later used to make surgical instruments. I am fairly certain that I have used surgical instruments made from metal that came from my hometown—and that's such a marvelous feeling.

Also, as significantly, the phrase reminds me of my godfather, who worked for one of those German mining companies.

★   ★   ★

Before I was born, Edgar Schwartz came to La Mira from

Germany to excavate the precious metals in the local mountains. The German company he worked for mined for metals all over the world. After they tested samples of soil from our area, they understood it was rich with nickel and silver, so they sent Edgar Schwartz to set up and run a mining operation.

Edgar Schwartz was red-haired, tall, about six-foot four, and muscular, with a well-trimmed beard. He brought with him six identical outfits of khaki pants and khaki shirts and wore one each day. They were custom-made to fit him perfectly. They were so well pressed that even when he was working in the dusty, dirty mines, they showed no wrinkles.

He had three different pairs of boots, all brown, thick, and military-looking, plus a brown belt.

Edgar Schwartz always wore a gun, which did not seem out of place as it was customary for men in the town to wear a gun or machete on the hip. Some locals carried concealed knives. Those who hunted carried rifles. There was plenty of game in our area—deer, quail, and *javelina*—which made for a good source of meat for people.

Edgar Schwartz had a long, narrow nose that began up between his eyebrows. He had fine, thin features and slightly long ears. He had a pleasant smile but would only smile when necessary. He seemed to never waste a smile. It had to be for a specific reason. Otherwise, he had a serious look.

He walked straight, never hunched over. His posture, stance, and walk resembled a soldier's.

He spoke excellent Spanish. He was very kind to people and loved children. He was married but didn't have any children. His wife was a teacher in Germany. His parents were also teachers.

When he first came to La Mira, he did not have a place to stay. My family offered him a small segment of the house to live in. He ate his meals with my family. He and my father hit it off really well. My grandfather also appreciated him, saying that he was a true gentlemen and a great philosopher. Even when he had living quarters of his own, he came to our house many times a week for socializing, dinner, and even breakfast.

When I was born, there were two Edgars in our town, Edgar Schwartz and me. I was named after him, and he was named my *padrino* or godfather. He returned to Germany when I was approximately two-and-one-half years old. Though many families hoped for this honor for their children, I was the only child to whom he was the *padrino*.

Edgar Schwartz returned to La Mira to continue the work that he'd started several years prior in the very beautiful, rich mines. As I was no longer an infant but an older child, I was able to spend time with him, and we became quite close. I was probably the only child allowed into the mines.

The mines had very large and long shafts, and anyone entering had to wear a hat and a headlight. There were little oxygen tanks inside the carts in case anything happened inside the mines that required additional oxygen.

My godfather once took me into the mines for a tour. It was quite cool down inside. It had a rustic and metallic odor. I heard the sounds of the rails, like a small train choo-chooing deep under the earth. He showed me various pieces of metals that they were excavating.

"Put your hand in here and feel these wonderful metals," my godfather directed.

I placed my hand in several pockets of the mountain. I viewed the different types of metals with their variety of colors.

He explained that some of the precious metals were quite heavy and more valuable than the ones that were lighter. Some of the metals would be used in factories in Germany as well as all over the world to make tools that would then be used to make life a lot nicer and simpler for all people.

"Edgar, it won't always be foreign countries, like mine, coming into your country to make use of your rich resources. Mexicans will come into their own and flourish. It will take some time, but it is going to happen," my godfather told me.

"I actually have inside information that my company will be required to leave in a few years when President Cárdenas decides to nationalize mining and other industries here. That means that Mexican companies will take over, and that's a good thing. That means Mexicans become the decision-makers over their own country's resources," he noted with a smile of approval.

Though I didn't exactly understand what he meant by Mexico nationalizing mining, I considered my *padrino* a philosopher, similar to my grandfather—although no one could really beat my grandfather when it came to philosophy.

When my godfather had dinner with us, right after dinner,

he and I would have our own conversations that would last a long time. He would teach me math as well as problem-solving skills, to the point that I knew a lot more than the average student my age. What he would do was choose a topic and then ask a lot of questions about it with each question leading to and instigating another. He made it feel like a game, but it was basically to open up a discussion and to help me think aloud and discuss things with him in order to solve a problem. It could be a math problem. It could be an engineering issue. It could be an exploration of underground sewer tunneling, something he had extensive experience in. At the end of the night, I felt as if my brain had undergone a good workout.

Frequently he said to me, "Never, never waste time. Time is precious like water. Don't waste it—even when you're asleep, you should be doing something."

"Like what?" I once asked.

He replied, "Sleep is essential because it's when you re-energize your body, mind, and spirit—which is very important for staying disciplined and productive during the day."

My *padrino* helped my grandfather develop a drainage and water system on his farm with a large well to water his crops. But it wasn't just my family that was touched by my *padrino*'s talents—it was our whole town. The people of La Mira revered him.

The local farmers had tried to raise cattle for beef and milk, but they'd never been very successful. Fortunately, there was never a shortage of fish, so we ate a lot of fish. We ate shrimp. Anything from the ocean we would eat. Even still, my godfather thought that he could make the beef industry work a bit better. He invested his own money and conducted trainings with many of the ranchers to create a cattle-breeding area and a system for better production of cattle so that there would be greater nutritional support in our town. The cattle ranchers often cited my godfather as a *regalo de Dios*, a gift from God, and commented how we were all very lucky to have him.

The German company and my godfather sharply disagreed with each other, so the two were not on the best of terms. The company wanted my godfather to bring a squadron of German engineers to work with him in the mines of our region. They insisted. However, my godfather insisted just as adamantly that he should hire Mexican engineers. They ended up coming to a compromise of sorts. They sent only a few German engineers, and he was allowed to hire some additional engineers from Mexico.

What was most wonderful about this was that many of the Mexican engineers my godfather hired were basically young adults from La Mira. They ended up getting good educations in the big cities of Mexico to become engineers; after that, my godfather hired them to return to their place of birth to practice engineering. They were extremely proud and excited to come back to our small town and live with their relatives while working and doing something fruitful in the mines of La Mira.

It was a wonderful thing that my godfather had done. It was another reason why our small town loved and admired him. Even as a child I could sense this admiration, and it made me feel proud that everyone around me felt as good about my namesake as I did.

My godfather loved the ocean. He frequently would come with us to the ocean, and we would all swim together.

I remember one time watching him under a tree near the beach. It was so hot, but the shade under the tree was wonderful and cool. I saw him staring at something. He was reading a letter from his wife. He looked a little teary-eyed and kind of sad.

When I approached him, he looked at me and solemnly stated, "At least I get a letter every six months from her. The mail is so bad. I wish I could do something for the mail system, but it's run by the government."

To reach the mines, Río Las Truchas, the river parallel to the Río Balsas, had to be crossed. While it was neither as wide nor as grand as the Río Balsas, it was still an active river. It had great fish, shrimp, and lobsters in its waters.

My godfather in conjunction with a team of dedicated Mexican engineers and workers constructed a sturdy bridge across the Río Las Truchas. While there had been a small, temporary bridge that the miners had been utilizing for years, it was not adequate for transporting the heavy metals on large trucks from the mines to the shore of the Pacific. There, every three months, the metals were loaded onto small boats and carried to a large ship that would then carry it all to Germany.

So, the engineers, workers, and my godfather, together as a team, got to work, and I witnessed the construction of the bridge from the onset.

It started with dynamite. One blast after another, they blitzed the edges of the mountain on each side of the river. These explosions caused huge amounts of rock and debris to break off the mountainsides and slide into the river.

My godfather explained to me, "With the dynamite, we're narrowing the river on each side. After we narrow the river, we're going to use metal and cement to create foundations for the bridge on each side. Then we'll build mighty pillars."

The sight of the dynamite blasting apart the mountain was wondrous. I thought to myself, "My goodness. All the things that I'm witnessing now—I wonder how many more spectacular things I will see in my lifetime."

I asked my godfather, "Padrino, have you ever blasted anything in Germany with dynamite?"

"Absolutely," he replied, "We used dynamite out there to do many things because in some areas we did not have resources to drill deep. We used dynamite for excavations."

He explained that they used dynamite to blast the rock out of large areas, so then they could use that rock as a source of footings for either buildings or concrete to stabilize buildings and bridges.

I was impressed with my godfather's intelligence and life experience. I even pondered to myself, "If I can be as smart as my godfather and my grandfather, then I should have no problems in life."

I saw the bridge to completion. During the months that they were building it, I became closer and closer to my godfather. I learned to appreciate everything that he would talk to me about and teach me. I felt, basically, like a sponge, retaining all he would say to me and the puzzles and problem solving he would challenge me with.

Finally, when the bridge was completed, I saw the mighty trucks fully loaded with mineral-rich rocks traverse it.

My grandfather was with me, witnessing the trucks' first crossing of the bridge. He told me, "Come on over and get right close to the bridge. See how it doesn't move, even with the weight of the trucks. You could have twenty trucks crossing this bridge, and it will never move. It is solid. Edgar, you know why it's well built? It's because an expert team of Mexican engineers and workers along with your godfather came together to build it."

And the farmers and ranchers in our area were also grateful for the bridge because they used it to get their cattle and goods across the river.

I looked up at my grandfather as he smiled and swallowed a bite of mango.

Wiping his beard, he added, "You, too, someday will do something great like your godfather. I'm certain about you. Yes, I'm quite sure."

3

Imagine a patient who can't swallow—who can't even stick her tongue out—because her neck is so swollen. The patient's neck has become so inflamed that she can no longer breathe. What's going on is the person has developed a large peritonsillar abscess, which is basically a pus-filled infection in a tonsil or somewhere in the throat that has grown very large in size.

Before a doctor can approach the abscess, the first thing is to address the person's inability to breathe. The patient must have a tracheostomy, a surgically created hole in the front of the neck and into the windpipe, to which a ventilator is connected in order to make breathing possible. Typically the patient must also be awake during the tracheostomy. Once this is done the doctor can drain the abscess that's in the tonsil or the back of the throat. After that, the patient can typically breathe again on her own. She'll have to take antibiotics for a time and should recover.

First as a medical student and then later as a practicing surgeon, when I encountered cases of peritonsillar abscesses, I couldn't help but think back to my childhood and to my father.

*   *   *

My father, Miguel Hernandez Cabrera, was a man of medium height, always neatly shaved, with thin features, a straight, long nose, fair skin, thin lips, and dark hair. He was a better listener than communicator, quite methodical and yielding in the process of conversation. He never said anything he did not mean, always keeping in mind accuracy as to what he would say or do. He was excellent at running meetings and carrying out administrative tasks. He was composed and not nervous at all when speaking to individuals or to a crowd though he did express himself rather slowly.

Although my father had completed several years of medical school in Mexico City, he hadn't graduated, so he wasn't a certified doctor. However, the people in our region so desperately needed medical care that they welcomed him into the community to practice medicine and dentistry.

It was not uncommon for us to get a knock on our door in the middle of the night because a lady had an infection in her neck or a child was bleeding from some type of injury or infection. My father never hesitated to go to their aid.

I thoroughly enjoyed watching him work.

My father had extraordinary skills in the practice of dentistry and in some areas of medicine. For example, it was not uncommon for people to develop peritonsillar abscesses or gingival infections that led to large abscesses in the glands of the neck. And though these patients typically could barely breathe, tracheotomies and breathing machines weren't options at the time. Because he had no way of addressing the breathing issue, my father tackled the massive pus-filled infection that was blocking the breath.

He put a long, thick needle into their mouth, telling the person, "You're going to bleed a lot through this puncture wound, but it's going to make you a heck of a lot better," and then he'd puncture the infection.

If not a needle, he would put his hand right into the patient's mouth and pop the abscess with his finger or with another kind of instrument. He'd tell them, "You're about to swallow a lot of pus, but you're going to feel a hell of a lot better."

With very little to no anesthetic, with scant instruments, without any machines or fancy equipment and supplies (not to mention electricity), and without an MD or a DMD, my father managed to aid people with everything from basic injuries to life-threatening problems.

My father's response: "If I were a real doctor, I would take credit for the procedure that I did, but, as it stands, I don't deserve the credit." He constantly berated himself that he hadn't completed medical school. When I heard him talk like this, I heard pessimism and disappointment.

Why didn't he finish medical school? My father had two great addictions—alcohol and tobacco.

His shame over not finishing medical school, combined with his pessimism, led him to drink even more. Everyone in my family, from my mother to my grandfather to my young siblings, was aware of his drinking and heavy smoking, but we didn't discuss it with him.

My grandfather rarely talked about my father, but I do recall one instance when he told me, "You know, Edgar, your father is a great healer. He helps a lot of people, but he doesn't help himself. He does wonderful things, yet he does not know it. He doesn't know all the people he has touched and all the people he has helped. He just doesn't know it. He sometimes wishes he were not here. He has expressed to me that he feels he should leave and never come back, or sometimes he hopes he would just die and people would forget about him."

My grandfather stopped and was quiet for a few seconds. Then he looked at me and said, "Your father is a great man, and you should love him dearly."

My father smoked practically every moment during the day. He smoked periodically during the night too. It didn't matter where he was, he smoked. When we went to the ocean, my father would be smoking when he was swimming. When water disturbed his cigarette, he would throw it away, and, instead of sticking around and swimming with us, he would return to the shore, open up a pack of cigarettes, and light another. I never knew him without a cigarette in his mouth.

I remember when my father was running a town meeting about how to get running water to homes, he had a lit cigarette that he was actively smoking. He had another lit cigarette on the side of his table. Then he had two more lit cigarettes ready in other areas of the room—in case he got up from the table for any reason. People laughed when he remarked, "What did I do with my cigarette?" Instead of going back to where he'd left one of the lit ones, he simply lit another.

Once my father was working with a patient who had a neck infection. He needed to inject some local anesthetic in order to puncture and drain the abscess that was obviously causing a significant amount of infection in the patient's body and neck. My father had a cigarette in his mouth with the ashes growing and growing at its tip. As he was puncturing the neck abscess, the train of ashes actually fell on top of the patient's head.

My father smoked every place he went, except inside the church because it was forbidden. On church days, he would light up as soon as he exited the church. Sometimes when he entered, he would forget that he was smoking. I remember seeing him talking to the priest inside the church. And my father actually took a puff. Only when the priest eyed him did he realize what he'd done. Immediately he apologized and put out the cigarette. My father really did not mean to be rude. It was his addiction.

One afternoon a man came to my father. He'd injured himself on a piece of aluminum. He had a ten-inch slash on his back that was spewing blood. The slash was smeared with sand and mud.

With a cigarette in his mouth as well as an intense concern for the patient's well-being, my father warned, "It's going to hurt, but we must get that wound cleaned." Then he poured 100 percent pure alcohol onto the gash. The patient released a loud scream.

My father attempted to comfort him, saying, "We have no other choice. To make it better, it is going to hurt—but then it will heal."

My father irrigated the wound copiously with hydrogen peroxide and alcohol and warm water that he'd had us boil as soon as the man had come to him.

To pack and dress the wound he used special cloth strips that my mother had made from bed sheets. What she regularly did to prepare for such injuries was cut up bed sheets into long strips and then roll the strips into coils, like masking tape.

Next he pulled out a roll of special, almost-transparent string, which I later learned was made of catgut. He was going to use this to make sutures to try to close the wound.

My father explained to the man that he had no local anesthetic to numb the wound area. It would take three weeks before he'd get more local anesthetic. "However, I do have this for you to drink," my father stated and then handed the guy a small bottle. It was some type of liquid morphine that the man drank before and during the procedure.

Before making the first suture, my father took a rusty, old clamp and cleaned it in hot water and alcohol. He placed the clamp on the wound area to help draw the two sides of skin closer together. All the while, blood was flowing strongly from the wound.

With a needle threaded with catgut in one hand and a clean cotton cloth in the other, my father wiped clear a space on the gash and then sewed a large, clamp-like suture in that space. With each bite of the needle into his skin the man released a cry of agony. My father did this eight times to make eight such sutures to close the wound and stop the bleeding. With each suture I could see the gradual disappearance of the flowing blood. My father could not close the gash completely, so he packed the area between the sutures with the cloth-like bandages to curb any flow of blood.

Once he'd finished my father told the man, "You're very brave . . . I guess that makes two of us. Anyway, I think you will feel better now."

This was one of the first surgeries I'd ever witnessed. And I was spellbound. Hooked. And though I hated his drinking and nonstop smoking, I wanted to be just like my father—only different. In observing him perform these small surgeries as well as draining abscesses in people's necks and mouths and in seeing the care he took to heal injuries with meager instruments and supplies, my father sparked my dream to study medicine. I wanted to learn those procedures in medical school too—only I wanted to graduate with an MD. Then I wanted to go farther—I dreamed of becoming a surgeon. I wanted people coming to me to seek medical care—only I wanted to be the kind of doctor who offered a warm smile, a pat on the shoulder, or a hug to my patients. I wanted to show affection, involvement, and warmth in my spirit, all of which he didn't have a talent for, both with patients and with family.

Though my father was ready to come to people's aid and he was gentle and kind with me and my brothers and sisters and he was a steady provider to our family—he was not affectionate. He neither showed affection to my sibling and me nor to people around him. He did not like to be touched. He never liked to hug, no matter the situation. We, his children, never sat on his lap or joked with him. He didn't touch our backs or hold our hands. My siblings and I were always jealous when we saw other children sitting on their fathers' laps.

Fortunately, my mother and grandfather were the opposite of this—affectionate, warm, and joyful.

When company left our dinner table and went home, my father would have a couple of drinks of what looked like brandy or cognac or some type of cheap liquor. I really wasn't sure.

"*Tengo que relajarme.* These little shots, they'll help me relax. They help me think more clearly," he would explain.

It wasn't one or two; typically, it was at least six.

I remember once I joked to my mother, "Mamá, sometimes I can't think clearly, so maybe I should try drinking too."

"*Mi hijo*, that's not proper to joke about. Don't say that to your father or to anyone. I don't want to hear about my children smoking and drinking. Do you understand what I'm saying?"

"Yes, Mamá."

"As a matter of fact, when you see grownups smoke, when you see them around the market smoking or drinking, you avoid those people and avoid those bad habits. I don't want you to do anything like that—ever. *¿Entiendes?*"

"Yes, Mamá."

I loved my mother. She always meant well.

My mother, Magdalena Hernandez, daughter of my grandfather, with her light brown eyes, bronze skin, and freckled face was a beautiful lady. She had a thin face with a precious smile. She was absolutely stunning when you saw her profile with her fine nose, slightly pronounced cheekbones, and well-measured chin. Her eyes, eyelashes, and eyebrows were regal. She had beautiful skin and gorgeous hands. Her nails were always clean. Her manners were exceptional. She was about 19 when she married my father, and she was many years younger than him.

How my mother cared and fed all of us children was an amazing task that she performed every day. No electricity and no gas meant that she prepared everything from scratch, including the fire that she cooked the food on. She made a fire every morning, every mid-day, and every evening to cook breakfast, lunch, and dinner. My mother could cook a meal out of nothing. She made great tortillas, and her beans were to die for. We shared everything and did not waste a thing. She carried my two youngest siblings, one wrapped to her back and the other to her chest, as she worked, moving as if she were not carrying any extra weight.

Although she'd never had an education, she was polite, a fantastic cook, and a remarkable mother. When I got sick with fever or any type of illness, she wrapped her *rebosa* around me and comforted me. Without that comfort, I think that my siblings and I would have died. It was our mother's nest and the comfort of it that kept us alive.

I never remember my mother once being sick herself. She had so much responsibility that it seemed like she simply couldn't get sick.

My mother worried greatly about my father and his deteriorating health due to the constant smoking and regular drinking. His appearance and features had become affected by the smoking and drinking. His skin became thin and yellow and hung off his frame as if a few sizes too large for his body. His cheeks were beginning to sink in. The bones below his eyes protruded, making it appear that either his eyes were shrinking or his eye sockets was expanding. He looked sicker than the patients whom he treated.

Although my father wasn't fazed by the sight of his patients' pus or blood, I noticed was that his persistent, deep smoker's cough did faze his patients. He would cough and cough and cough—to the point of awkwardness and embarrassment—in front of his patients. Those of us in the family were used to these extended coughing episodes. However, I could tell that the people he worked on were astounded and very uncomfortable with his state of health. To me it seemed that they recoiled from him—that if it weren't for the fact that they needed his medical help, then they would avoid him at all costs.

I felt sorry he experienced such agonizing and suffocating discomfort in his chest and throat. When I realized some patients only tolerated his presence because they were desperately in need of his medical skills, I cried for him in silence.

While the bridge was being built, my father and mother came with me to visit Edgar Schwartz and see the team working. I'd discussed the bridge construction with my mother, and this was her first time on site.

On the visit, my father decided he wanted to go into the mineshaft. Because my godfather was aware of my father's constant smoking and its evident toll on his health, he advised my father against it, but my father was a stubborn man. He insisted that he get to go in.

Despite my *padrino*'s timely warning, upon entering the mineshaft an emergency occurred. My father couldn't breathe—he began asphyxiating. He was given oxygen from an emergency tank and then spent twenty minutes afterwards in a raging coughing frenzy.

I got very scared. My godfather and mother were very concerned too.

When we returned home after the visit, my father lit a cigarette and sat in quiet contemplation smoking.

My mother, who was a very shy, quiet woman, turned to him, lamenting, "Miguel, I don't think you learned anything from what happened to you . . . You're going to end up killing yourself, and you're going to end up killing the family."

4

"She's not making much urine, and that's a bad sign. Her kidneys have shut down, and we've asked an nephrologist to come by and see her," the chief resident explained to me. I was a young medical student, doing my rotations at this time.

The patient, a woman in her mid-thirties, had contracted septicemia—in her case, because she'd given birth a week prior, the septicemia was, more specifically, postpartum sepsis. What this infection entails is a dangerous bacteria infecting blood vessels and preventing them from constricting. With the blood vessels dilated, the blood pressure plummets to dangerously low levels—and eventually causes death. Septicemia and postpartum sepsis were—and still are—rare in the US and developed countries because of the availability of antibiotics and excellent medical care; however, even now it still sometimes occurs.

To keep the patient alive, we had to give her antibiotics to kill the bacteria and medications to keep her blood pressure elevated. The patient was on a respirator and had bags of fluids and antibiotics hanging around her bed. She was also on dialysis.

When the chief resident noted, "The baby's doing really well at home, and the family is anxious to get the mother back home, but I'm not sure that's going to be possible," I realized it was this woman whom the grieving family I'd seen in the waiting room was connected to.

The woman ended up spending three weeks in the intensive care unit. She was on dialysis to drain her kidneys and remove water from her system. She was on multiple antibiotics to try to kill the dangerous bacteria, and due to the side effects of the antibiotics and the medications to keep her blood pressure up, she ended up losing two of her toes and three of her fingers. The multiple intravenous and dialysis catheters ended up scarring her body, but ultimately, she survived and got to go home to her baby and her life.

In the 1930s, '40s, and '50s, postpartum sepsis was a leading cause of death in Mexico where access to antibiotics was very limited. I remember clearly that many children from my childhood lived with their grandparents because their mothers had passed away from postpartum sepsis. There were tragic cases of postpartum sepsis in my family too.

★   ★   ★

In addition to my siblings, Jorge, Surama, Pedro, Lupe, Asunción, Reyna, and Manny, I had many half-brothers and half-sisters from my father's previous marriages. I had six older half-siblings from my father's two previous wives both of whom sadly died from postpartum sepsis.

Out of my seven full siblings, three were older than me— Jorge, Surama, and Pedro. Jorge was living in Veracruz, Mexico, with our older half-brother Alberto who worked as a professor of anthropology at the University of Mexico in Veracruz. Surama lived with one of our older half-sisters in Zamora, a town up north in Mexico. Pedro lived with our older half-sister Olivia and older half-brother Neftali near Phoenix, Arizona. Miguel, our older half-brother, lived in the city of Phoenix. I had an older half-sister named Raquel who lived in Mexico City. As a child, I had not met many of my half-siblings.

"Edgar, we have a surprise for you. Your half-brother, Miguel, will arrive today from the United States. He's looking forward to meeting all his little brothers and sisters," my mother told me one morning.

Miguel Hernandez was in his early thirties. He stood about five feet nine inches tall and was a handsome man with smooth facial features. He had exemplary manners and radiated an enchanting charisma.

When Miguel arrived in La Mira, family and friends crowded around him. The scene was absolutely fabulous. He reached for Lupe, Asunción, Reyna, and baby Manny to hug them. Warmly they embraced this older half-brother whom they were meeting for the first time. Friends that had known him since he was a child greeted him too.

Everyone around him wanted to partake in hugging him, making him comfortable, and welcoming him back home. There wasn't a single person around him that did not want to embrace him and make him feel comfortable.

Instead of coming forth with my brother and sisters to hug this older half-brother, I shrunk back, ducking behind my sisters, and stared at him. I couldn't understand myself; even at eight years old, I considered myself mature, brave, and ready to face anyone—to discuss anything and ask many questions. But suddenly, it felt as if I'd been zapped by a strong magic. I stood frozen in awe. My brain knew I wanted to greet this fantastic older half-brother and hug him tightly—but my body felt stunned as if overcome by an unearthly enchantment. I couldn't look him in the eye, but I also couldn't look away from him.

He seemed like a celebrity, a movie star. He almost seemed like he wasn't real—like he was beyond real, super-real. And I felt too humble, too unworthy to be acknowledged by such a presence. I really didn't understand what had come over me, and I felt powerless to the enchantment.

I saw him embrace my grandfather very warmly, and they talked for a while. Next he embraced my mother, and then my mother introduced him to my godfather. The two were meeting for the first time.

My heart pounded as if it were going to jump out of my chest. An anxiety came over me, and I couldn't shake it off.

I continued to hide from him—and watch him keenly in my hiding.

My younger sister, Reyna, encouraged me, "Edgar, come on over and say hi to our brother."

When I realized I could no longer hide, I went to my grandfather, who always gave me a feeling of strength and protection—and I didn't know what I was trying to be protected from—perhaps this overwhelming sense of unworthiness I felt in the pristine presence of this super-real man. I continued feeling bewildered yet overcome by my behavior.

Noticing my strange desperation, my grandfather took my hand with great gentleness and turned to Miguel, announcing, "Miguel, you must meet Edgar, my right-hand man and helper. There's nobody in this town like him. I think you'll find out what a special young man he is. I am so proud of him, with everything he does—and guess what? He is an excellent student at school. When you hear what his teacher, César, says about him and what our friends in town say about him, you are going to be so proud of him too."

My grandfather went on to say that I was the hardest-working child in town. He also confided to Miguel, "Edgar is the love of my life."

Miguel looked at me and gave a warm smile. My grandfather also smiled such a wide smile that the skin in his lower face stretched to where the wrinkles there seemed to fade away.

My grandfather looked to Miguel as he smiled, and again I noticed the pounding of my heart—I still felt frozen by awe in the presence of this remarkable figure of a man.

My grandfather continued to stay by me.

My godfather, in his perfectly fitting khaki pants and khaki shirt, joined us.

Next, my father approached.

And so I found myself standing in a circle of fine men. I stared at my father, who had tears in his eyes, as he welcomed Miguel back home. My godfather radiated competence with his tall bearing and intelligent eyes. With a hand on my shoulder, my grandfather glowed love, tranquility, and calm strength.

Miguel, moving nearer to me, said, "*Mi hijo*. My son, come here. Come close to me."

And just as unexplainably and overwhelmingly as that anxiety and feeling of unworthiness had come upon me—it disappeared. Total composure set in my body and spirit, and I moved close to Miguel.

Miguel put an arm around me, and I smiled for the first time with pride. I felt special. He made me feel like I belonged with him. Also, after he put his arm around me, I felt that I'd known him for a long time.

My whole being shifted from feeling high anxiety and the desire to flee—to feeling complete ease and love.

A signature move of my grandfather was putting his arm on the shoulder of anyone he really liked. This too was Miguel's signature of affection and respect.

And so I stood with my grandfather's arm resting on one of my shoulders, and my older half-brother Miguel's arm resting on my other.

"Edgar, please take Miguel to the house and show him the room we've prepared for him," my mother told me.

Our house was made of adobe and had smooth dirt floors. The floors were cool, and I loved walking on them barefooted.

However, when showing Miguel our house, I found myself embarrassed about the dirt floor. I was afraid that my brother would be disappointed in what we had for his accommodations—a small mud-brick room with dirt floors.

Then I became afraid he'd ask about the bathroom. Our bathroom was an outhouse. I never even knew the possibility of a bathroom inside a home, so why would I be embarrassed? Why would I be afraid? I didn't know why, but I was.

Looking at me, Miguel asked, "Is this your room?"

"Yes, but now it's yours."

Miguel sat down on the bed, a square, wooden frame with a half-inch thick, circular *petate* for a mattress.

"This is quite comfortable," he noted.

I knew he was being polite.

"Where will you sleep?" Miguel asked.

"I'm staying with my sisters and my baby brother in the other room."

In this way, with his simple questions, warm manner, and kind observations, Miguel helped me to relax.

When I feel comfortable, I talk, and so I began talking. "Miguel, are you coming to the ocean with me and Abuelito tomorrow? I'm going to miss a day of school, but don't worry. It'll be fine because I'm three lessons ahead right now. I'm usually ahead anyway, and César, my teacher who is really great, he won't mind if I take a day or two off, so I can be with you."

"Edgar, thank you for inviting me to the ocean with you. Yes, I'd like to go. I haven't been back here for many years. Like you, I grew up here, so I must make time to visit the many people here who knew me as a little boy. There are so many people in this town who were so good to me, and I must greet them. I must show them I remember them and appreciate them. Does this sound good to you, Edgar?"

"Yes, Miguel. I understand that you have many people to visit."

I noticed that his shoes were shiny. His pants were beautiful with belt loops, a zipper, pockets, and careful seams—not like the white sackcloth drawstring pants the kids and men of our town wore. And he was wearing socks, which I certainly was not used to seeing.

All of us kids wore *huaraches*, which are leather sandals. Their soles were constructed of actual pieces of old tires. Sometimes, when we walked on wet dirt, we almost left the tracks of actual tires. They were comfortable and solid. And we didn't wear socks with them, so seeing socks was noticeable to me.

I asked Miguel more questions, "Do you speak English?"

"I speak some English, enough to do my work and get by. But I want to get better at it."

I confessed, "I would love to learn English."

Miguel assured me, "Don't worry—someday you will. Just wait your turn, and you will see. Something will happen."

"Miguel, why have you waited so long to visit?" I inquired.

"It takes time and money to make the trip here from the United States of America. I have a job, and people depend on me, so I don't want to take time away from work too often. And I have a car—"

"You have a car?" I interrupted.

"Yes, I have a car. And it needs new tires and certain repairs, and I didn't have enough money to put on the car and on the visit, so I decided to make the visit. I'll save money for the car later. I would rather spend that money making this trip to meet you and visit the family. It's important to me to make this visit."

At these affirming words I found the courage to say, "Miguel, let me tell you about our bathroom. First of all, it's outside like everybody's bathroom in town, but since my godfather designed it, it has a lot of features that make it special."

I went on to explain to him everything about our bathroom. I explained that it was so unique that I had taken a lot of people in town on tours of it. I even remembered thinking that I should sell tickets to people to come and see it because it was that much of a novelty, and so many people wanted to see it.

Its walls were made out of palm trees and leaves. We had plenty of palm trees in our town. We had palm trees everywhere you went—on the side of the road, in backyards, in front yards. From any place in the town, you could look around and find palm trees, except when you left town. Then you started seeing other types of trees.

The bathroom walls, composed of slabs of palm trees, were covered with a smooth mud mixture. We mixed mud with hay to create a kind of mortar that had a lot of strength, and then we applied that mortar in between the slabs of palm trees. These sturdy walls secured our privacy.

Because my godfather had worked so much with tunnels and also had developed septic tanks, he decided that for our bathroom it would be far better to tunnel the waste about twenty-five feet away from the source, into a cement tunnel or shaft that would serve as a kind of septic tank. He said that the waste could stay in the shaft for years as long as we took care of it. We needed to clean it periodically with acid.

My godfather knew everything about chemicals. He seemed to know every chemical known to mankind. He taught me about acids—hydrochloric acid, nitric acid, sulfuric acid.

With this special design our outhouse provided excellent hygiene. It didn't smell. Potentially harmful bacteria were minimal. Also, the structure could endure rains and offered great privacy. In my opinion, it was the cleanest outhouse you could ever find.

I was there when my godfather and several workers built it. My godfather was so nice. There wasn't anything he would not do for us. He had energy. It seemed like for him a day was 48 hours, not 24 hours. He did so much and accomplished so much in a day. Everyone that knew him told me, "You're lucky that he's your godfather. He is absolutely a genius. He knows everything."

I also explained to Miguel that we had a tap outside that gave us water from a well. In the bathroom there were several buckets filled with water. When you used the bathroom, you used the water from a bucket for flushing, and then you had to fill the bucket so that if anybody else came after, then they would have a bucket to flush with too.

As I told my brother about my godfather and our outside bathroom, it seemed that I talked for a long time, and my brother listened to everything that I was saying, showing interest and attention.

When I finished explaining the outhouse, Miguel said, "I can't wait to see it. It so happens that everybody has to go sooner or later."

And this is how I knew that Miguel was not only kind—he

had a good sense of humor too.

He went on to joke, "I noticed when we were first meeting, you wouldn't look at me or speak to me. And now, you won't even let me get a word in."

I thought that was pretty funny.

Early on in spending time with my older half-brother, I came to realize what a fine man he was. He had a good sense of humor. He expressed himself well. He was kind. Also, he had exceptional manners. When I opened my mouth to say something, he would suddenly stop speaking in order to listen.

My mother had tried to teach me such good manners when she'd once warned me, "Edgar, you need to stop interrupting people when they speak. You need to settle down, and you need to wait your turn until they ask you to speak."

I had tried to explain to her, "Yes, but I'll forget what I'm going to say if I wait."

She had replied, "You have to learn better manners."

Miguel's manners were remarkable. He would talk softly, and he would listen. Even with me, a child, he would never interrupt. He would just listen and listen and listen.

I did not want to say goodnight to him, but eventually my mother came to the room to tell me it was time I went to sleep.

Before leaving, I inquired, "Miguel, may I touch your luggage?"

With his permission, I picked up his brown leather suitcase that had a leather belt strapped tight around it. I stroked my hand across its thick leather exterior. Although there were many scratches on it, the leather felt soft and smooth like the saddle of a horse.

"How long have you had this suitcase?" I asked.

"My employers in Phoenix gave it to me. It was a gift. They are very kind and generous people that I hope you'll meet someday. They own a jewelry store, and I work for them making jewelry. If you like, you can look inside the briefcase, Edgar."

When Miguel opened the suitcase, a particular fragrance hit my nose—inside it smelled exactly like Miguel. I touched several of his shirts and some pairs of his trousers. And he had a shaving kit in a small plastic casing. I saw a toothbrush inside and toothpaste. His things appeared exotic and magnificent to me.

"How long will you be staying here?" I ventured to ask.

"Not too long, but I want to spend as much time as I can with all of you. I want to get to know all of my siblings in Mexico. We'll have a good time while I'm here, but I'll need to return back home to Phoenix, Arizona, to get back to work."

Although I'd known he was only visiting, not staying permanently, his articulation of this fact did not sit well with me. I left the room and couldn't get his comment that he would be leaving out of my mind. Although I knew it was the truth, I refused to believe it.

I was so charged with energy and inspiration from meeting my older half-brother that I barely slept that night. Tossing and turning, I could only think of my half-brother Miguel and how I hoped he'd let me accompany him wherever he went the following day.

Very early in the morning, I heard Miguel showering. As he was shaving, I emerged, tired and with bloodshot eyes, to clean my face and wait. I smiled at him a couple of times as he was shaving, and he turned around and winked at me.

All the while obsessive thoughts tumbled in my brain, "Should I ask if I can go with him around town today? Will he be upset? Maybe I shouldn't ask him—but I can't imagine not going with him. He can't go on visits without me. I want to know where he's going."

I walked around, paced the cool, dirt floor multiple times, trying to make it obvious that I wanted to go with him but without outright asking. I was becoming upset that he had not invited me.

"Maybe he thinks I should go to school? Perhaps that's the reason, but I told him yesterday that I'm three lessons ahead ..." My brain searched to understand why he'd not invited me. I ran through multiple reasons why, but none satisfied me. I simply had to go with him, and I was not going to accept his going alone.

I'd been so sure that immediately when I woke up he would tell me, "Get ready to go, Edgar. I'm going to take a shower and shave, and you're coming with me," but that had not happened. The apprehension was killing me.

My mother, who was awake and making a fire, told Miguel, "I will make coffee and some breakfast for you."

He responded, "No, it's okay, Nena." Nena was short for

Magdalena, my mother's name. Then he continued, saying, "Edgar and I are going to visit Chucho. He invited me over."

When I heard that, all my agitation and tiredness dissipated. I felt totally revived; my enthusiasm was high. I was thrilled.

I wanted people to see me with my brother at all times. I felt proud to be with him, and I could not wait to get out of the house.

Once out the door, Miguel took hold of my hand. Then, after holding my hand for a few feet, he let it go and put his arm around me, across my shoulder, almost like I was no longer a child.

Where I grew up, adults hold the hands of children. When a person put their arm on your shoulder, it meant that you were grown up and you were an adult. So, when Miguel put his hand across my shoulder, it made me feel grown-up and mature.

We went to visit Chucho. He was short, thin, and strong, with a thick mustache. Like my grandfather, all his life, Chucho had been a farmer. He never wore anything other than the colloquial dress of our town, the sackcloth shirt and drawstring pants. The skin on his face and body was identical to my grand-father's—leathery and thick with sandpaper-looking hands. He also wore a machete as my grandfather and about all the farmers did, strapped to his left side at the hip. At sundown each day, the local farmers, walking home from their fields, often in single file, made striking silhouettes with their machetes protruding off at one side, like a line of canoes, each with a paddle dangling off to a side. It was unforgettable to witness.

Chucho had twin daughters but had lost his two sons, one from an infection and the other from falling off a wild horse. His wife died from postpartum sepsis that she'd contracted when giving birth to their twin daughters. Though she had seven children of her own, my mother cared for Chucho's twin girls, sharing with them the little milk that we had from our home, and this meant the world to Chucho. He constantly said he was indebted to my mother, and there was nothing he would not do for her. He always said that his girls were alive because of my mother, and anything that her children ever needed, he would be there at anytime to supply. Chucho was a man of his word. And he was like family to my family.

When Miguel was a teenager, he'd had a dispute with our

father and apparently had lived with Chucho for two months because of it. Chucho had been instrumental in bringing about a reconciliation between them. Our community didn't believe in holding a grudge. Unity was an important factor in our lives.

In La Mira ranchers and farmers first consulted with Chucho before doing business deals. All the ranchers and farmers respected him wholeheartedly. He knew the buyers from several cities. These were the buyers that would purchase crops, meat, and produce from local farmers and ranchers to sell to city companies and businesses for further production and retail. Chucho knew everything about these buyers—their needs, their prices, and how to handle them—so local growers first consulted him before making any deals.

Often, all the farmers and the ranchers would meet with him at his home to discuss strategies for business. He talked about pricing and the time for selling crops, advising, "When we are together, we are in control. When we falter, the buyers will pull us apart." Chucho was way ahead of his time in this regard.

In addition to being a successful farmer and strategic business planner, Chucho was an accomplished gardener. The plants and flowers adorning his home were exquisite. The flowers, shrubs, vines, and trees framed his entry, lined the corridor, and shaped the courtyard to make his home into a small estate. His garden with its red, orange, and pink flowers, tropical shrubs, and tall coconut palms smelled luscious and offered plentiful shade in addition to pleasing the eye. His gardening skills made our town proud.

When Miguel and I walked through the courtyard, Chucho approached us, smiling, and took off his machete. He hugged us both and then said a few words to Miguel. He brought us into the kitchen where we smelled something absolutely delicious cooking on the fire.

It was dried jerky mixed with eggs and simmered in a red hot sauce and then served over white rice. It's a traditional breakfast called *aporreadillo*. Another way of eating it is with beans. Miguel, in particular, thoroughly enjoyed the breakfast.

Miguel told us that he made the same breakfast in Arizona. And while he could find all the ingredients and spices there, it just didn't taste as good. Somehow the food in our town tasted better.

Miguel and Chucho talked about everything, including my father's health. It was pretty obvious that everyone, including my mother and many of our loved ones and friends, knew how ill my father was and how his condition was worsening on a daily basis. He truly was a sick man.

Unlike many other people that would say my father had "just a little cough" or that he was "just sick but not that bad," Chucho refused to play down my father's health. He told Miguel the truth. He admitted that many times my father's coughing scared him. Chucho argued that my father was likely a lot sicker than people thought. My father was able to hide things, and it seemed that when he got to the point that he was going to have an especially terrible coughing spell, he would walk away and endure it privately, so as not to scare people and to save himself some embarrassment. But he'd reached the point where he could no longer hide because the awful coughing was happening more and more frequently.

Chucho softly told my brother that he'd witnessed an episode of an absolutely relentless, scary, horrifying coughing fit of my father. It happened when Chucho brought a man who'd fallen off a carriage and injured his leg to my father to close the wound on the man's leg. While my father was cleaning and closing the wound, he started coughing severely. Additionally during the fit his color changed from blue to gray to purple to ash.

"Miguel, the man whose leg was wounded became so frightened of your father. I didn't know what to think myself—I couldn't tell if it was the man or your father who needed the most help. Really, I was horrified. I didn't know what to do, and that's why I wanted you to return to see for yourself what's been going on," Chucho lamented.

As they talked, I stood quietly, imagining how my life would be if I lived with Miguel in the USA. I saw myself jumping into a car with Miguel in the driver's seat. I imagined rolling down the windows and the cool air hitting me as I sat next to Miguel as he was driving.

Miguel and Chucho talked for several hours, but to me it felt like minutes since I was immersed in my daydream about living with Miguel in the United States of America. I imagined many things—how it would feel to live there, to go to school there, to learn English, to eat their food. It was one thought after another—a racing thought process of desire and imagination. I wondered, "Can this dream come true, or is it just the imaginings of a kid?"

After talking with Chucho, Miguel and I met up with my grandfather, so we could all visit the ocean together. One of the extraordinary occurrences that Miguel wanted to witness, and that everyone enjoyed watching, was the exploding waters of the great Río Balsas and the smaller Río Las Truchas slamming together and then smacking their way into the Pacific Ocean. This happened at Melchor Ocampo. Truly it was a spectacular scene, with the whacking and whirling water sending mighty waves exploding upwards about thirty feet in the air, as the rapid, vicious river water tumbled into the ocean. It was as if a water bomb had been detonated.

We sat, relaxing against some large trees, about eight feet in diameter, drinking coconut water and eating the flesh right out of the coconut itself. My grandfather said that the same trees had been there since he'd been a child.

Miguel and my grandfather talked the whole time, mostly about my father and his poor health. I couldn't really hear all the specifics, and in many ways I didn't even want to hear about it. They talked about what they could do to get him to stop smoking because they knew that that was the culprit behind his illness. They couldn't come up with any solutions.

My brother admitted, "Even if we had something to offer him to make him stop, I don't think he'd do it. Sadly, it seems he's on a mission to die." My brother and grandfather continued to talk with a mix of puzzlement and frustration in their voices.

I looked at my brother frequently as he was talking. I found his manner of speaking unique. He would stand back to make a point and use his two hands to show emphasis. He never raised his voice, but it was the movement of his hands that signaled his agreement or disagreement with what was being discussed.

Then he became quiet and seemed dazed, almost like he was looking at something in another dimension of space and time. When this happened, my grandfather signaled me to let Miguel rest, so we moved a distance from him to the sandy shore.

My grandfather and I sat in the sand, looking at the ocean and watching the day turn to night. We looked at the moon and felt a caressing breeze.

My grandfather confided, "There's something about Miguel—I can't quite put my finger on it—but he's worried about something."

I was convinced it was my father and his terrible health that was worrying Miguel, but when I suggested this, my grandfather disagreed, "No, it's not that. It's something else."

"The moon's just not right," I heard my grandfather go on to say.

My grandfather advised me to enjoy my time with Miguel because soon he would be leaving.

I did not want to hear that. In fact, I didn't want to hear anything about Miguel leaving, nothing whatsoever. When my mother would say, "Miguel, you will be leaving soon," or someone would ask him, "When are you leaving?" I just wished they would not say it. I wished they would just be quiet and let him decide when he wanted to leave. I didn't want him leaving. Thinking about his departure was very upsetting to me. I wanted to think of anything except that.

When I awoke the next morning, Miguel had already left. I asked my mother where he'd gone, and she said he was out visiting.

I, personally, did not want him to visit anyone. I wanted him to stay with us at home. I didn't care for him to even talk about going to visit this person or that person. I felt very possessive of his presence.

I told my mom, "I don't even know why he has to go see those people. He's here to visit us and not to visit anybody else."

"Edgar, you've got to remember he hasn't been here for years. He has a lot of people that love him. They're people that knew him when he was a child. He has to do that. That's just the way that you do things when you become a kind person. You appreciate people around you."

Needless to say, her explanation didn't suffice.

Though I'd hoped I'd be with Miguel that day, I ended up going to school. I didn't pay attention to anything that was going on in class. It seemed like people would talk to me, kids would talk to me, and I wasn't even there. I was consumed with my brother and worried about him. "Where is he? What if something happens to him? Who exactly is he visiting? Are they taking care of him? Are they treating him well?" I just couldn't wait to get out of school, so I could search for him.

When school was out, I ran home, but my brother was not to be found.

"Where's Miguel? Where is he?" I asked my mother with fear in my voice and my eyes.

She responded, "What's the matter with you, Edgar?"

With ever-shortening breaths, I managed to say, "I just don't know where he's at. Where is he? Did he leave? Did he go back to the United States?"

My mother assured me, "Your brother would never do that. He's somewhere in town. He was born here. He knows a lot of people here, and they want to visit with him. He's not going to be here long. He'll be leaving soon, so he has a lot of visiting to do."

I sobbed to my mother, "He's not leaving. He can't leave. He won't leave. He can't leave. I won't let him leave."

Then I ran out of the house and proceeded to search for him in a state of high desperation. I didn't want anyone around him but me. Although I loved a lot of the people he was visiting, I just didn't like him to be without me.

I was completely overtaken by his persona, his appearance, his manners. I was crazy about him. I loved everything he did. I loved everything he said. I loved the way he said it. There wasn't anything that he could do that could disappoint me.

Finally, after I'd been searching for several hours in a panic, a lady touched me on the shoulder and told me, "Your father and Miguel went to the mines to see Señor Schwartz. They are at the mines."

Upset and defeated, I returned home.

Seeing my face, my mother chided, "*Mi hijo*, you look very ugly when you are upset."

Immediately upon saying that, she gave me a kiss and asked, "You want to return to the United States with your brother, don't you?"

"Yes," I admitted and started to cry.

My grandfather who had witnessed this whole scene reassured me, "Your brother is a beautiful human being, and someday you'll both be together."

To my mother he asked, "What are we going to do when Miguel Senior passes away? It's something that I've been talking to Miguel Junior about."

I wasn't fazed by my grandfather's question to my mother. It was something that I knew would come. I just didn't know when.

Perhaps my dream of leaving with my brother to the United States was simply a way to escape the pain of my father's impending death and the pain of not knowing what would become of the rest of us after he died. No matter the reason, I was entranced by my older brother and the possibility of living with him in the United States of America.

That evening, Miguel gave me an American dollar.

I looked at the dollar, declaring, "This is beautiful . . . It's so thick, not like Mexican bills. Mexican bills are really thin. They look cheap compared to this dollar."

My brother explained, "It's not that they're cheap. It's just that one American dollar is worth 12.5 pesos."

I asked, "So the thicker the bill, the more it's worth?"

"Yeah, I guess you could say that," he responded.

"A $5 bill or $10 bill or $50 bill must be really, really thick," I remarked.

"Sort of. They're certainly worth a lot of money. But the peso certainly has value too."

Miguel said that when he'd crossed the border, he'd exchanged dollars to pesos but had accidentally left one dollar in his wallet, and he wanted me to have it.

I took the dollar, looked at it several times, the front and the back, through the sides, and up in the light.

"Who is the man on this bill?" I asked.

"It's George—in Spanish we say 'Jorge'—Washington, the first President of the United States. Every bill has the face of an American President on it," Miguel explained.

"Miguel, when you work, is this what they pay you with?"

"No, it's a little more complex than that. They actually give me a piece of paper called a check with a number that tells how many dollars that check is worth. Then after that, I cash the check to get dollars or save those dollars in a bank."

I didn't know much about finances—and I'd never heard of a "check" or a "bank" before. I wanted to know more, but my mother interrupted, telling us it was time to get ready for dinner.

Before getting up, Miguel added, "Someday, Edgar, I'll talk to you more about what it takes to earn a dollar. I predict that in the future you are going to be earning lots of dollars."

When his friends came over for dinner, I felt more at ease. I sat on his lap, and he laughed with me. I loved my older brother, and I could tell he loved me and loved being with me too.

5

During my surgical training, I was to perform a surgery on an older gentleman who had a hernia. Mr. Williams already had had an operation for lung cancer in which his trachea and vocal cords were removed. He breathed with a permanent replaceable breathing tube called a tracheostomy tube. This also meant that he'd lost his voice.

By putting lit cigarettes to the small hole in his neck, Mr. Williams managed to smoke right through the tracheostomy tube. Though he could not taste the smoke, his body demanded the nicotine.

When I saw Mr. Williams smoking in this way, in complete disregard to his obviously failing health, I was sadly reminded of my father.

★   ★   ★

A week into his visit with us, for the first time Miguel witnessed my father battling out a horrific coughing spell. It was worse than the episode he'd had at the mines.

My father coughed and coughed and coughed. Meanwhile, his whole body turned blue. He seemed to be choking. His face was frightening. His eyes were sunken in, and his eye sockets got bigger and bigger and bigger. With all the shuddering, shaking, and thumping, it didn't seem possible that his frail, degraded body could continue to support him. He seemed to be coughing out his last bit of life.

My youngest sister and baby brother were terrified and hid.

Miguel was very afraid and rushed to comfort my father, to try to help in some way, but my father pushed him away. This back and forth went on repeatedly, sometimes pausing, but then

Miguel would try to approach again. It was a ghastly scene.

Though this was the worst coughing episode I'd yet witnessed, in a way I felt used to it and not as rattled as I would have expected.

After my father gulped down a small jolt of liquor, the coughing subsided.

Miguel stepped outside, and my mother followed. She went out to talk to him, discussing all the concerns she'd been holding back, her worries about the children, the family, their livelihood, and my father's likely fast-approaching death.

I was not privileged to this conversation, but I could sense the urgency.

The following morning Miguel asked me, "Does our father cough like this all night long?"

"Yes," I admitted. "I have gotten used to it, and I think all of us have as well."

I wish Miguel hadn't seen it because it changed him in the last days of his short stay with us. He became worried. His spark was gone. That illumination that he'd had around him faded. He did not want to leave the house, but that part of his change was fine with me.

The next day at school, I heard other kids talking about my father, saying terrible things: "Mr. Hernandez is a walking skeleton," "My parents said he's forgetting things, that he's losing his mind," and "I heard he's going to die any day now."

My teacher, César, told me he'd like to speak to me after school.

César Fuentes, my teacher, came from an outstanding family of teachers. His grandfather, his father, and all his brothers and sisters were fine teachers. They taught in various areas in southern Mexico. They were great and talented individuals with one mission in mind—to make their students learn and become fruitful citizens of Mexico.

If all of Mexico had teachers like César and his family, no child in Mexico would be illiterate. The Fuentes had such a passion for teaching that by simply listening to them alone, you would learn something. Their words alone seemed to enter the mind and straighten it out. They communicated a compassionate message to students that we conduct ourselves in the best manner, learn, and become educated so that we grow into capable and responsible adults, and ultimately, we'd make our families and our country proud. César was an excellent teacher.

My father was instrumental in getting César to come to our community to teach. At one time my father was *presidente* of the town, which is sort of like being a mayor or head of a city council but not exactly. The *presidente* runs town meetings that address issues like children's immunizations and schooling. When the meetings addressed teacher recruitment, they were really full because the community's primary goal was educating its children". As *presidente*, my father did a lot of work to encourage César to live and teach in our town.

My father always told my siblings and me that our teachers were like our second parents and that we should learn to respect them as such. My father was right—César was like a second parent to me.

He was a young, energetic, dark-skinned, and exceptionally good-looking man. His teeth were so bright white he could have made a commercial for a toothpaste company. His smile was powerful. He rode a bicycle. We would see him around town, traveling from one place to another on his beautiful bicycle.

He wore white, short-sleeved shirts always. The upper button of his shirt tended to be open, exposing the shiny skin of his chest. His biceps protruded below the rim of the short sleeves.

César was extremely talented. He played the trumpet, violin, guitar, and accordion, and he could sing beautifully. At my grandfather's birthday party, César had sung "Ave Maria," and it was quite moving. He had a very interesting voice, even when he talked, and you wouldn't know whether to feel sad or to smile. It was difficult sometimes to respond because his voice was so beautiful.

He was a man of affection. He embraced all of his students, especially when comfort was needed. He did not like us to call him "Mr. Fuentes." He wanted to be called "César."

César taught the second, third, and fourth grades, and seemed to know all the ingredients a child needed to get a good education. Because he felt that our class should be like a family, he had each of us take an oath at the beginning of the school year. We promised that if any of us fell behind in our studies, we would admit it to the class and collectively the rest of us would work to help that student catch up.

César argued that while competition could be healthy, because there were many factors and circumstances of life that affected a student's performance, we must be sympathetic and we must unify as a group so that all of us could come together and assist any of our classmates in need of extra help.

César had looked around when he was telling us this, saying, "It could be you . . . It could be one of you or you or you," pointing at each of us individually, "that falls behind and needs our help." We all agreed that we should work together and help each other.

He was an outstanding teacher and an outstanding human being.

After school César told me, "You know that I've known your brother Miguel for many years. I met with him yesterday, and he told me that he wished he could take you back to Arizona with him . . . but he thinks the family would fall apart without you here."

I was taken aback.

César paused for a moment and then continued, "I told him that I totally agreed with him."

"How is it both of you think of me in this way?" I asked.

"You know that if you were to leave, it would break your grandfather's heart. Not only that, Edgar, you have to remember, your family needs someone to brighten their lives. I think they would miss your never-ending and constant talking, something you do not just with your family but with everyone. Everybody in town adores you. Everyone likes the way you express yourself, and they say that you're mature in the way you see things in life. And your mother would miss you terribly too."

That night, instead of relaxing and dropping into sleep, my mind churned and mulled with so many questions and possibilities. "Even if I can't leave with him now, what about in a year or two—could I move to the US with Miguel? What will happen to my mother and me and my siblings when our father dies? My godfather has given me an open invitation to go to Germany with him. Do I want to go to Germany? Would I rather move to Germany or the US? Surely my parents would let me leave. After all, my older brother Jorge is in Vera Cruz with our half-brother Alberto, Pedro is in Phoenix with our half-sister Olivia, and Surama lives in Zamora, so what's wrong with me going somewhere too? Maybe I should stay here. It would be so difficult to leave my grandfather."

My true feeling, deep in my mind and heart, was that I wanted to go to the USA with Miguel, and my dream was to have all my siblings and my mother eventually go to the United States too. That was really my true dream in life.

The following day I decided to talk to my grandfather.

"Abuelito, I guess I've gotten used to Papá's coughing and his sickly appearance, so I stopped thinking about it. But now with Miguel and Mamá so worried, I'm wondering what you think."

"*Hijo*, I am so sorry you and your siblings and Miguel have to witness your father's coughing fits. That's a scary thing to see. But I must tell you—I fear this is only the start of your father's decline. He is going to get worse and worse. We must prepare for his death."

He continued, "Soon the time will come for Miguel to return to the United States. I know how you've grown to adore him in the short time he's been here, but you know he must return to his responsibilities."

I did not want to hear about Miguel's departure, about his responsibilities, about his need to buy new tires for his car. I wanted him to stay. I refused to accept that my brother needed to go back to the United States.

I gave no response to my grandfather's comment.

I decided to go to the mines to see my godfather.

"Edgar, it's only a matter of months before I return to Germany. Because of that bill President Cárdenas signed to nationalize certain industries, the German company I work for won't be doing any mining in Mexico anymore.

"And I agree with President Cárdenas. The Mexican people should be the ones to manage the fine minerals and resources of Mexico. I know Mexican engineers with their tremendous work ethic and great intelligence can do the same work my German colleagues and I are doing. I'm not worried at all about the mines. But I sure will miss Mexico."

The way he was talking to me, it sounded like my godfather was leaving the next day—and that this was his goodbye speech to me.

He added, "And I'll tell you something, Edgar, it will be

the saddest day of my life when I leave Mexico. I've grown to appreciate the culture, the people, really everything here. At one time I thought I would stay in Mexico forever. I love it here. And I love you and your family. I'll say it again—I've told my wife so much about you, and the both of us welcome you to come live with us and go to school and then university in Germany. Nothing would please us more than for you to return to Germany with me."

His words saddened me. While I was thrilled that he believed in me enough that he and his wife invited me to be in their family, still—with my father's poor health and my meeting my wonderful half-brother Miguel so suddenly and just as suddenly he'd be leaving—it made me sad that my beloved godfather had to depart soon also. There seemed to be so many changes about to take place that I felt overwhelmed.

My godfather went on to state that he predicted changes in my life would be coming and that he thought that wherever I decided to go, I would be a successful young man with a great future. He reminded me to be patient.

"Life is interesting, and there's a lot of doors that will open for you. They'll open when you least expect it. As I see it, Edgar, you belong to something unique in life, and I don't think it's here in your town. But still, your family does need a young man around to help out and to keep the family happy and smiling.

"And your grandfather—he puts all other grandparents to shame. They could not compete with him, as he is a fine gentleman and a philosopher of life.

"I know how attached you've become to your brother Miguel. He's a fine man, an exemplary man. I visited Chucho and learned that the reason Miguel came down to visit is because Chucho wrote him about your father's health and how worrisome it has become. Chucho also told me that your brother is having him sell a small coconut farm he owns, and most of that money is going to your mother, so she will have something in case something happens to your father."

"I didn't know. Miguel didn't tell me this," I told my godfather.

"I figured he didn't—so I'm telling you. Your brother is a fine man—a rarity. And I want you to be very strong when he leaves. It is necessary for him to return to the United States, so you must be brave and strong to help your brother have a good departure."

Then he gave me a hug and told me he needed to return to work.

My godfather's talk got me thinking about my brother and his moments of intense quiet and contemplation—like the time he'd become so withdrawn and quiet at the beach. I no longer felt it was my father's health he was preoccupied with. I think he was worried about how the rest of us in the family would make ends meet without my father around.

The dreaded day finally arrived.

My grandfather cooked two young goats. Also there was corn, vegetables, watermelon, and guavas from his farm. It was a goodbye celebration.

But I didn't feel celebratory. My eyes were red and swollen from crying.

A large truck arrived. Two long benches lined each side of the truck's bed. This is where the passengers sat, facing each other. The bed of the truck had a scaffolding over it onto which was strapped a yellow tarp to protect the passengers from the dust, heat, or rain.

This was the truck that would take Miguel away.

Then I saw the driver—pot-bellied with a crooked mustache. He had food stains on his shirt, and his big belly seemed to stand out at least ten inches from his chest. I hated his appearance. I hated his sloppiness. I hated him, and I hated everything about him. I even hated his truck.

The sound of his voice bothered me tremendously, I hated it. I disliked the tone of his voice. He had a weak voice for such a large man. I hated everything that was going on, and I hated everything about this driver.

Then I saw the other passengers. There was a man with his wife—I assumed it was his wife. I didn't like the guy at all. And I didn't like the wife either. I found her unattractive. I thought the man was the wrong proportion for her—she was a really large lady, and he was a really tiny man. They made an awful-looking couple. I couldn't bear them.

I noticed another passenger, a lone, skinny, balding man who seemed confused. He kept looking around, almost like he wanted to step down out of the truck, but he wasn't sure. He made several gestures like he was about to climb down. He seemed like a bumbling idiot.

The driver placed a wooden stepladder at the end of the truck. I even hated that. It was wobbly. It didn't seem safe to stand on.

I pretty much hated everything.

I wanted there to be a short circuit and next a loud BANG! Then suddenly the truck's engine would be on fire, so we would all have to evacuate the scene. I wanted the driver to fall on the ground and start coughing like my father, and then everyone would be afraid to ride anywhere with him and we'd all go home.

I couldn't believe these crazy, devilish delusions I was imagining. It was just that I did not want my brother to leave.

I'd never wished ill on anyone before in my life. I'd never even hurt anyone before—I just didn't want my brother to leave.

From a distance I watched the goodbyes. The scene reminded me of Miguel's arrival, the way he'd been surrounded by people and the way I'd kept my distance. I saw Miguel converse with my godfather. Then they shook hands. Miguel hugged other friends and acquaintances. He then talked to my grandfather who wept as he hugged Miguel.

My grandfather then came out to where I was and placed his arm around me. I tried to resist more crying, but I could not hold back. I really could not control myself.

My brother knew he would have to deal with me sooner or later before departing. Amidst the hugs and handshakes, he occasionally glanced in my direction, as if saying, "I haven't forgotten you. I'm coming."

He talked to my mother for a few minutes.

Finally the moment came. I felt special, like I was onstage, frightened, yet full of emotions and full of tears. Then I suddenly stopped crying. My tears dried up as Miguel approached me. My grandfather left me to be alone with Miguel.

"Edgar, I loved returning to my hometown. I loved seeing my family and old friends again. The ocean and the food—it's been so wonderful. And you—you've been the highlight of my visit. I know a lot about you that you don't know that I know."

I quickly perked up, asking, "Really?"

My brother kneeled down slightly and put both his hands on my shoulders. He took his right hand to tap me on the chin, so

I'd lift my head up and look him in the eyes. Then he told me, "Yes. And when I come back, it'll be because I'm coming to get you to bring you to America."

He gave me a hug. Next he walked back over and kissed my mother and father. Then he stepped into the bed of the truck and sat at the end of the bench.

The fat driver got into the driver's seat.

When I heard the sound of the engine, I thought I was going to faint.

As the truck drove away, my brother waved at us, as if saying, "Goodbye for now, and I shall return someday."

I'd had the most fun of my life when Miguel was with us. And with his promise of someday returning for me, I very much felt that I would not be living in my small town for much longer. I was eight years old and knew I belonged elsewhere. And as my grandfather and godfather both had told me—I knew I would become something.

6

I was in surgery in Phoenix when I received a message on my beeper. It was from my son, Miguel, asking me to call home.

"Miguelito, you asked me to call?"

"There's a letter for you, Dad."

"Look at the return address on the envelope. Tell me who sent the letter, *hijo*."

"It says it's from the American Board of Surgery."

I had at least another five hours at the hospital, if not more, before I could make it home. I knew it would be a long five hours, filled with lots of anxiety and anticipation. This was the long-awaited letter, announcing the results of a grueling surgical board examination.

As soon as I got home, I immediately opened the letter. It read, "Dr. Hernandez, congratulations on becoming a board-certified surgeon."

Feelings of relief and accomplishment engulfed me as I hugged my son.

I paused a moment, recalling another long-awaited letter sent so many years ago.

★   ★   ★

With his hand trembling, my father held up a letter. "A letter from your brother," he announced to the family before lunch.

It was already several months since my brother had left La Mira to return to Phoenix, Arizona.

"Please read it now," I voiced.

With his hand possessed by uncontrollable tremors, my father awkwardly dropped the letter onto a table and declared, "We'll read it during dinner."

Looking at the date that was stamped on the edge of the front of the envelope, my father noted, "Besides, it's been weeks since the letter was written."

Since Miguel had departed, Chucho had sold Miguel's small coconut farm, so my mother was able to put away that extra money for a time of need.

My godfather had started wrapping up his work in the mines in preparation for his final departure to Germany. He continued dining with us frequently.

César had continued helping me grow in mind and spirit. He liked to go fishing in the river, and I went with him. Also we visited the mines. All the while, we talked, and he was constantly teaching me.

Though we couldn't have imagined it possible, my father's coughing episodes had actually worsened. He'd begun pulling up black globs of blood during the long coughing fits.

One night, I woke to use the outhouse and then returned to sleep. In the morning when I got up, I noticed that my feet were traced in dried black blood. I realized that my father must have gotten up also during the night to go to outhouse. He must have expelled blood onto the ground that I later stepped through.

I realized for certain that my father would not live for much longer. He had lost a significant amount of weight. He was having a hard time breathing, a hard time walking. His strength was poor. His appetite was poor. However, his appetite for cigarettes and his favorite liquor remained steady.

Then, in church one Sunday morning, my father became quite ill. He had a high temperature. He became quite pale. Then he fainted. We were certain that he would die that day.

But he didn't.

It was 1958, and we knew of no other form of long-distance communication than letters. La Mira didn't have electricity, except for the twice-yearly use of a generator, or telephones or telegraphs. At that time I never knew that telephones existed. Since we knew no other form of communication, Miguel's letter meant so much to us.

Perhaps not for my parents and siblings, but for me the hours dragged that afternoon. As every minute seemed to slow, my anticipation to read my brother's letter increased.

Much to my delight, my sister Lupe commented to me that

she too was anxious to hear what the letter said. She told me that Miguel was a beautiful older brother.

We sat around the dinner table. For light, we had two homemade lamps, one on each end of the table. Each lamp was constructed from an empty Tecate beer can. The can was filled with kerosene, and a small rag was stuck in the can with one end of the rag sitting in the kerosene. We lit the top of the rag. These makeshift lamps were the only source of lighting in our home. The light was smoky but enough for us to read by and to function with at night.

When my father said he would read the letter aloud, so all of us could hear it—Lupe and I looked at each other and smiled in anticipation. I moved to sit at the end of the table next to my father, so I could read the letter myself as he was reading it.

I found myself moving closer and closer to my father. However, the stink of cigarette smoke and his unkempt attire kept me from getting right next to him. He also smelled of liquor, and he seemed nervous. He was shaking even more than usual. He pulled the candle closer to him.

My father examined the envelope, its front and back, and flipped it around in his hand a couple of times, sort of tapping it onto the palm of his hand. I think he did this in attempt to shake the tremor he had.

"Papá, can I hold the letter?" I asked.

When Lupe nodded her head in agreement, I added, "Actually, can each of us take turns holding it?"

The letter moved down one side of the table, from person to person, hand to hand, with each of us examining it closely, and up the other side of the table. When I held it in my hands, I felt delighted—as if I'd landed a winning lottery ticket.

We were having meat with chili and beans, and as we passed it along, the letter moved right over the plates. By the time it got back to my father, it was smeared with beans, salsa, and my baby brother's fingerprints.

My father took a piece of cloth and cleaned it, so the letter inside wouldn't get stained once the envelope was opened.

My father was antsy in his seat, repeatedly shifting positions in an attempt to find a comfortable way to sit. Apparently his back was hurting him. He asked my mother for some aspirin.

My mother retrieved a large bottle of aspirin and gave him two tablets.

She told my father, "Miguel, your pain must be getting worse. These make the twelfth aspirins you've had today."

He gave her a look and then took a swig from a large bottle. It was a yellow liquid that looked like tea but was liquor.

After inhaling deeply on a cigarette, he proceeded to open the envelope. Once he'd opened it, he paused to take another drag on the cigarette.

Next he withdrew the letter. It was a single sheet of paper. The envelope was small, so the letter had been folded on itself twice in order to fit.

I saw the worn-out skin on my father's hand, thin like paper. I could see the bones and tendons through the skin. His skin looked like a translucent piece of plastic. His arms were thin, and I could sense being so near him the delicacy of his skeletal frame and the extensive drooping of the skin around his face.

The deterioration of his entire body and facial features were especially apparent when he neared the light of the candle. It seemed like his face was melting.

He coughed a few times. We all looked at each other, hoping he would not have an asphyxiating, lengthy coughing episode.

He ironed out the letter. Then he cleared his throat and began reading.

My heart started to pound as if trying to jump out of my chest. I placed my elbows on top of the table to settle my heart and my thoughts and to listen to my father read.

I should add that during a normal mealtime, this position of the elbows on the table was not acceptable to my mother, especially during dinner. My mother had no schooling, but she had learned great manners when she worked as a maid for a group of federal workers in a camp in southern Mexico.

The letter started with greetings and wishes of good health for everyone in the family. Miguel expressed his wish that our family was joined together in happiness and that our father's strength was good. He conveyed to my mom his appreciation for the commendable way she took care of us, children, and our father. He thanked all of us for the wonderful reception he'd received when visiting. He noted that he'd returned safely to work in Arizona, that he was in good health, and that he missed us terribly. He said that he'd also written letters to my grandfather, César, and Chucho.

I noticed my father was getting quite close to the end of the letter, but Miguel had not thus far mentioned me by name.

I was in a panic, lamenting to myself, "Miguel has forgotten me. Miguel forgot me. He forgot the promise. He forgot our connection." I released a long sigh in an attempt to slow my galloping breathing and sprinting heart.

My father paused to cough. He cleared his throat and took a couple of drags from his cigarette.

At that Lupe and I exchanged sad glances.

Then, looking down at the letter, he smiled and proceeded to read, "Please tell Edgar how much I treasure our conversations and the good times we had at the ocean."

Joy melted over my body.

The letter closed, "Sincerely, your son, Miguel."

Though delighted with the mention, I also felt an acute disappointment. "Why didn't Miguel say he would be coming back for me? Why didn't he say that he wished I could be with him in the United States?" my mind demanded.

My father looked around the table, observing, "It sure is nice to hear from your brother. I'm sure he will write again soon telling us that he'll be marrying, that he'll be having kids of his own. After that happens, we probably won't hear from him again. He'll just get too busy."

My mother responded, "Even if Miguel marries and has a family of his own, he'll never forget us."

At these comments, I became awash inside myself with tumbling emotions—dejection, desperation, sadness, guilt, selfishness. "What will happen—to us, to him, to me?" I quietly wondered.

The next day at school I asked César if he'd heard from my brother.

César said he'd receive a letter from Miguel and that we would talk after school.

"I don't know why everything I want to know has to wait," I thought, "All this waiting is a kind of torture."

César started class by saying that it was a good day to talk about what countries do throughout the world to make people's lives better. He talked about various countries and how their policies and economies affected all of us in the world. When he mentioned that the United States was a rich nation and a leader in wealth with a growing economy, I couldn't stop imagining myself living in the United States, benefiting from its many opportunities but also contributing to its wealth.

He talked about European countries as well, and I immediately thought about Germany and my godfather. He talked about the influence of rich countries on the world. He talked about poor countries and how they depend on either neighboring countries or foreign countries for assistance and for sharing their wealth, technology, and health findings.

I didn't know how a teacher in a small town could know so much and discuss so much with us, his students. I was convinced no one knew more than my grandfather, no matter the topic. However, César was a close second. He spoke clearly and with enthusiasm. He said Mexico had a long way to go before it would catch up with other countries. He said Mexico was full of wealth and had a lot of resources, but we lagged behind in our education system and also in our technology. He said a country's economy fuels its people's success and the quality of the available education. If the economy was poor, education suffered. He said that many Mexican people traveled to, or wanted to travel to, the United States for a better future. They thought the US with its rich economy offered a better education and a better standard of living.

César admitted to us that he often considered going to the United States himself, but he felt that his heart and soul were, and should be, devoted to the education of young Mexican children and that we needed him.

His smile with his pristine white teeth made his statements even more pronounced. He truly demonstrated his passion for teaching. He said he knew a teacher that had gone to the United States and then returned several years later to become an even better teacher. He said that the teacher now taught his students the English language. César explained that many Mexican children learned the English language for one purpose—to increase their chances of obtaining a good job in Mexico or of traveling to the United States to work or live permanently.

It was an unbelievable discussion for us fourth graders. My classmates and I were mesmerized with the talk. It was a notable day.

While he was talking, I imagined myself speaking English

and then going to the United States, or learning English once I lived there with my brother and started school. Since I'd met my older half-brother, my dream was to study in the United States and live with him.

César told us that in the United States, because of its wealth, the opportunities were unlimited in terms of education. He said the American educational system was the best in the world. He admitted that it sounded critical but that our educational system in Mexico was at least ten years behind the times. In a sense, he seemed to be arguing that education, technology, and knowledge trickled down to Mexico from our more developed neighbors in the north, the USA and Canada.

Towards the end of the discussion, I could honestly say that all of us in the room felt that it was the most exciting conversation we had ever heard from our wonderful teacher. For me, it both strengthened my dream to go to the US and, at the same time, took my mind off the great anticipation I felt about talking to César later that day.

After school, César and I went outside to sit underneath a big shade tree. There César talked to me about the letter Miguel had sent him. In the letter Miguel praised César for the wonderful teaching he gave to all the children of La Mira as well as to me and my siblings, specifically. He told César that we were lucky to have him as our teacher.

César told me that Miguel also wanted to donate a small amount of the proceeds from the sale of his small farm to the school, so the school could get some necessary items. We desperately needed chairs. We had tables but no chairs, and Miguel had witnessed us carrying chairs to school each morning and returning home with them in the afternoon. So, though we had tables, we had no chairs, and my brother wanted to change that.

I recalled that Miguel had told me he needed new tires for his car, yet he was giving some money to our school for chairs. I was moved and understood more keenly why I loved him dearly. My brother was generous. I didn't know a thing about a person having wealth because no one in La Mira had abundant money, but I knew one thing—Miguel was a very generous and caring man.

"César, did Miguel say anything about me specifically in the letter?" I asked, daring to be direct about what I most wanted to know.

"No, Edgar, he didn't mention you specifically. He did say that he hoped to come back and visit us again soon," César replied.

"Oh," I responded in apparent disappointment.

"Edgar, be patient. You are only eight years old. You have a big life ahead of you. And with all my heart I believe that someday you will do something great."

7

It was 1993, and my wife and I were at the movies together watching *Tombstone*. I love Westerns, and I was hooked, totally immersed in the world of Doc Holliday, Wyatt Earp, and Johnny Ringo. Val Kilmer performed a terrific Doc Holliday—playing poker at a saloon, drinking, smoking, joking, and somersaulting his pistols like it was nothing. Then came something I really hadn't expected—Doc Holliday started gasping and coughing. Without warning he coughed up a mass of black blood globules. The bloody mass shot out of his mouth down onto his chest, his shirt, his boots, the floor, and all the while he was turning blue in a struggle for breath.

My body broke out in a drenching sweat. My easy breath just as quickly turned into rasping inhalations as if I couldn't take in enough air. My heart rate had skyrocketed. I swiftly stood and made a staggering exit out of the theater.

I was having a panic attack, a true and classic panic attack.

That unexpected scene in the movie had zapped me back through time to one of the most devastating and frightening moments of my life.

★   ★   ★

My father was pacing the house and coughing as he played with baby Manny. His coughing grew in intensity and frequency as if he were fighting to discharge some kind of creature from his insides. Then suddenly his roaring cough emitted a paint splatter of blood across the floor, the wall, the furniture—like nothing I'd witnessed before. Black blood mixed with soft blobs of organic matter poured from his mouth as if some faucet of death had been turned on. His skin turned ash gray. With every cough the chunky black trickle of blood turned into a hard stream that jetted forcefully out of his mouth instead of dribbling down his chin.

I could not have been any more frightened.

The coughing, the dripping, the jetting, the spurting, and the labored, diminishing breath did not stop, even after forty minutes.

I was aghast, but all the while I played with Manny, trying to keep him occupied, as my father sputtered and spurned in a wrestling match with his insides. I didn't know what to do.

Once a lull occurred, I sprinted out of the house, leaving my little brother crying on the floor, as my father lay there, preparing himself for the next round.

I ran as fast as I could to the market to look for my mother.

I saw her, carrying a basket of fruit and vegetables on one arm. In seeing me racing to her, she sped to me.

I screamed, "It's Papá! It's Papá! *¡Esta pasando!* He's dying! *¡Hay sangre por todas partes!*"

My mother demanded, "*¿Dónde esta el?* Where is he?"

"*En la casa.* And Manny is with him."

She dropped the basket and dashed towards home. I jetted after her.

When we arrived, he was lying on the floor with his shirt, chest, face, and hands awash in thick, black blood. It looked like the scene of a slaughter.

Manny lay near him on the floor, wailing, his eyes wide and petrified.

On her knees, my mother began wiping the blood from my father's face, from his chest, from his hands.

"*Agua.* Fetch him *agua*, Edgar," she ordered me.

"No water . . . Rest. I just want to rest," my father managed to utter.

He looked extremely ill, exhausted, and emaciated. He must have been seventy pounds lighter than he once was. His cheeks were exposed and looked no more than skin and bones. I knew he was dying. This was the end.

Yet, somehow he recovered.

The following day, it was business as usual. My father was smoking again as if nothing had happened the previous day.

I didn't know if he knew he was dying or if he was waiting

for the right time to die or if he did not care or if he was in denial. Maybe it was a combination.

My mother discovered he'd been secretly taking some type of medication. It was an oral suspension usual taken by the spoonful, but he was just drinking it down straight from the bottle.

As if hit by a bolt of lightning, my mother revealed, "It's some type of strong pain medication your father gives to patients when he has to do a procedure on them."

The violent and bloody coughing episodes continued more and more frequently. My father's activity level dramatically decreased. He moved less and less. Eventually he did not go outside the house at all. His appetite was poor, and his overall ability to move became so restricted that it was striking and pitiful to see.

I continued spending time with my grandfather, my godfather, César, and Chucho. Except for my grandfather, the others were not blood relatives, but they could very well have been, for we were close like family. I knew I could count on them for anything that I needed, and I could talk to them about my father and his impending death and the future of my family.

It had been a year and a half since Miguel had visited, and I was nine years old. With my father's health at such a low, combined with the fact that Miguel had never written that he would return to bring me to the USA—making the future of my mother, my siblings, and me seemed so uncertain—I decided that when my godfather returned to Germany in two months' time, I would seize the opportunity—I wanted to go to Germany with him.

I needed to discuss my decision with my parents.

In response, my father stated, "*Hijo*, I am going to die soon, very soon. At this point, there's nothing anyone can do about it. It's unpreventable. I know it, and so does everybody else."

I thought I would cry at his words, but with so many years of despair and tumult surrounding his health and so many tears already shed, no tears spilled from my eyes.

My father continued, "I trust your godfather, trust him completely. I know nothing bad will ever happen to you as long as he is with you. He'll care for you like you're his son. You'll get a great education in Germany, and if I had to bet on someone becoming successful, it is you. Go and make us proud."

My mother agreed, saying, "I want the best for you, *hijo*, and it will be best for you to leave with your godfather. No matter how far away you go, we will reunite again."

They both smiled at me.

The smiles on their faces made any doubt and anguish vanish from me. I felt content about the decision. My parents' belief in me made me feel grown-up, and I was determined never to disappoint them.

I talked to my godfather, my parents, and César. All of them supported my decision to go to Germany. There was one last person for me to talk to—the true love my life, my most beautiful Abuelito.

After I told him my plan, my grandfather responded, "There's no future for you here. You have a great teacher, but even he can only teach you so much. You need to go and learn at a higher level. A child's dream can never be denied, especially when you've dreamed it long enough, so go, *hijo*. Go and follow your dream."

Over dinner, between drags on his cigarette and shots of liquor, my father asked, "Who's hiding my bottle?" He turned to baby Manny, "Are you hiding my bottle?" Next he looked at my sisters, asking, "Or is it you three?" Then he looked at me, "Maybe it's you." He decided, "No, you wouldn't do that. It must be your mother."

Then he stopped, took another drag and another drink, and smiled at all of us. He seemed in an extraordinarily good mood. Plus, his hands weren't shaking. He seemed more at ease than he had been in years.

His skeletonized body was rigid, almost like it was frozen. Though he did not move very much as he spoke, he smiled warmly and gazed at us almost with teary eyes. Then he smoked. With each drag of the cigarette, he exhaled, blowing the smoke up into the air like a happy dragon. He'd never done that before. He seemed euphoric.

It was a great pleasure for the rest of us because our father never laughed and played like this.

I thought, "Maybe it's the liquor. Well no, it can't be because he's been drinking for a long time. Or perhaps it's the pain medication he's taking. No, that can't be it either because he's been drinking it for quite some time too—unless today he happened to drink a lot more than usual. Perhaps that's why he's so jolly."

Although we were taken aback by his new look and mood, we joined him. We laughed about very silly things that we had never imagined him even smiling about. And he was actually laughing too. We all were a bit puzzled but at the same time thrilled.

He turned to me, asking, "Edgar, remember when I was working on that patient—working on an abscess in his neck—when a long log of ash from my cigarette suddenly dropped and fell right on the patient's head?"

"Yes," I responded.

Giggling, my father admitted, "At the time, I was so apologetic. I was so embarrassed—but for some reason, when I think of it now . . ." Cracking up with laughter he had to stop speaking. Finally, he managed, "When I think of it now, I can't help but laugh!" And then he broke down in another fit of laughter.

When his giggles subsided, he announced, "I think it's time for us to go to bed." He turned to me and touched me on my shoulder. He did the same to my three younger sisters and my little brother, looking each of us in the eye and then saying goodnight with a warm touch of the hand on the shoulder or cheek. It was a pleasant dinner and a lovely goodnight.

In the morning I heard my mother crying. When I saw her, I immediately knew what had happened.

"Get your grandfather, and call your godfather as soon as possible," she directed me.

My grandfather and my godfather immediately began making funeral arrangements.

The news spread, and family, friends, and neighbors came to our home to offer their condolences. Our many visitors showed genuine grief and sympathy. César was one of the first to come over. He attempted to console my mother and expressed his kindest sympathy for the loss of my father. Then he left to go across town to send a telegram to Miguel.

Later César returned to tell us that he'd received news that Miguel was in the hospital with a serious infection and was not able to travel. Miguel's doctor would not allow him to leave the hospital for six to eight days, at least, but as soon as he could, Miguel would be coming.

We proceeded with the burial because it could not wait.

I was surprised that I did not cry. When I asked myself why, I realized that I knew how greatly my father had been suffering and because of that, his dying seemed a kind of mercy, a relief from his pain.

Because my father often asked César to sing "Ave Maria," César sang this song at my father's funeral. César sang with such spirit and heart and love that he brought everyone at the funeral to tears, including me. Chucho stood, embraced by his twin daughters, with tears streaming from his eyes. My godfather and grandfather stood on either side of my mother.

At the burial I looked at my mother who was weeping, and I felt such intense love for her. With my gaze I tried to tell her that I loved her. She smiled back at me as if she'd heard my whisper. Similar to me, I think she understood that my father's death was for the best because it meant his suffering had ended. She told us that she hoped his journey would be a good one and that he would be amongst angels.

It was a lovely funeral and burial. There were many flowers. All kinds of friends came together, and they all, personally, one-by-one, expressed to my mother their sincere friendship and their unending support for her and the family.

I don't think that anyone in our small town had anything but wonderful and lovely things to say to my beautiful mother. My mom was humbled and smiled at everyone. In fact, she didn't look sad, she looked happy. She looked happy because everyone around her made her feel loved and supported. It made her happy that our family would go on, even though my father had died.

I noticed that I felt taller, more mature, and wiser though I was only nine years old.

My grandfather and I visited the ocean together, and on this visit I truly felt in my heart, mind, and spirit that I was leaving soon. I would miss the wind, the breeze, the moon, and the wonderful walks and times I'd spent with my amazing grandfather. All of this I would profoundly miss—and I could already feel the sadness of saying goodbye.

While walking the wet shoreline together, my grandfather told me, "Your dear brother is coming soon, and you'll be going back to the United States with him."

"How do you know that?" I asked in response.

"I know so, and I know you believe it to be the truth too."

He added, "This will be the beginning of a new life—of challenges and success—for you, *hijo*."

8

I was working in the ER when a young woman was brought in. She was dressed as if on her way to play tennis—wearing a handsome white and red outfit and brand-new tennis shoes. She'd been hit by a drunk driver and was killed instantly, so when they brought her to the ER, she was dead on arrival.

"Judy, I need to speak to her family immediately," I informed the nurse.

"From what we could gather from her possessions, Dr. Hernandez, we think she's from out of state. We think her family is in Virginia. We found their phone number in her address book."

I picked up the phone, took a deep breath, and dialed the number.

"Mrs. Hinton, this is Dr. Hernandez in Phoenix, Arizona..." I began and then proceeded to explain that her daughter had been brought to the hospital but had been pronounced dead.

When I stopped speaking, silence presided over the line. All the while, I could only imagine the devastation the mother must be feeling and the sense of helplessness because not only was her young daughter killed, but this woman was clear across the country, so far away.

Finally, the silence broke.

"What happened?" Mrs. Hinton asked. "Who hit her? Did they arrest the driver? Why did this happen? Are you sure it's my daughter?"

I answered, "Unfortunately—yes."

"I can't speak . . . can't get my voice out. My husband is here and devastated with the news . . . Can we call you back?"

"Yes, ma'am. Please call me back. I won't move from here," I promised and gave her my number.

For me this conversation, which was brief and spontaneous, was absolutely draining, and I knew that for the Hintons it was significantly worse.

When they called back, they told me they were flying to Phoenix and would arrive late at midnight.

Hours later, around midnight, Judy informed me that they had arrived and were waiting for me.

When I appeared before them, Mrs. Hinton asked, "Are you Dr. Hernandez?"

"Yes ma'am, and I'm so sorry . . ."

Mrs. Hinton had fallen to her knees and shook with tears. She leaned toward me, grasping my legs, my knees.

Her husband moved to lift her and hold her.

"Do you think she suffered?" Mrs. Hinton asked between tears.

"From my experience as a surgeon, she probably died right on impact and did not suffer much," I offered. It was not any real consolation, but they asked me, and I was obliged to respond to their question.

I escorted them into the room. We moved aside some curtains to reveal the body of their beautiful daughter. We'd tried to clean her up as much as possible, covering her neck where she had a huge gash that most likely had resulted from the blow that had severed her spine. The nurses and I had tried to hide all of the devastating injuries.

I remembered I'd said to the nurse, "Not only is it awful to lose a loved one, but to be so far away and not be there to comfort her was probably the most devastating thing that this couple could imagine."

Telling family members about the death of a loved one or telling patients about incurable conditions—it's the most difficult task for doctors. It has been and will always be very difficult for all parties.

When I think back to my own father's death, I am grateful that he lived a long and full life. At least he didn't die young. I also think of my brother Miguel who experienced a particular kind of suffering that only relatives living very far away experience when they get news that one of their loved ones has died.

★   ★   ★

Miguel arrived in an old green bus with the words "*Transporte de Michoacán*" written on its side. We all were there to greet him.

Much to my surprise, I experienced no pounding heart or quickened breath. I had no apprehension or anxiety. I felt total tranquility at Miguel's arrival. My mother, however, did not let go of my hand.

My brother exited the bus.

Once again, my beautiful brother was here.

After his first visit two years prior, he'd only written four times and none of his letters spoke anything about me going back with him to the United States. Many times I'd lamented to my grandfather, "Miguel's forgotten about me completely." He always assured me that Miguel was indeed thinking of me and was trying to figure out how to get me there. "The signs are there and written in every one of those letters that he will come for you," he would reassure me.

Miguel was weeping as he walked to us. "I am sorry I wasn't here. I am so sorry," he uttered. He explained that he'd had an abscess on his neck that had penetrated up into his scalp and required two surgeries. We could see the two large cuts on his neck and scalp and the bandages in those areas.

I hugged him. I cried. My grandfather also cried.

Miguel asked that my grandfather and I accompany him to the cemetery.

When we arrived at the cemetery, Miguel approached the fresh plot inscribed with my father's name and fell to his knees.

"Papá," Miguel began, "I beg for your forgiveness because I wasn't here for you at your funeral. I am so sorry about my absence. And years ago, when we had an argument and I moved out of the house and lived with Chucho for a while—I am so sorry. Please forgive me.

"It was Chucho who talked me into going back home, and I thank Chucho for his patience, his kindness, and his advice to return home.

"Papá, I will miss you greatly, and although I have been away for many years, I always thought of you. You were always on my mind."

At this point my grandfather and I began to walk away to give Miguel some private time at the graveside, but he turned to us, saying, "Don't leave. Stay here by my side."

He told my father, again as if conversing with him, "I will be taking Edgar with me back to the United States, and I want your blessing."

I looked at my grandfather, smiled, and hugged him. Then I went to my brother and hugged him. I cried for a while. I hugged him again, and I continued to cry.

My grandfather placed his right arm around my shoulder as a sign that he approved.

We were scheduled to leave in five days.

I needed to think about how I was going to tell my godfather that I would not be going to Germany with him. This was probably the most difficult thing that I needed to do. I admired him and loved him, and I thought that he would also be a great father to me, as I knew my brother Miguel would be too.

My mother and grandfather said they would talk with him, but I told them, "No, I am now grown-up, and I will speak to my godfather myself."

The day after Miguel's return, my godfather came over to visit my brother and apologize for not being at his arrival. He explained that he had many things that he needed to do in the mines in preparation for a load of precious metal that was to be shipped out of the country in two days' time. I told my godfather that I wanted to go to the mines with him and help him. He welcomed me with a smile.

The following day, after breakfast, I set off to the mines to visit him. My brother could not go, so I went with Chucho. Chucho said that he would come with me but would wait outside. There were a couple of farmers that he wanted to visit in that area. He also confessed that he was claustrophobic and did not like to go into the mines. This was fine for me because I wanted to talk to my godfather alone.

When I got there, I put on the hardhat and protective gear, and stepped into a cart with my godfather. We proceeded into the mineshaft.

"It's good to see Miguel again if only for a few days," my godfather stated, as if supplying me an opening because he had already anticipated why I wanted to speak to him.

"Padrino, I've decided that I'm not going to Germany with you. I am going to leave with Miguel back to the United States," I told him.

He had a hardhat on and headlamp, and we were in the dark mineshaft. All this made it difficult for me to see his eyes, but I could tell he had started to cry.

He stopped the cart and with tears in his voice said, "Edgar, I am very happy for you. You belong with your older brother. And at the same time, I am sad for myself. You will be in the United States and I'll be in Germany and I will probably never see you again.

"You have a great future ahead of you, Edgar. Already, you are a grown-up, an old young man. You have already endured many tough things in your life, but overall, those experiences made you grow up. When I look at you, I see a grown-up, not a child. I love you."

Then he put the cart in reverse, and we exited the mineshaft.

Before I left, we hugged again. He cried and I cried.

He said to me, "You know, who would not want you as their son? You're a dream boy for any father. I wrote my wife and told her I was bringing a son with me, and she was delighted. She will also be happy that you are going with your brother to the United States. I think she will agree that you belong with him."

Returning home from the mines, I didn't say a word to Chucho. I felt lonely, sad. Heartbroken is probably the best word for how I felt.

The last few days went by quickly. My mom seemed very happy like a huge load had been taken from her shoulders. She told me to write her letters, be obedient, be smart, be a good student, and remember always that my teachers in the United States were the same as in Mexico and I should consider them like second parents.

She bought me a small toothbrush and a comb, advising, "Take a shower every morning. Brush your teeth and comb your hair. It is very important you take care of your teeth, so you can eat well and grow well. Your hair must always be in place, neatly combed. Your hands and nails must be clean and cut just like César emphasized in school. You should act just the same as when both your teacher and I are with you."

I looked at my mom and felt like crying, but I didn't know if I had any tears left.

The day before my departure, my grandfather took me to a shop, explaining, "*Hijo*, we're going to get you a new, crispy white sackcloth shirt. It's important that you look good for your trip. Your *huaraches* are still in good condition. I think they'll last you a bit longer. Once you are in the United States, you probably won't be wearing them anymore. I image you'll start wearing shoes."

We enjoyed our last coconut popsicles together, which were a favorite of my grandfather's.

"Never forget all these wonderful things that you and your *abuelito* enjoyed together, like these wonderful coconut popsicles. Always remember me and the good times we had together," my grandfather told me.

The following day, we were set to go. The entire town was there. Even the chubby driver with the stained and rumpled clothing. He owned the truck. Sometimes buses would come, sometimes trucks would come. It just happened to be this driver again.

However, this time, I didn't feel angry at him. I'd hated him the first time because he'd taken my brother away. This time, I realized he was actually a very nice man.

I shook his hand and told him, "I'm leaving with my brother on your truck. I'm going with him to the United States of America."

"Wow, aren't you lucky!" was his response.

Then I embraced my mother. She was smiling, not crying. My grandfather hugged me and said, "You know what to do."

I replied, "I know."

I hugged and kissed my sisters and brother.

Then Miguel took me by the hand and helped me up into the back of the truck. I sat at the end of the bench, and Miguel sat next to me. He held my hand.

From that point on, my brother and I became one. He became my true father.

PART TWO

9

The paramedics brought a young boy and girl into the burn unit. The children had just been rescued from a burning truck, so the nurses and I assumed that they'd been in a driving accident.

To make them comfortable the children were given pain medications, and then the assessment took place. It was apparent to me and the other residents that the children did not have life-threatening burns. They were mostly first- and second-degree burns that could be treated with ointments and temporary graphs, but no surgery would be necessary. We made the children comfortable, cleaned them, warmed them up, and put the dressings in place.

After that, I exited the unit to find the parents—and the first thing they did was apologize.

The father began, "Doctor, doctor, we are so sorry. It is our fault. We've been living in the back of a truck."

I realized then that it wasn't a road accident but something else that had resulted in the burns.

"We bought a heater and set it in the bed of the truck. We plugged the electrical line into a nearby house. We hung a large tarp to make a kind of tent over the bed of the truck. And we noticed that the tarp was stained with oil and it smelled a little like gasoline in places—but we were desperate to keep warm," the father explained.

"When all of the sudden we woke in the night and our little boy and little girl's clothes were in flames. They were screaming. We were screaming too. It was chaos. My wife and I wrapped them in blankets and brought them outside to try to kill the fire on them. Our kids were crying, and we tried our best."

The mother inserted, "Doctor, we love our children. We'd

never want to harm them. We are so sorry we used that dirty, stained tarp. It was a bad decision, but we'd never hurt our children on purpose. I am sorry, sir."

"Yes, doctor, I'm sorry too. Please forgive us. We had nowhere else to stay," the father added.

"Mr. and Mrs. Blannon, you don't need to apologize to me or to anyone else. You don't need to offer any explanation. My role is to make your children better. At the hospital we just want to help all of you. And that's what we're doing with your children. Luckily, they won't need surgery, but they'll likely need two or three weeks in the hospital to heal properly," I explained.

All the while I couldn't help but think how this humble couple who deeply loved their children and who also lived from hand to mouth reminded me of so many people in the Mexican town where I grew up. And the tarp over the back of the pickup truck—that brought me back to many decades earlier when I'd made the first leg of the journey out of La Mira and up to the United States.

I wondered if Mr. and Mrs. Blannon would even believe it if I told them that I too sat in the bed of a pickup protected from the elements by a shabby tarp. Luckily, my tarp stayed intact and we didn't experience any problems from it—but the minimal safety the tarps offered and their ramshackle-ness certainly were similar.

★   ★   ★

Looking up from the bench seat, I noticed the crude wooden scaffolding that framed the overhead space above us in the bed of the truck. The thick canvas tarp covering the wooden frame appeared to have originally been white but had been painted yellow and green. There were ten passengers total, five on each side. Canteens of water and small packs of dried coconut were available to us.

Looking down, I considered my brother's shiny shoes versus my *huaraches*. It dawned on me that my footwear was somehow an embarrassment, not that Miguel had ever given any indication of this.

My brother certainly dressed handsomely and smelled good.

The driver had even complimented him, saying he was wearing very nice clothing and sharp shoes. Of course, I thought of the driver as a lousy dresser with a sloppy appearance. But I recognized he was a hard-working man, and being a driver, it wasn't necessary that he dress well. He just needed to drive carefully, and for that, everybody gave him credit.

My mother would always tell us, "Your clothing may not be great. It may not be expensive, but it will always be clean." She also regularly stated, "It's much better to be clean with old clothing than to be dirty with new clothing."

My brother had given no indication at all that he was dissatisfied with my *huaraches*—the possibility had just swooped in and taken hold of my brain. In fact, my brother was very considerate in his treatment of everyone, no matter their clothing or appearance. Miguel maintained good eye contact when he spoke. He would never look at anything else, no stealing glances down at my footwear, instead maintaining his gaze on my face when we talked.

This reminded me of César, who had taught us, "When older people talk to you, you always look them straight in the eye to show that you're listening and understanding all that they're saying to you. Make sure you acknowledge what a person is saying to you. You can do this with a smile, a nod, or you can verbalize that you clearly understand and appreciate what the person is saying."

I think my teacher was right, and Miguel certainly abided by this practice.

Looking up from our feet to his face, I saw that my brother had closed his eyes and was very quiet.

A man sitting opposite us pulled Miguel from his pensiveness by inquiring, "*¿A dónde van?*" Where are you going?

Miguel replied, "We're traveling for the next five days."

"You must be going to the border—*la frontera.*"

"*Sí, eso es correcto,*" Miguel confirmed.

Miguel went on to explain that he lived in Phoenix and had come to get me and that we'd be immigrating to the United States in the next ten days.

The man smiled, saying, "You two are extremely lucky."

Miguel then turned to me to ask, "Can I see your birth certificate?"

I opened my small bag, and there was my birth certificate and also an official letter from my mother in an envelope.

Miguel cautioned, "These are very important documents, so we must protect them. Once we can access our luggage, let's be sure to put them in my suitcase."

After that, he and the man talked for hours. Listening to their conversation made the time pass faster.

Personally, I didn't feel much like talking. I was already missing my grandfather. As far as I could remember, I saw my grandfather every day of my life. I would wait for him after school on his return back home from the farm. The best treat was when we'd get popsicles together. As soon as I greeted him, I could tell he was tired and probably hungry, but he always had time to have a popsicle with me. We would sit together and talk. He would tell me what he did on the farm that day, and I would tell him about school.

I was also thinking about my *padrino*, hoping that he was not upset about my decision not to go to Germany with him. I wanted him to be safe while working his last weeks and days in the mines, especially because the mines were so dangerous. Though my *padrino* was always strict about following regulations so that accidents could be prevented, a few miners had gotten hurt. Luckily no one had ever gotten killed. I just didn't want anything bad to befall my godfather.

Then I started to worry about everyone, all my loved ones, my sisters, my little brother, my mother, my friends, my teacher, Chucho . . . To stop my anxious mind from worrying, I tried to nap, but the rocky, dirt road was very bumpy, making napping pretty much impossible. The bumpy, dusty, unpaved road seemed endless.

I told Miguel, "I can't see anything beyond our truck because of all the dust getting pulled up. I wonder if we could even tell if there's another car behind us."

"Because it's so rough, it isn't a road that many people come through, so we probably won't have many—or any—cars behind us," he replied.

Occasionally, I could make out a farmer with a donkey or groups of farmers in their white sackcloth clothing walking alongside the road. I felt bad that we were throwing all that dust on them. I hoped that our driver would slow down, so they wouldn't get smothered in dust.

After a few hours of talking, Miguel and the other man's conversation subsided.

Then Miguel began speaking to me. "This is going to be a very long trip. We'll change to a bus in the next town, which should be in about three hours. I know this has been a cramped and harsh few hours, but soon it will be better. The bus will be a lot more comfortable with soft seats."

As long as Miguel seemed happy, I was very much okay.

He continued, "It's going to be several days to the border. We'll do some paperwork and wait a few days to get your visa. After that, we will cross and be home."

"Miguel, what's a visa?" I questioned.

"It's a special document issued by a country with your name on it that says you are in the country legally," he explained.

Miguel then removed a card from his wallet and showed it to me, explaining, "There are different kinds of visas. This is mine. It's called a green card." It was a thin card that sat in a protective clear plastic sleeve. It had zigzag lines running across it horizontally.

"Notice that it states that I'm a legal resident of the United States. That means I can live and work there as long as I like. It is one step below citizenship. After five years or so, if a person with a green card is in good standing and has no problems, like their police record must be real clean, then they can apply for citizenship."

A man across from Miguel asked if he could see the card. Miguel reluctantly showed it to him but did not let it go from his hand. Others in the pickup showed interest too.

Miguel continued, "You realize how difficult it is to get a card like this?" At this point he was speaking to everyone in the back of the truck, for we were all mesmerized by what he had to say.

"It took me close to three years to get this card," Miguel admitted.

"Will I get one like yours?" I asked Miguel.

"Yes, but first yours will be a temporary one. Then you can get one later on like mine.

"In addition to the green card, there are other types of visas. One is a work visa that allows a person to work for a limited

Edgar H. Hernandez   83

amount of time in the US, and then they must return home or apply to get it renewed. The other is a visitor's visa that allows a person a certain amount of weeks in the US. After that, they must leave. There is also a student visa. This allows a person to stay in the US while they're attending school full-time, but they must file a report every year promptly to get it renewed.

"I am so blessed to have this green card. It has opened so many doors for me in the most wonderful country in the world. I'll never take it for granted."

As my brother spoke, everyone listened with rapt attention as if they too were yearning to make it to the US where they hoped to find plentiful opportunities for creating a good life for themselves and their families.

Admittedly I felt extremely proud of Miguel who seemed to know so much and share that knowledge so graciously with all around him. I put my arm around his to embrace him. He smiled and gave me a quick wink.

To Miguel and to everyone in the pickup truck, I confidently announced, "I'll get my visa in seven to ten days, and then we'll cross the border to be home in Phoenix, Arizona."

Some people smiled; some laughed.

Miguel noted, "Edgar, it might be a bit tricky to get your visa so quickly, but I know it can be done. I managed to get mine, and I helped your sister Olivia and your brother Pedro get theirs three and a half years ago. I have some experience getting visas."

In a quieter voice, Miguel continued the conversation just to me, saying, "I bought a house in Phoenix. I'm still working on it, making some renovations, and I have a lot more to do. But soon, it will be a home that we can be proud of and comfortable living in. There's a school close by too. So, soon, you'll meet your new teacher."

I smiled and got close to him.

I tried not to ask him too many more questions. My mother had reminded me to be polite and not speak until I was asked questions or if the discussion required me to participate. She told me not to volunteer personal information to other travelers and to always be polite. Admittedly, she got a bit repetitive, saying this same thing to me many times in the days before I left.

Even when I was about to board the truck, my mother

warned me, "I'm still nervous thinking of how you might annoy people by talking too much and asking too many questions. Please just sit tight and mind your brother. I know how you can ask too many questions and how you can get going talking a lot."

It seemed she had coached me well because my brother commented, "You got very quiet. You must be missing everyone."

He was correct, but I didn't elaborate.

At the same time that I was missing everyone and missing my town, I was also overcome with excitement about the new life I was about to start in the United States with my brother. In a sense with each mile that passed, my happy anticipation for the future increased a notch while my sadness and worry about leaving my family and town decreased a notch.

"I don't know about you, Edgar, but I am starving. With the many goodbyes I said this morning, I didn't have a chance to eat much."

"I'm okay. I had a banana and milk with my sisters and Manny this morning," I told him.

And that got me thinking about my siblings more. Somehow, I didn't think they realized what was going on. They probably thought I was coming back, either in a few months or a year or two. And I knew they would soon find out that I probably was not coming back, maybe never. I really thought this was a trip with no return.

Through a small window separating the cab from the bed of the truck, the driver informed us that we would be stopping for a short break.

Los Coyotes, the village that we stopped in, was even smaller than my town. It had a gas refueling station and a small cantina-type restaurant there.

We descended from the bed of the truck and walked to the restaurant. After we sat down, my brother took out his handkerchief and wiped his forehead. Then he took the same handkerchief, turned it around, and patted my forehead with it.

"Let's have a cold drink and relax for awhile," he suggested.

A young lady approached and asked for our order. She was very pretty and smelled really clean. Since my mother emphasized personal hygiene and a tidy presentation, I found I enjoyed noticing and even smelling clean and neat appearances.

I told my brother, "She is cute."

My brother responded, "Yes, she is, and, as you like to say, she also smells good."

The young lady had a long braid of dark hair going down her back. She wore a charming dress with thousands of roses printed on it.

She returned with two cold Pepsis and my favorite—bean tacos.

The bean tacos, of course, made me think of my grandfather. He made the best bean tacos. He'd take a tortilla and apply a smear of beans onto it. Then he would fold it and drop it onto hot coals. With his hands he would turn it over on the coals one or two times until the tortilla was slightly burned. He'd retrieve it from the fire, gently pry it open, and quickly sprinkle cheese right onto the hot beans.

He taught me to hold a jalapeño in one hand and the bean taco in the other. First I'd take a bite of the taco. I'd chew it and taste it. Then I'd take a bite of the jalapeño and chew it and taste it. I'd alternate between the two and try not to sip any water because then I'd wash away all the delicious flavors.

And boy was my grandfather right—it was heavenly eating bean tacos this way.

Once we finished the small meal, the young lady came to us, saying, "My father thinks he knows you."

"Who is your father?" Miguel inquired.

Suddenly, a man approached us. He had a great-looking Emiliano Zapata-like mustache and big, bushy hair. "Are you Miguel Hernandez Cabrera's boy?" he asked.

"Yes. My name is Miguel just like my father."

"I know you because I remember that you came through here before on your way back to the United States. And I know your father, I mean—I *knew* your father."

With tears in his eyes, he continued, "I want you to know how badly I felt when I heard about his passing. The passing of Miguel was really sad for me and for many others in this small town. Your father was a good man. He certainly could drink—probably too much for his wife and kids to bear—and he smoked himself to an early grave . . . but he was good to me."

While I believed this man had insulted our father, Miguel maintained his composure. He didn't bat an eye.

"It is due to your father that I became successful in this little town. He did a lot for me."

With that, the man hugged Miguel and then me.

As we drove away, the man waved goodbye to us. His daughter stood by his side and waved too.

When they were out of sight, I asked, "What did our father do for that man?"

"Many years ago, our father accompanied me on this trip up to the border, and like we did today, he and I stopped in Los Coyotes. There that man came to our father asking for medical attention. The man's hand was severely infected. Apparently, the man had beaten his wife—punched her in the mouth and landed his knuckles into her teeth. Not only did he mess up his wife's mouth, he also hurt his hand. Our father agreed to help him—and also helped his wife—on the condition that the man swear he'd get his act together and stop hitting his wife. Apparently the man has lived up to his word."

I listened dumbfounded and then felt proud of my father. Though the man had pointed out my father's shortcomings with alcohol and cigarettes, when it came to taking care of people and his own family, my father was a most honorable man. I felt lucky to receive such a keen reminder of my newly dead father's caring and valiant nature.

I wanted my brother to tell me more about his life, but I didn't want to badger him with the many things I was wondering about—did he ever have a mustache? How long did it take to learn to drive? How long did he have to work to have the money to buy a car? Could he read and write in English? Did he know other Mexicans in the United States that had become American citizens too? Were there tortillas and bean tacos in the United States or was it some other food? Did he agree with César that the US had a good economy and opportunities? Did he have a bathroom in his house in Phoenix or was it an outhouse? Was there electricity in his house in Phoenix?

I held in my questions and tried to be a good listener. I trusted that I'd get to know him and he'd get to know me because we'd have a lot of time together.

He told me he worked as a silversmith making Navajo jewelry.

I asked, "What does that mean—'Navajo'?"

He explained that the Navajo were a tribe of native people in the United States, similar to the Purépecha and the Tarascans in Michoacán and the many other indigenous groups throughout Mexico.

I told him, "There are probably 175 different indigenous groups in Mexico, and probably about that many or more languages and dialects; however, their numbers are decreasing."

"Edgar, how do you know that?"

"Because my godfather and I talked about it."

"I think you're probably right. In the United States, there are many native people with different backgrounds and different languages too."

Miguel next explained that in 1955 when he was first trying to get his papers together to immigrate into the United States, he was in Nogales, the border town where he and I were going to cross into the United States. Because getting the proper documentation and paying for it was difficult, he ended up finding work in Nogales at a jewelry store.

An American gentleman named Bernard Lambert got to know him because he was interested in some of the jewelry pieces Miguel had made. Mr. Lambert was so impressed with Miguel's work that he offered him a job in the United States. My brother explained to Mr. Lambert that he didn't yet have immigration papers or the money to pay for the process but was working on it.

Over a few weeks my brother got to know Bernard Lambert and his wife, Margaret, fairly well. They came to really like each other, so much so that the Lamberts sponsored Miguel's entry into the US and helped him attain the needed paperwork.

Bernard and Margaret Lambert owned a store that sold Navajo jewelry in Phoenix, Arizona. After sponsoring Miguel with the immigration requirements, they promised him and the US government that he'd have a job waiting for him in Phoenix. This facilitated his immigration.

He explained, "Bernard and Margaret are truly wonderful human beings. And really, I owe them both my life."

When he'd arrived in Phoenix, he lived in a small apartment above the jewelry workshop. "We'll be living there for a while until I finish renovating the house."

He explained that everyone called Bernard "Doc" because

he had a dental degree and once was a dentist. However, once he'd started practicing dentistry, he found he didn't have the patience and steadiness of hand needed to repair people's teeth. After he broke the teeth of some patients, he realized he was creating more problems than he was fixing, so he decided to stop practicing dentistry.

Then he got into the jewelry business. Mr. and Mrs. Lambert owned the biggest Indian jewelry wholesale company in Phoenix and had over forty employees, all Navajo Indians with the exception of Miguel.

"As a matter of fact," Miguel confided, "I speak better Navajo than English. Because I spend forty or more hours a week with 39 Navajo men, I'm fluent in the Navajo language."

Finally, the truck arrived in a small, charming city with cobblestone streets. The air was cool, not as humid as it was in La Mira. At the city center there was a shady park with many benches and large green trees.

It was late afternoon, so first we found some accommodation near the bus station, and then we got some dinner.

After dinner, we had ice cream. It was the first time that I tasted ice cream, and I was in heaven.

My brother told me, "Just wait, once we get to the United States, the ice cream is even creamier, richer, colder, and tastier. I will buy you five different types of this American ice cream."

"Five different types—that exists?"

"Yes, there's strawberry, chocolate, coffee, mint, vanilla."

I asked, "What's 'vanilla'?"

"Vanilla is a flavor . . . but I can't really explain it. It's different than strawberry or orange or pineapple. It's its own thing. I don't know exactly what it is or how to explain it. You'll just have to see."

"Oh, okay," I responded, a bit confused and dissatisfied with the explanation.

After ice cream, we walked back to our room. Miguel put his arm around me, almost like he was protecting me. It made me feel really good.

In the morning at the bus station we observed nearby vendors opening up the doors to their stores. Some placed signs, produce, or other items they were selling in the space in front of their shop. It seemed a daily routine.

Just as Miguel had promised—we were going to ride a real bus for this leg of the journey. I actually recognized the bus we got into because it looked like the one my brother had been on when he'd arrived in our town just about a week earlier. These kinds of buses only entered our town occasionally, depending on the weather and time of year. When it rained, that bumpy, dusty road we'd spent the previous day traveling on would become a river of thick mud that only smaller trucks could get through.

This bus was called *"Sonorense,"* which indicated that it traveled to the northern state of Sonora.

My brother explained, "We will be changing buses at various points on the journey today and stopping to take breaks. Because they all look alike, you need to be careful not to become confused and get on the wrong bus. What you do is notice the number at the top corner of the bus's windshield and get to know the driver. You want to be sure to get back on the correct bus after a break.

"This bus is taking us to a bigger city. And guess what? The city has electricity. It's got streetlights, and there's even lights that control the traffic. You'll see the lights turn green, red, and yellow. Green means that cars can go. When it's red, cars must stop. The yellow means cars just take it easy—they can move forward or stop, depending on what makes the most sense."

Honestly, I didn't know what he was talking about.

He continued, "The city that we will arrive at is called Uruapan. It's the second largest city in Michoacán. Then, later, we'll enter another state called Jalisco."

I told my brother, "Everything is coming together. Many of the engineers that worked in the mines with my godfather went to school in some of these cities and states. The capital city of Jalisco is Guadalajara, and it is the second largest city in the country."

"You are correct, Edgar. And eventually we'll be passing through Guadalajara. But first, Uruapan. Get prepared for a long trip because it's going to take about ten hours to get to Uruapan. At least the ride will be more comfortable than yesterday's since we are in a bus with cushioned seats. The seats are so nice that we can easily take naps on the way. You'll really like Uruapan too. It is picturesque with old buildings and great open markets."

I couldn't wait.

The bus was full of all sorts of passengers that appeared to come from different backgrounds. Some were well-dressed and looked like business people. There were a lot of people with beautiful jackets of different colors and different stripes. Some people looked like farmers like my grandfather in white sack-cloth drawstring pants and a shirt of the same material. Some of them also wore machetes like my grandfather on their belts. The bus was loaded with fruit the farmers were taking to the markets of Uruapan—avocados, tomatoes, guavas, apples, and bananas of various sizes. They were hoping to sell them for a higher price than what they'd get in their villages. A lot of the people that were on the bus were well groomed and tidy.

"Soon, Edgar, you will see a television and a telephone."

"What are those?" I asked, puzzled. As a nine-year-old child from a town in Mexico in the year 1959, I'd never heard of these things.

My brother explained, "A telephone is a machine for talking to someone like they are near you, yet they are very far away."

I found this quite scary. I had seen a radio that my godfather had, but it wasn't scary the way this telephone sounded. I was unsure that I even wanted to see such a thing.

I had experienced electricity before, but it came from generators and was used rarely, only at special events in La Mira. For example, there were some generators in our town plaza to create electricity for night events. My godfather also had several generators to create power in the mines. One of the subjects he explored with me was how batteries functioned and how electricity was conducted to provide lighting. He had warned me, "Don't touch those thick black wires. They're full of juice, and they can harm you." I knew what he'd meant by "juice" because I'd seen someone touch one of those wires, and they got burned badly.

As we moved farther and farther from my town, I'd think of the beloved friends and family whom I was leaving behind and whom I already missed so much. I did not want to think about them, but it seemed that as soon as I would talk about something, then someone would come back into my mind.

My brother pointed out the window I was sitting next to, saying, "Look at the river. Do you know what river that is?"

"Yes," I replied, "It's the same river that passes by our town, the Río Balsas. Abuelito told me to look for it. He said a long time ago, he was passing by the river on his way to the farm when he spotted a bottle floating in it. The bottle was plugged with a piece of cork. He pulled out the cork and found a note inside. Even though Abuelito can't read or write, he somehow understood it was a note from a boy and girl in Uruapan. I don't know what the note said, but it delighted Abuelito when he discovered it and thought of all the miles it had traveled to reach him."

I went on to joke, "Miguel, do you think the driver will stop to let me drop a bottle into the river to send a note to Abuelito?"

My brother laughed at this suggestion.

My brother started a conversation with a young couple. He learned that they were going to Uruapan to go to school.

When they asked about us, my brother responded, "This is my little brother, Edgar. He and I are going back to the United States."

At that half a dozen passengers turned to look at us. "Yes," my soft-spoken brother repeated, "we are going to the United States of America to a place called Phoenix, Arizona."

The faces peering at us looked amazed and intrigued as if they were wondering, "How can we get there too?"

After ten hours on a very dry, dusty, bumpy road, we finally arrived in Uruapan, a very impressive city with many fancy old buildings, cobbled streets, beautiful stores, and impressive open markets.

When my brother and I got off the bus, I couldn't contain myself, taking in everything around me, almost as if the whole city were spinning. I had never seen such a beautiful place. There were green trees throughout. I noticed stalls loaded with the loveliest-smelling fruits and produce. I saw fruits that I had never seen before—pears, apples, peaches, and grapes. These were nonexistent in the small town where I was born. The air temperature was noticeably cool. The clouds seemed loaded with water and ready to break forth with rain at any moment.

Miguel advised, "Let's get to the hotel and take care of accommodations. We're going to have another long ride to-morrow to another city called Morelia. If you think this city is beautiful, wait till you see Morelia."

I asked, "How is Morelia more spectacular than this city?"

"For one thing, Morelia is the capital city of Michoacán, so it has fancy government buildings. And there are a lot of universities there, so it is full of the energy of ideas and learning. It is busy every day and night with Mexican students eager to pursue an education in order to become professionals. Soon you will see what I mean about Morelia."

At the hotel, to the right of the desk counter, stood a large box with a curved piece of glass making up one of its sides. Music and conversation and people in shades of gray appeared in the glass. It was a television.

I had heard people in my town discuss music and film stars, like Cantinflas, Ignacio López Tarso, Meche Barba, Pedro Infante Cruz, Jorge Negrete, and the Soler brothers. People talked about them, but we never saw them, so now in catching a glimpse of the venue of the stars—the television—it was amazing, almost like a dream.

In addition to the television, there were cars in abundance. Just standing inside the hotel we could hear layers of honking from cars, honking that sounded ceaseless to my ears. While the hotel staff prepared our room, Miguel and I walked outside, and there before us—a multitude of boxy, metallic, wheeled rats racing around a maze. It was approaching dark, so headlights started turning on in the cars. It was marvelous to see and hear the multitude of squawking cars with brilliantly lit orbs beaming from their fronts.

Our room was on the highest floor of the hotel, and looking out the windows from up there, I felt like I was miles up in the air. In reality the hotel was only three to four levels high, but to me, the height was staggering. Out the windows I could see the many beeping cars with their glorious beams of light shining before them. Also I saw shimmering strokes of light being discharged from the windows of other city buildings. A city with electricity at night—I'd never seen anything like it before in my life.

With disbelief in my voice, I asked my brother, "So Morelia's even bigger and prettier?"

He replied, "Absolutely. There are bigger buildings, and the buildings are more elaborate. You'll be surprised at how beautiful it is. I promise you. And one more thing, in Morelia, we're going to have hot chocolate."

I knew chocolate, but "hot chocolate" I had no clue about. I figured it must be nothing short of delectable.

"And then wait till we go up north into the United States. You're going to have a drink called a milkshake. Imagine ice cream mixed with milk to make a thick, cold, creamy slurry that you both eat and drink at the same time, and you can get flavors added in like chocolate, strawberry, and vanilla—yeah, I know you still don't understand vanilla. But in about a week, you are going to be having a milkshake."

Just when I thought I couldn't be even more puzzled, surprised, or delighted—I learned about the milkshake.

Once downstairs, we sat at a table and ordered food. It ended up being a fantastic dinner. We had a delicious soup made of chicken broth with brown rice and chopped lettuce with a little lemon juice and salsa sprinkled in. Then they brought my favorite—bean tacos. Miguel had a mole, which is a spicy chocolate sauce that goes over chicken. Moles are very tasty and have always been a favorite food of mine.

As we were finishing our dinner, Miguel asked, "Remember I told you about a telephone?"

"Yes."

"Do you see that object on top of the counter? That's a telephone right there. You can pick that telephone up and call any place in Mexico. As a matter of fact, you can probably talk to anyone in the world."

"Do you think we could take a closer look at it after dinner?"

After dinner, we approached the device. Miguel explained, "You pick the telephone up here and dial the numbers here. Everybody has a different number. When you get to Phoenix, you'll have a number."

"Really? I will have my own number?" I asked excitedly.

"Well, not exactly your own number, but we hope that we'll have a telephone in our house once the house is fixed—and that telephone will have a number. We'll also get a television."

That was unbelievable—our own telephone and our own television too!

"All sorts of movies and shows are on TV in Phoenix. There are American movies and—actually, there are no Mexican movies on TV, but in the near future, there probably will be. There is a Mexican theater in Phoenix, and we can go there."

We went outside and walked towards the central square, taking in the busy nightlife lit by cars, light from windows, and even the occasional street light. It appeared so exotic to me.

The plaza was majestic with its many lights and trees and cobbled walking paths. Many people were strolling about. There were grandparents, grandchildren. There were children with their parents, families all holding hands. They sat on benches in the park and ate ice cream. There were ice cream vendors all over the place, so we ordered some ice cream. I had coconut ice cream, which I found creamier and smoother than the coconut popsicles I enjoyed with my grandfather. My brother had pineapple ice cream, which was also delicious. I was having the time of my life.

The blowing of car horns woke us in the morning.

"Edgar, let's get moving and not waste any time because the bus to Morelia leaves right at nine. It won't wait."

We purchased our tickets with time to spare.

As we walked along a long, ornate corridor with an open courtyard on one side, the alluring smells of freshly baked breads, rolls, and pastries reached our noses. It smelled so delicious.

Miguel, who loved Mexican pastries, decided, "It's going to be kind of a long ride, about five hours, so let's get some *pasteles.*"

After purchasing some pastries, we boarded the bus. Since we were only the second and third passengers to board, we had an almost complete selection of seats to choose from. I ran all the way to the back and did some cushion-testing to find the perfect seats.

"Boy, they're all really soft. This bus is a lot nicer than the others," I called out to Miguel.

"Yes, the buses will get nicer the farther we go up north," he replied.

As always, I chose a window that offered an optimal people-watching position. I always imagined that I would see my grandfather walking along the side of the road coming from his farm, but it seemed the farther north we traveled, there were fewer and fewer people on the side of the road who looked like traditional farmers like my grandfather. I would see more business people, people on bicycles, and people in cars.

In addition to watching people outside the bus, I made sure to look at every passenger boarding the bus. They all were very polite. They would greet each other, *"Buenos días,"* *"Buenos días,"* *"Buenos días."* I could hear almost every passenger exchanging greetings. It seemed they wanted to sit down, get comfortable, and strike up a conversation because they knew it would be a thoroughly boring ride if there was no talking.

I noticed a pretty lady wearing a dainty cap. It seemed in Uruapan many men and women wore fancy hats and elegant jackets. My brother explained that the city of Uruapan had a lot of textile factories, and salesmen would bring fabric from Uruapan to bigger cities to sell. Then they would return, place more orders, and leave again with more fabric to sell. This was everyday business there. And that probably explained why we were seeing so many men and women wearing handsome clothing and hats.

The young lady with the beautiful, purple hat sat in the seat right across the aisle from my brother. As soon as she sat down, she dropped her purse, and my brother picked it up and gave it to her, which seemed to break the ice for a long conversation. I slept for the first hour or two, but I could hear them talking. They talked about everything. She was a hairdresser, worked in a beauty shop, and also manufactured dresses. She said that women would come to see her, and she would take measurements and make dresses for them, usually for weddings or other special occasions.

As we traveled, the roads got nicer. As a matter of fact, in the smaller towns and villages we passed through, I saw electrical poles with long, drooping wires running between them, something that I had never seen before.

"Soon we will be in the beautiful city of Morelia, but first, we're going to be stopping in a slightly smaller city called Zamora. That's where your sister Surama lives, and we are going to see her for a few minutes. They give us about two hours there because they have to load and unload goods from the bus and wait for new passengers. Once we arrive, I'm going to run and find Surama and bring her over, so she can meet you. I want you to wait for us next to the bus."

At the Zamora bus station, I waited twenty minutes for

Miguel to return. When he finally came back, he was walking with a beautiful lady.

"Edgar, this is your sister Surama. She lives here, and she's going to university here," Miguel said by way of introduction.

Though Surama was my sister, I was a baby when she'd left home, so I never knew her. She was ten or twelve when she left. She left to go to a convent, but that didn't pan out.

Surama hugged me and gave me a kiss, saying both to me and to Miguel, "You must stay here. You have to stay here. You can't leave."

My brother explained, "We have to leave because I have to get back to work. I only have a short amount of time, and I've already stretched it."

The bus driver announced, "If you're going to Morelia, it's time to board!"

Miguel and Surama hugged. Then she gave me a hug and a kiss and told me that someday we would see each other again.

My brother was very quiet for a while. He didn't say anything for thirty minutes, and I didn't want to bother him. Though I had a lot of questions about my sister, I decided to wait until later to inquire. I think he was probably sad that Surama couldn't come with us. I wasn't sure exactly. What I did know was that she was beautiful, she was in a good place, and she was safe, and all that made me happy.

About fifty minutes into this hour-long ride, the road started ascending and the bus climbed higher and higher in altitude. At the summit I could see a spectacular city at a slight descent before us. The whole scene was absolutely sensational. The road going into the city was surrounded by large pine trees, trees I had never seen before—tall, thick in diameter, with dark green tassels.

I asked my brother, "What type of trees are those? I have never seen them before."

"It happens that in Morelia it gets really cold, and it even snows. In these types of places where it snows, you find pine trees. You're not going to see them in Phoenix. But up north past Phoenix, there's snow, and you'll be able to see the same kind of tree."

Pine trees surrounded the Morelia bus station too. After getting off the bus I walked to one of the trees and pulled a small branch down to my face. I breathed in the unique scent of pine—crisp, woody, sappy, tingly effervescence—a scent I had never before experienced.

When I returned to Miguel, I promptly asked, "So there's trees like this to the north of Phoenix? How big is Phoenix? Is it bigger than Morelia?"

"Yes, Edgar, it's bigger than Morelia. Phoenix's buildings are bigger, and there are more of them. The difference is that Phoenix is flat, it's spread out, and it is terribly hot during the summer, something that you'll adapt to with time."

He went on, "To deal with the heat, we have swimming pools. We swim in swimming pools."

That was something else I had never heard of before, so he explained to me what a swimming pool was. Again, it sounded unreal, dreamlike, this United States of America.

We arrived at our hotel and found seats in some interesting chairs. They were made out of wood, but their seat bottoms and back portions were made out of cowhide. You could even see the fur sloughing up in certain segments of the leather.

I could tell that my brother was exhausted. I didn't know whether it was due to all the conversations, all the people he had met, all the hours on the road. I didn't know how much rest he'd gotten during his stay in La Mira. He was probably still exhausted from doing the trip to arrive in La Mira, but he'd had to make this return trip before adequately recovering, like he was doing a double trip. I could tell that he needed to rest, so I clamped down on my conversation and questions.

After a small dinner, Miguel made sure that we went out and got some hot chocolate. In Morelia to make hot chocolate they took a tablet of chocolate. It was about a half-inch thick and two inches in diameter. They put it in hot milk and let it disintegrate. It made an outstanding hot chocolate and had just a hint of cinnamon. And we didn't just drink it. We took a non-sweet bread and dipped it into the hot drink. After soaking it a bit, we could bite off some of the bread. In this way we ate and drank the thick, warm, chocolate-cinnamon drink. It was delectable.

The following day, we woke to a gorgeous morning. On our walk to the bus station, I admired the wide cobblestone streets dotted with lampposts. Large trees and lots of flowers decorated the streets. I saw many gardens featuring all sorts of different colored flowers. Morelia smelled so clean and fresh. Even the slight wind carried with it the aroma of sweet blooms.

Our destination after Morelia was Guadalajara, the second largest city in Mexico and the mecca of some of the biggest and most prestigious universities in the world, according to what my brother and many people that were traveling with us told me. At the bus station we met many people that had relatives studying a variety of different professions at the University of Mexico at Guadalajara.

As we sat waiting to board the bus for this eight-hour ride, my brother told me, "It's going to be a fascinating trip today, Edgar, because we will be traveling along the edge of one of the biggest lakes in the country—Lake Chapala."

I told my brother, "I know about Lake Chapala because Abuelito told me everything about it. He said he fished in it when he was young, but he said it took almost a month for him to reach it from his home village. He told me he caught healthy, white, tasty fish."

"He told you the truth, and you will be able to taste the fish because we're going to stop and have lunch by the side of the lake. You'll be able to see how pretty and big the lake is."

On the bus ride I saw fishermen fishing along the side of Lake Chapala and also out in the lake. I saw many people packing fish to take to market.

A gentleman sitting near us told my brother that this lake could possibly feed the entire country for several years. I thought that was interesting. I, personally, did not think that people would like to eat fish every day. I, for one, preferred to eat beans every day. But I realized this wasn't the point of his comment, so I didn't share my opinion.

Miguel explained that Guadalajara was the second largest city in Mexico with very tall buildings and glorious, wide streets. "You won't find any cobblestone streets there. Guadalajara's streets are smooth and black. They are so smooth that you could roller skate on them without tripping."

"Miguel, do you think I might be able to get a pair of roller skates sometime once we settle down?" I asked.

"I'll see what I can do."

After that, he was kind of quiet for a few minutes. I could tell that he was deep in thought.

One thing I noticed about my brother was that he some-times stared out into the open sky, as if in a trance. Sometimes Miguel was so deep in thought that he became totally oblivious to everything around him. I knew not to disturb him when he was in this state.

A man sitting nearby shared that his son was attending university in Guadalajara. "He's studying to be a lawyer, and eventually he hopes to go to the United States. I've got a very good friend that works in the American steel business, and my friend promised to help my son immigrate if he wants to do more studies in the United States."

When I heard him say that, I told him, "Sir, I'm going to the United States with my brother, Miguel. He lives in the United States, and he's got a really excellent job. He owns a Ford car."

The gentleman replied, "I would like to meet him."

I felt like telling the gentleman, as my brother had said ear-lier about the skates, "I'll see what I can do," because somehow, all of the sudden, I didn't want anyone bothering my brother just then. I felt very protective of him because he was in a with-drawn, concentrated state.

Eventually my brother turned to the gentleman and said, "I'm happy for you and your son, sir. You should be proud of him. Studying law and wanting to go to the United States are great and noble goals. I think he will do very well. As I say to my brother, Edgar, if you set your mind to something you really want to do, it will become reality. It just depends on how badly you want it. My brother, Edgar, someday will go to university also."

At these words I felt very happy. I felt my brother's great af-fection for me and his recognition of my deep desire to become someone of importance in the United States.

My brother had an ability to make friends—with anyone, anywhere, any time. If there were a competition regarding making friends with strangers, my brother would beat anybody easily. He wasn't shy, but he was soft-spoken. He always looked people in the eye and communicated in a way that I saw as unusual yet interesting and inspiring.

In every contact that he made on our entire journey, I noticed his open, kind facial expressions and the gentleness in the way he shook hands and embraced people. He conveyed love. He conveyed affection. He conveyed trust. He conveyed sympathy. Because of that, I think he was able to make friends quite readily, a talent shared by too few people.

Once we arrived at the Guadalajara bus station, this gentleman insisted on buying us dinner. He was an extremely polite, well-dressed man, with very nice manners. He seemed to be educated too.

After dinner the gentleman accompanied us to the train station. In saying goodbye, my brother gave him his address in Phoenix and told him if ever he visited Phoenix, he'd be happy to open his home to him as a friend of the family. They embraced like they'd known each other for a long time.

We bought our tickets and boarded the train.

While I had seen pictures of trains, I had never seen one in real life or ridden on one, so I was very excited about this part of the journey.

My brother explained that as we slept, the train would take us way up north and we'd wake near the border.

All night, I could not sleep due to my excitement about the ride and my anticipation about our final destination. I knew we were getting closer and closer. My animation seemed unrestrained.

I was not worried when my brother told me he would place me in a school in Phoenix, Arizona, soon after we arrived. He said I would have to learn English really quickly, so I could do my schooling and not fall behind. This challenge did not bother me. In fact, I was looking forward to it. I remembered that my godfather was born in Germany and spoke German, yet he became fluent in Spanish.

I tossed and turned, thinking of what my teacher would look like, what type of friends I would meet, and how it would be to speak English fluently. I imagined myself riding a bicycle, roller-skating, and playing baseball, things I had wanted to try but could not do because we didn't have these options in La Mira.

I think I only slept one hour, and I woke happy and ready to go. I had a smile on my face when I woke. I took a shower, combed my hair, and brushed my teeth.

I'd thought the train was going to take us directly to Nogales, the border town, but that was not the case. The train took us to Hermosillo, a charming town that was filled with red flowers. Every place that I looked, I saw flowers in bloom. I think that that was the reason they named it Hermosillo because *hermosa* means beautiful and in this town there were lovely flowers along the streets, along the sidewalks, and in every home. Miguel explained to me that it was a huge agricultural town with lots of booming agriculture-related businesses.

From Hermosillo, we had to take one more bus to reach Nogales. After that, we would finally cross the border.

On the bus Miguel explained that he had made arrangements to have a few individuals help us with the process of immigration. "These people are well educated, experienced, and have very good intentions in helping us immigrate. It's their business, helping people with the documentation. They've helped me in the past, and I trust them completely."

This concept of immigration was a curiosity to me. I didn't know what was required to go across the border. I knew we needed documents and that we had documents, but I did not understand all the specifics or why we'd need to hire professionals to help us.

In our travels I'd heard bits and pieces about difficulties communicating with the American immigration officers and how all the regulations could be confusing. I wondered how long it would take us to get the documents I didn't yet have. Also I wondered what possible problems could occur. I kept my questions to myself, but I remained vigilant.

"Edgar, this is our final bus ride. We should arrive in Nogales by nightfall. Early tomorrow morning, we'll visit a very important man who is very tall and very skinny. He's as experienced with helping in the immigration process as he is tall—so we are in good hands. He's a professional accountant and also has a business helping people gather the correct documentation for immigration. He's very competent. So we don't have to worry. Let's get some rest until then," Miguel told me.

Finally, we arrived in the busy and fast and noisy city called Nogales.

As Miguel had told me, it was a very important commercial border town with an abundance of traders and buyers for home-building goods, such as timber and tiles of all types. Americans went to Nogales to buy unique roofing materials, internal home materials, and ornaments made out of wrought iron.

"Americans come to Nogales and buy these materials. Then they resell them to other people in the United States who use them to construct large, fancy homes called 'mansions.' Nogales is a city where a lot of people do a lot of business. People are making a lot of money here, and they work really hard at it. It's a very active, productive city as you will soon see."

And Miguel was correct. I soon discovered for myself the ceaseless hustle and bustle of Nogales.

10

I was sitting at my desk, writing notes, as I waited for my next patient. I knew he was a man with a diagnosis of breast cancer, and we were to discuss the mastectomy I'd be performing on him.

When he entered my office, I was immediately struck by his height—he must have been at least six feet, nine inches tall—and the particularity of his features. He had strikingly thin facial hair, equally thin facial features, and his arms and legs were very, very skinny and seemed disproportionately long relative to his torso. His fingers resembled overly long and delicate twigs.

I realized that this man likely had Klinefelter's syndrome, a not uncommon genetic disorder that only affected men. It wasn't until I was in medical school that I learned the name of the syndrome, Klinefelter's, but it was when I was a child in 1959 that I'd first encountered it when I'd met Aurelio.

In the way he spoke, moved, and gestured, this patient reminded me so much of Aurelio. He seemed an American replica of my Mexican supporter, expert, and friend. This patient provided a welcomed reminder of an exceptional man that had done so much for me and my family many decades earlier.

★   ★   ★

Early in the morning, we went to meet Aurelio, the immigration documentation professional.

Aurelio's assistant told us to go ahead into his office and that he would be in shortly to see us.

Soon after we sat down, Aurelio entered. He was so tall that he had to hunch down to fit underneath the door entrance and avoid hitting his head. In addition to his extraordinary height, his face was noticeably skinny and long. He had drooping eyes, drooping skin, and very long arms. His wrists stuck out approximately three inches beyond the end of his shirtsleeves.

My brother stood to shake his hand. Then he introduced me to Aurelio.

When Aurelio spoke, he spoke very softly. In listening, I thought I might have a hearing problem. I just couldn't hear him most of the time. My brother later confided that he had to pay very careful attention to what Aurelio said because of how quietly Aurelio spoke.

We started by socializing. Aurelio wanted to know the details of our trip, almost as if we were related to him or were really good friends.

Aurelio asked, "What do you think your father died from?"

My brother, still sad from the loss, explained, "We don't know. He was a heavy smoker and a heavy drinker so that likely factored into his death."

Aurelio sighed and took a long, deep inhale. He flattened his hand out on his desk and responded, "I'm familiar with situations like that. People who drink and smoke a lot typically don't live very long. They often live very miserable lives. I hope this wasn't true for your father."

Aurelio would pause when he spoke to take in multiple short, deep breaths. It seemed he was contesting for air, and coordinating speaking and breathing was a challenge for him.

Then we moved onto business. "There are a lot of people trying their luck at immigration," Aurelio began.

He said this as if he didn't endorse immigration, like it was truly a gamble for anyone trying to gain entry in the immigration process. He seemed to suggest the success rate wasn't very good.

With this opening statement, my hope deflated some. I decided I was not very impressed with Aurelio.

"Tell me about the financial situation of Edgar's mother and the rest of the family."

"They will be okay for a while," Miguel responded.

"What do you mean 'for a while'?"

"They have enough money and so forth to last them for a fairly good amount of time."

Aurelio explained, looking my brother straight in the eye, "You understand that the process of immigration is evolving, becoming more and more complex every day. It seems that it's taking longer and longer to do things. It's taking longer to process applications. It's taking longer to be called after your application is processed. It is not as seamless and straightforward as it was even in just the last four or five years since you did it, Miguel."

It took Aurelio a significant amount of time to get these words out. Plus, his movements were noticeably slow. I thought to myself, "This man needs more energy, something to rev him up, so he can move faster and talk faster—and talk louder." Also I figured he must have been born with this slow manner.

My brother remained patient.

Aurelio then asked, "Okay, what specifically is going on? What do you need?"

"We need to get documents for my brother to immigrate."

At that Aurelio looked at me and asked, "So, you want to go to the United States?"

"Yes sir," I replied.

He turned to my brother and asked, "When you were here several weeks ago, we talked about your job. Do you still have a job?"

My brother responded, "I think so."

Aurelio raised his hands and warned, "You better, or this will never work. Your brother will never get a visa."

My brother explained that his boss was a man of his word. Apparently Mr. Lambert had told Miguel that he could take six weeks off or longer to do whatever he needed to do, and it would be fine.

Aurelio responded, "Well, they tell you one thing, and then they do another."

My brother retorted, "Not Mr. Lambert. He and his wife, Margaret, are different. They are kind, and they would never lie to me. They always keep their word. They always tell me, 'Miguel, you are one of our best workers, and we love you very much.' I have complete confidence in my boss."

"We'll see about that," Aurelio maintained. "You need to call him and get his status on your job. That's very important. You will need a letter, so don't waste too much time talking to him, okay? Forget about formalities. It is very important. You have got to have a letter regarding the status of your job. The letter must clearly state how long you have been working for him, how much you make, and how secure your job is."

Aurelio then started writing a list on a piece of paper. It took him quite a while to write everything down.

My brother and I behaved like we had all the time in the world, yet we desperately wished Aurelio could speed up.

Finally, he completed the list. He stood and, hunching over us like a palm tree, handed the piece of paper to my brother.

"Get this done, the sooner the better," Aurelio urged.

My brother glanced at the list and then thanked Aurelio.

Before we departed, Miguel asked, "What is the fee? I'd like to pay you now."

"Later. Just get these things done. We'll deal with it later. We have a lot more work to do."

With that response, I revised my initial thinking some, "I guess he does care about us. He's not here to make fast money out of us."

There were seven items on the list:

One—a letter from Miguel's boss regarding job security, length of time he had been working for Mr. Lambert, and his current salary.

Two—proof of Miguel's housing. Rental agreement or documentation of home ownership.

Three—a letter regarding Miguel's financial status and potential debt.

Four—a police record.

Five—if Miguel owned an automobile, proof of ownership.

Six—letters of reference from three coworkers.

Seven—a character reference from a church or a friend outside his work.

Aurelio advised Miguel to make some phone calls immediately. He directed us to another room that had five telephones in different crevices on the wall. A sign read, "Pay the attendant prior to using the phone. The attendant will connect you to the number you are calling."

With Aurelio's permission, Miguel proceeded to make some calls.

Naturally, I was delighted to see a room full of these futuristic talking machines. Plus, I'd get to watch Miguel use one!

It was on one of these calls that I heard Miguel speak English for the first time. To me, it sounded good. I didn't know how it would sound to other people. He seemed to stumble only a little as he was talking, but I didn't know any better since I didn't know a single word of English myself.

We learned that it would take about ten days for all of the letters and documents to get to us in Nogales. My brother was surprised that it wouldn't take any longer.

During the ten days of waiting, I thought that my brother would become frustrated, but he didn't seem to or, at least, he didn't show it.

Finally, we had every document except the police record from the Phoenix Police Department to show that Miguel had no criminal history. When Miguel called a trusted friend in Phoenix who was helping to gather the various documents, he learned that he needed to go personally to the police station to get the police record. It couldn't be done by a friend or by mail.

He hung up the phone, paused a moment, and turned to me to say, "Here is the situation. I have to go to Phoenix to take care of that final document, but it will be fine because I can bring my car back, and then we can drive back together. We'll end up saving time."

He explained that he would talk to Brenda, Aurelio's secretary, to see if she could check up on me at the hotel.

"Miguel, don't worry about me. I'll be fine. I'll be smart and take care of myself. I just want you to go on to Phoenix, be careful, and return safely and not worry about anything."

"I'll talk to Brenda and Aurelio. They'll help you if you need anything."

By that time, I'd started feeling much better about Aurelio. I realized that his manner and his physique were quite unusual, but I knew that he was sincere in caring about the people he worked with. The more we met with him, the more I warmed up to him.

Occasionally, he would put his arm on my shoulder. I always felt that when people put their arms on someone's shoulder, it meant something—they liked you, they cared about you, and they wanted to protect you. It was something that the men who had cared most for me in La Mira—my *abuelito*, my *padrino*, and Chucho—had done. It made me feel special when Aurelio would tap me on the shoulder or put his hand on my shoulder to make a point.

I was thrilled to see Miguel when he returned three days later.

I also got to see his beautiful 1954 Ford Fairlane. It was a very light green color. It had two doors, luxurious white leather seats, a very shiny steering wheel, and shiny hubcaps on the tires. It had circular headlights in the front, and long, rectangular red lights in the back. The tires were even painted white on their sides. It was a stunning vehicle. I was dying to get into it and take a ride.

Miguel brought me a "real" shirt and a "real" pair of pants too. I only had the two outfits of white sackcloth that I'd brought with me for the trip. I would wash one outfit every two days in the hotel sink, and as they were drying, I would wear the other shirt and pants, switching off every two days. My mother was very serious about cleanliness, and she would definitely die if she knew that I was wearing dirty clothing. She just would never accept that.

Most importantly—my brother had all the necessary documents.

We immediately went to Aurelio's.

Aurelio scanned all the documents for a final review. He looked at every piece of paper, page by page, line by line.

Finally, he looked up at my brother and announced, "You did a great job. These letters speak very highly of you. I am impressed."

With a smile my brother stated, "I told you that I have a really good boss. The Lamberts really love me. They're really good to me, and they're excited about my brother. I told them everything about Edgar, and they're just dying to meet him. Margaret was delighted when I told her about him."

Those words certainly affected me. This lady who didn't even know me already wanted to meet me.

Aurelio looked up and said with enthusiasm, "You know something? I think things are looking very good for both of you."

Considering that Aurelio had been so skeptical when we'd first met with him and he generally didn't show much enthusiasm, his optimism meant something.

He continued, "Okay, everything looks good. Let's have a

look at the birth certificate. Plus, you have a letter from Edgar's mother, giving you total power of attorney regarding Edgar."

After looking at these, he concluded, "Your documents are complete. You did a great job. Let's go."

On our way to the Consulate, Aurelio reminded us, "You'd be surprised that over half the people waiting at the Consulate not only don't have all the documentation, but they don't even know what documentation they are supposed to have. They are waiting and waiting and have no clue what they are doing. So many folks think they can get a visa with a birth certificate and maybe one other paper. It just doesn't work like that. Then they run from one place to another like a chicken with its head cut off, wasting time, money, and energy. By the time they decide to consult with me, they hardly have the will to pursue the necessary legwork required or the money to finance the extended weeks and months they'll have to wait in Nogales for the correct documentation to arrive."

Once at the Consulate, we walked in and took a number. I looked around and noticed the room was almost completely full. There were young people, single people, married people without children, other couples with children, and some very elderly people. There was a couple, a very old couple, and the man resembled my grandfather with his weathered skin, long, white beard, and white sackcloth clothing.

I couldn't help but think of Aurelio's words and wonder, "Do these people have their complete documents?" I imagined them getting the runaround, spending money, and becoming very confused. I looked at the children that were scampering around in there, and I felt sorry for them. I was hoping that everything would go well for them. I wanted everything to go well so that they could immigrate and pursue lives of great possibility and prosperity—as I imagined I would be doing. I worried about the children, and I worried about all the people that were around us.

Somehow though, I wasn't worried about myself. I thought that we had everything pretty much in line and we would just fill out all the applications, give them our documents, and then they would approve it and we would be on our way in the next few days.

Aurelio told us that when everything was all set in an application, it usually took 24 to 48 hours for them to review it, depending on its complexity. He felt very confident that we had everything we needed.

I felt some anxiety as we sat and waited. My brother reassured me, "Just relax and think about when we go across the border. We'll get into the car and we'll drive across. On our way to Phoenix, we'll get a milkshake. It's going to be a great time."

My brother turned to Aurelio to ask, "Why did it seem so much easier for me back in 1955 to immigrate?"

"Because your American boss had money and a stable business. He put his name and his business down as your sponsor. You didn't have children. You weren't a child yourself. You had no issues or responsibilities, so your circumstances were relatively simple to approve. Not everybody has such a simple application, and not everybody is so lucky having a Mr. and Mrs. Lambert standing at their side to tell the American investigator that they vouch for you and that you are going to work at their business straightaway."

My brother smiled and replied, "Yes, Aurelio, that makes sense. I get it."

Then Aurelio put one arm around Miguel and the other around me, saying, "It's time for me to return to the office. The Consulate won't allow me to be there with you. Don't worry— the officers are all fluent in Spanish. They don't need me there to be a translator. The only people that can go into the interviews are relatives that have already immigrated, like Miguel or a boss or sponsor. For me, I'm just a middleman trying to do my job. As soon as you're done, come directly to the office. By then they should have given you a set time to return."

As Aurelio made his exit, almost everybody turned to watch him walk away. He was like a mighty tree surrounded by plants and saplings. With each stride his arms swung in great arcs. When he looked around, his neck and head moved like that of a lizard. Before finally exiting, he made a slow turn to look back at us, smile, and wave his left hand in farewell, and again, the end of his sleeve came near his elbow.

I made conversation with several of the people waiting their turn in the large room. I talked to a teacher who said it had taken him three months to garnish all the documents needed to start his application. Other people there seemed to have little clue about the documentation. Some were given guidance by friends or strangers they'd met in the streets and markets of Nogales. I really felt that some of them were completely lost.

I concluded one thing—communication was a real problem for them. Many didn't know how to read or write themselves. Many didn't know how to articulate the kinds of questions to ask to determine the documents they would need.

I explained how they could find Aurelio and that Aurelio might be able to guide them. I told them that he would outline all the required documents and evaluate the documents they already had.

Finally, our number was called.

Miguel and I walked down a hallway and entered a small room. Into the room entered a pretty lady with golden hair. She pulled forward two chairs, so we could sit, and she asked for all the documents. She spoke perfect Spanish. She arranged all the documents and began examining each one.

She told my brother, "You have very nice letters, sir, and you should be proud of all the things your friends and your employer said about you."

Then she asked about my father and his death. She said, "I'm sorry about your loss."

Next, she asked about a death certificate. Basically an official certificate of death had to be filed in La Mira and then transferred over to a larger city for proper recording. That larger city was Uruapan.

My brother pointed out, "I wouldn't think a certificate of our father's death is necessary considering we have an official letter from Edgar's mother granting me power of attorney over Edgar. This grants me total responsibility for him."

"I'm sorry, but we have to have a copy of the filed death certificate. This certificate has to be signed by the filer in the city of Uruapan, Mexico. Without it, it suggests that Edgar's father may be alive and not in support of that letter from Edgar's mother granting you power of attorney over him."

"How long do you think it takes to get a death certificate filed, so we can get a copy to you?" my brother inquired.

"God only knows—it could take months to a year. I have seen that occur. It's a lengthy, exhausting process," she replied.

It felt like a lightning bolt of bad news had just struck us.

My brother looked at me and asked, "Why didn't Aurelio know this?" He was puzzled.

The immigration officer continued, "It all looks very good except the lack of that certificate, so we will have to hold off the process."

She returned the documents to my brother and pitched the application away without writing anything on it.

"Come back when you get the certificate, and we can, hopefully rapidly, process the application. Hold onto the documents. They are your responsibility."

Miguel inquired, almost pleadingly, "Since we are so close, can't you at least start the process and keep the documents on file until the last item comes in?"

She gave a very blunt "no."

Miguel was stunned, and I didn't know what to say.

My brother remained polite. He looked at her, shook her hand, and thanked her for being so generous with her time.

As we returned to that big room, I stared at the many hopeful occupants, waiting. I prayed that their experience would not be as disappointing as ours.

Aurelio expressed aggravation and sympathy when we told him the news. He agreed that it could take months and as long as a year to get the certificate on record.

"Let me talk to someone about this, get their opinion," he told us. With that he picked up the telephone and made a call. He talked to the person for quite some time.

All the while, Miguel and I were in extreme agony, with so many thoughts and worries running through our minds about what to do next.

Finally, Aurelio put the receiver down, scratched his head, and looked up, down, and all around the room—anywhere but at us.

We knew the news was bad. Whatever he'd learned from the other person was not going to be in our favor.

"Miguel, I just don't know what to say. I've never had a case like this before. I'm very, very sorry . . ."

My brother and I looked at him. We knew he spoke with real sincerity. He seemed very caring, and it was apparent he felt really bad about the whole situation, like he was responsible for letting us down. He had seemed so sure that there would be no obstacles. I think he was as stunned as we were.

However, something needed to be done as soon as possible, probably the sooner the better, because time was running out for my brother. He needed to get back to work. He needed to submit car and house payments.

Aurelio turned to me, remarking, "In a way, young man, you are very lucky to be where you're at because you know exactly what you are lacking and how and where to get it— though you will have to wait. There are many people out there that have no idea how to proceed. They're spending money and time, and they're confused. Some can't even read or write, and it makes things extremely difficult for them. Sometimes they just give up, and they go back to their towns or stay here in Nogales and make some kind of living because they don't have the resources or tenacity to pursue their dream. I hope that you are not looking to give up at this time."

Aurelio paused for several seconds. Then he continued, "Please listen very carefully. Try to be open for a moment. Let's entertain something that could work on a temporary basis, but you both will have to be strong and listen to what I have to tell you."

Miguel and I leaned in even closer to hear what he was going to propose.

"I am in the business of aiding individuals to achieve legal entry into the United States, and my oath forbids me to do the contrary. However, a temporary illegal entry may buy us some time while we wait for the recording of this official document in Uruapan."

Startled, my brother interjected, "Are you suggesting that we cross him illegally?"

With a shameful look on his face as if he had just committed a crime, Aurelio responded even more softly than usual, almost like the words could not come out of his lips, "Unfortunately ... yes."

My brother retorted in exasperation, "I have never told a lie, and this will never happen."

Aurelio responded, "I beg your pardon, and—with all the respect in the world—something like this will happen and per- haps very soon. Now go, go and consider the whole situation."

My hands were sweaty. My brother's face was bright red and

perspiring. He rubbed his head in frustration to the point that his hair was uncharacteristically out of order.

He turned to me and announced, "I need to make a call. Go to the hotel and wait for me. I will get back there shortly."

While I was waiting for my brother, worried thoughts churned in my mind. I imagined all those people waiting in that big room, waiting to see the immigration officers. Like me, they had filled their reservoir of hopes and dreams with this one grand plan—going to the USA—but some couldn't read or write. They had very little money. The process and documentation was a huge beast that they could never satisfy. And once they went in for the interview, that beast would tear a hole in them and begin devouring their dreams.

I did not know what our financial situation was like. Maybe it was identical to theirs—maybe we had very, very little money too. I didn't think that we had a problem with communication, as they did. My brother conducted himself well. He understood what was going on, he could read, he could write. Of course, it was all self-taught because he didn't have a first grade education.

Lately Miguel had seemed much more anxious. "Perhaps," I decided, "he has some serious financial difficulties—that are probably due to me. If he didn't have to deal with me, he'd be fine."

With that, my mind started spinning, weaving a tight and complex web of anxiety. "Are my mother and the rest of my family okay? Are my sisters and my brother well? Do they have enough money to eat well? Do they have enough to live on?"

Then I started thinking that perhaps it was a mistake for me to be here. Suddenly it felt self-indulgent and selfish for me to try to go to the United States. "Why am I thinking of myself? I should be thinking more about the rest of the family, my sisters and my brother, rather than thinking only about myself."

I imagined my mother feeding my siblings as she coughed, hot with fever, and was barely able to function herself. That's all I could think of—how my mom persevered through her own ills, sacrificed her own needs, to take care of the rest of us and make the rest of us feel safe.

The tempest of anxiety and worry in my head made my body feel sick and weak. My breathing had become quick and shallow. My blood rushed strong with dread. I wanted to run away but didn't have the spirit to run. I was having a panic attack.

And then tears exploded out of my eyes. I cried and cried. My whole body seemed to shake and convulse with the avalanche of tears.

In my crying the thought came to me that perhaps my brother had left me. Perhaps he'd lied to me. Perhaps he'd said, "I'll be back," but he would never come back. Such wicked ideas spun through my mind.

I was feeling worse and worse by the minute, almost like I was losing hold of reality. I found myself repeating, "It's a mistake for me to be here. I know it's a mistake. My dream to go to the United States is completely selfish."

I firmly felt that it was a true mistake. I continued to cry. I called out softly on several occasions, "Abuelito, Abuelito, what can I do? Please forgive me."

I'd always gone to my grandfather in times of distress or serious concern. He always had an answer for me, but this time, my grandfather couldn't help me. He just couldn't hear me. Or I just couldn't hear him.

In this state of apprehension, I paced the floor of the hotel lobby and ventured outside numerous times, hoping to spot Miguel returning to the hotel. I would stand in the lobby for a while; then I would run upstairs to the room several times, back and forth between the lobby and the room upstairs. I didn't know how many times I'd done this, yet Miguel was nowhere to be found.

It was not until approximately two hours later that I saw him from the window, walking towards the hotel.

I didn't know what to do. "Do I run down to meet him or do I just stay here in the room and wait for him?" I was in a state of real confusion.

I found myself jetting down to the lobby and sprinting out the door towards him.

I could tell when he looked at me that my panic was evident. He opened his arms wide and caught me in a big hug. I cried and cried.

"I thought you left me for good," I gasped between sobs.

He too had started weeping, but he managed to articulate very clearly, "I will never leave you. You hear me? Do you understand me? I will never leave you."

With my emotions in chaos I couldn't respond—scared yet

happy; desperate yet appeased; guilty yet relieved; excited yet exhausted; hopeless yet yearning. I deliberately tried to slow my breathing and regain some calm.

"Miguel, I'm sorry. I got really scared. I was convinced I'd made a mistake to leave my mother and sisters and brother. Then I started imagining you wouldn't return. I felt like I was waiting and waiting so long—too long."

"Do not worry, *hijo*. I had every intention of coming back. I had several things I needed to do."

"I'm sorry Miguel that I caused so many problems. I thought that this would be easy, but now I know, it's not."

"Edgar, what do you say we go get some ice cream?"

"Yes. Great idea."

With his arm around my shoulder we began walking.

He told me, "I spent a while talking with Mr. and Mrs. Lambert about our situation and the additional documentation. I told them everything. Now I want to tell you what we decided. Before I tell you, know that you're going to have to be very strong. Do you think you can do that for me? Do you think you can be strong?"

"Yes. I will be strong, no matter what."

So Miguel continued, "I talked to them about my money situation. I'm about two months behind on car payments. Also I had to stop remodeling the house I bought because I ran out of money. By this time I assumed I'd be working and you'd be in school in Phoenix. Since that isn't the case, plus this additional documentation issue—I'm a bit worried. Mr. and Mrs. Lambert were generous enough to give me a loan to help us out right now. So that brings me a lot of relief. They are the most generous people I've ever known. They are going to really like you, Edgar. And Margaret said again how she can't wait to see you."

As Miguel told me this, I found my mind and body beginning to settle. Even still, I was pretty sure something else was going on—that Miguel still had some bad news to share. It seemed like he was purposely taking a slow, careful route to deliver the bad news.

Really, I already knew what it was. And I'd already told him I could be as strong and as big as he wanted me to be.

By this time, we'd enjoyed our wonderful ice cream, and it was time to return to the hotel.

But rather than start walking, Miguel faced me with his eyes closed and stated, "I'm going to take you across to the United States illegally. It's something I never thought I would have to do, but there is no way that I can allow you to return to La Mira."

"Miguel, I'm not scared. I will do whatever you want me to do. Anything you need me to do, I will do," I replied.

"Edgar, I promise you that sooner rather than later I will get your legal papers. This is only a temporary fix and I need you to be strong and I need you to do this. I feel very bad about asking this of you, but someday we will make it up and do things right. I promise you."

"Miguel, I know. I understand."

"This is how it is going to work. Across from the blue restaurant that's next to the Consulate, there's an entry-exit gate for pedestrians. There is an American immigration officer who works that gate, and you will ask him if you can walk through to the US side—and he's going to allow you."

I wasn't sure how or what he meant by this. Why would an American immigration officer whose very job was to protect the gate from illegal crossings allow me to walk through it?

Miguel continued to explain, "You're going to have to work hard over the next few weeks to make it happen. It's not going to be easy, but after the hard work, the actual crossing should be a simple task."

I wasn't sure whether to be frightened or excited about the challenge. I still didn't understand exactly what my work was going to consist of. I didn't understand a lot of the plan. What I did understand—I knew that it was very wrong what we were about to do.

"Please, never think ill of me, Edgar. I will make it right. Sooner or later, I promise I will make it right. Let's go over to check the entry-exit gate where you will cross."

When we arrived in the vicinity of the entry-exit gate, Miguel pointed out, "You see how many people cross through it every day? The restaurant is very busy. I think the officer working the gate right now seems like a nice guy—much friendlier than other officers. He looks like he's got nice manners, and he loves to eat. I've noticed that he's always eating."

At that moment, the officer was eating tacos and leaning on

a bench. A few people approached and showed him some type of passport or identification, and he waved them through. All the while he just kept on eating and smiling. There was a good nature about the man.

"I see what you mean. He seems to be outgoing. I think that I'm going to like him, and I think he's going to like me real soon because he likes to eat what I like to eat—bean tacos."

My brother asked, "How do you know that?"

"I can tell that's what he's eating now because I've been eating bean tacos all my life. I am an expert at identifying them."

My brother said to me, "You're going to do this by yourself. I'm sorry, but I think this is the best and safest way. If it fails, nothing will happen to either of us. You won't get in trouble."

"Alright," I agreed. "Let's do it, so I can get to Phoenix."

The following morning, we met with Aurelio to discuss the plan about crossing the border illegally.

Aurelio said he'd spoken to a teacher about teaching me English, a two- or three-week crash course. He said the teacher spoke excellent English and could teach me the basics so that I could communicate with the American officer guarding the entryway. Aurelio had negotiated a payment of fifteen dollars for the crash course.

He noted, "Your plan, along with the crash course in English, is cheaper and safer than hiring a risky *pollero*. [*Nowadays *polleros* are typically referred to as *coyotes*.] A *pollero* cost several hundred dollars, yet many people end up in big trouble when they encounter a problem during a crossing with a *pollero*. For instance, you and your brother would have to be separated, and if you ended up getting caught somewhere in the desert or on a highway and were deported, you may never see each other again. *Polleros* are bad news."

Aurelio felt good about me learning English to communicate with the officer. The idea was not that I would try to become fluent in English—obviously that couldn't happen in three weeks—but to simply learn some basic phrases to befriend the officer. Then if the officer felt comfortable with me as a so-called friendly kid who talked to him a bit every day over a few weeks, then maybe he would allow me to go through the gate to run a "quick errand" across the border.

My brother agreed, "Aurelio, your idea about Edgar taking

the English course is excellent. And Edgar, I know you can do it. You are a fast learner. César told me that you could memorize item after item faster than any student he ever taught. Even when Caesar was in the big city, he had very fast learners, but he never saw anyone pick things up as fast as you. Not only can you learn quickly, but you retain what you learn too. You're going to do great."

Aurelio then repeated that the plan was the smartest and safest way because if it failed, nothing would happen to me—the officer would simply deny my request—and also nothing would happen to my brother.

My brother went on to say, "I've only agreed to this dishonest act because both Edgar and my survival depend on it. If I waited here with Edgar for a year, I'd lose my job, my car, and my house. With those things lost, Edgar would have no chance of gaining legal entry. If I go to Phoenix and send Edgar back to La Mira, I worry that I'd never have the opportunity to go and retrieve him again. I worry he'd lose his chance, and all our work so far would be for nothing. So, though our plan is wrong, it is still the right decision. And Aurelio, I promised Edgar and I promise you that someday I'll make it right. I'll get legal status for Edgar. And I'll never break that promise."

Miguel repeated, "I'll make it good. I promise I'll make it good."

It took me a week to learn a few English phrases and sentences—*Nice. Excellent. Good morning. Hello. Goodbye. Hi, how are you? My name is Edgar. What's your name? It is nice to meet you. Have a good day. Take care.*

As I walked about Nogales, I found myself repeating English phrases. Then I made sentences. I mixed words and tried to play around with them. I sang the phrases—anything to make them stick. I was trying very hard to have all of the English words stay with me so that I could communicate with the border entry officer as soon as possible.

In the afternoons across the street from the entry-exit gate, I started playing soccer with a group of children. I made sure to direct smiles at the officer when I could. Occasionally, when the soccer ball landed near or bounced off of the chain-link border fence, he would signal us to move a bit farther away so that none of the people passing by would get hit. Everyone loved soccer in Mexico, so neither the officer nor anyone else got really annoyed at us.

After making it pretty obvious that I was going to be around for a while, I decided it was time to make a more direct impression on the officer, so he would know who I was specifically, as there were several kids who played in this area. My goal was for him to single me out to run errands, like bring him lunch, sodas, and snacks. I was going to make every effort to get closer and closer to him, and I was truly hoping that we would become friends, but I also knew that sooner or later I would betray the friendship.

After dropping some English phrases on him—*How are you? Good afternoon. See you later* (followed by a wave of the hand)—I took it up a notch with comments like *I like your badge* and *Do you want me to get you something to eat?* There were two restaurants across the street as well as nearby street vendors for me to fetch food from.

One day he asked me in English, "What's your name?" I froze for a second because I wasn't sure he was talking to me. Then I replied, "My name is Edgar." I had no idea how I came out with this complete answer. I surprised myself. It just popped out naturally.

Then he asked me if I could get him an orange drink from across the street, and he spoke in Spanish, "*Quiero una bebida de naranja.* You know, Jarritos." He was referring to a brand of soft drink popular in Mexico called Jarritos.

I told him, "*Hablas español muy bien,*" which means, "You speak Spanish very well."

He replied, "*Tu inglés tambien es bueno,*" meaning, "Your English isn't bad either."

I was surprised to hear him say that.

Also, I realized that since he spoke excellent Spanish, I was probably wasting my time trying to make friends with him using bits and pieces of English. So, I quickly responded to his request in Spanish, saying, "*Si, voy por el.*" He handed me some change.

On my way back from buying the orange Jarritos, I started to worry, "What if he makes more conversation with me—and it's in English, but I don't know the words—what am I going to do?"

When I returned, a man was speaking with him, so I handed him the drink and his change. He didn't pay too much attention to me, which I was glad about. I didn't say anything because I didn't want to interrupt his conversation or get tangled up in a conversation in English.

I continued to practice my English, but I often thought, "What for? He speaks Spanish really well." I figured that the more English I learned now, the easier and faster my school experience would be once I was in Phoenix, assuming I made it there. Plus, Miguel had already paid my English teacher upfront, so I might as well continue with the instruction.

For us to make it the three weeks in Nogales, Miguel sold some jewelry pieces he'd made and brought over from Phoenix. He also managed to get a temporary job at the jewelry store in Nogales where he sold those items. He said a jeweler was having some surgery and would be out for those three weeks, so he was offered a job. It wasn't just about making a little money; my brother took the job because he liked to keep busy too.

As each day passed, I was making gains with the immigration officer. I brought him lunch several times, and I thought we were slowly and cautiously becoming friends. Luckily, it was July and August, so there was no school on. Had it been the school year, he would have been wondering why a nine-year-old was roaming the streets and not in school.

The instructor informed me that I was learning English at a very rapid pace, but what the teacher did not know was how much I practiced. Words, phrases, questions, anything that came to my mind, I would repeat over and over and over and over during breakfast, lunch, dinner, before going to sleep, in bed. My brother would tell me, "You need to get some sleep," because I would talk and talk and talk, over and over, anything I could think of in English.

I even practiced with American tourists in Nogales. They would shop at many of the stores, looking for bargains or particular items not available in the USA. I talked to Americans coming to Nogales to visit dentists. I practiced and practiced without resting. Anybody that I could talk to in English, I would talk to. After a while, I thought I was becoming annoying to people, but I didn't really care. I was on a mission.

My teacher didn't know all the practice I was doing outside our tutorials. He told me I was able to have conversations he would never have imagined possible, "For such a short period of time, you can undertake conversations that it would take most people months and months to achieve." I was delighted that I'd made such progress, but I knew it wasn't due to good luck.

The teacher was really a nice man. He even told me that it was the easiest fifteen dollars he had ever made teaching English. He said it was too easy. "I feel so guilty, like maybe I should give the money back to your brother . . . but I guess I'll keep it," he confided with a twinkle in his eye.

I also started to make a little money by helping Americans who crossed into Nogales on foot to go shopping. I helped them by carrying items from the store to the entry-exit gate. I carried items to the gate, and they would give me a quarter or fifty cents. Sometimes even a dime. I appreciated everything they gave me. I never asked for anything or expected anything. I just wanted to talk to them to practice English. I was learning to put my classroom English to use, and I was increasing the amount of English I was learning.

I was impressed by how kindly the tourists treated me. It certainly hit me that it would be very easy to make a living in the area if a person were willing to put in the work. I was earning a few dollars a day just helping the tourists.

When I gave Miguel the money I made, he told me, "Make sure what you're doing to earn the money is right. Make sure that you're not taking advantage of people, accepting money for a task that is really too easy and should be done as a favor."

"I would never do such a thing. I just enjoy talking to them. I never ask them for money. And if I'm carrying something small, I refuse any compensation."

Finally, the day for the momentous undertaking was near. The plan—I would ask the border entry officer a very simple question and then walk through the entry-exit gate. It seemed easy, and I thought I was sufficiently prepared to do exactly what I needed to do.

My brother asked me, on the day before, "Are you okay with everything we discussed so far?"

"Yes," I responded.

"Are you certain?"

"Yes, I am," I assured him.

"Because if you don't want to do it, we can go back to La Mira, and I will return for you after we obtain the needed papers. In fact, we could go to Uruapan and wait for the certificate to be placed and filed, or we could commission someone to bring it to us here while we wait here in Nogales."

I told him, "No, I want to go ahead. I am definitely mentally prepared to do it."

"Okay," he said. "It's tomorrow then. If it works out and you are allowed to cross, I'll be waiting for you at the Safeway grocery store in my car. And if it doesn't work out, return to the hotel. After four hours, I'll know it didn't work, and I'll come find you there."

Strangely perhaps, I wasn't concerned. I felt soundly confident.

We went to bed, and I did not practice my English anymore. I slept deeply.

The following morning came. At breakfast my brother looked me in the eye and asked once more, "Are you okay?"

"Yes, I want to do it. I will meet you across, as planned." I felt total tranquility.

My brother said, "If it doesn't go well, they're not going to harm you. He's just going to say a simple word—no."

Miguel got in his car and drove away.

I made my way toward the gate. It was about one block in distance from me.

All at once, I noticed my heart was beating faster and faster. I felt perspiration release in a wave from all over my body. My jaw became tight, like it was stuck shut, and my teeth clenched together as if they'd been wired tight.

In the short distance of a single block, my cool calmness morphed into a full-on panic attack. Total fear enveloped my body, something I hadn't anticipated.

I'd envisioned everything going smoothly. I'd been so sure of myself. Now I was fighting to move, breathe, and think normally.

"Maybe they'll send me to jail. Maybe my brother won't be there. Why are we doing this? This is totally dishonest. I can't believe I'm doing this. I'm trying to deceive an honest guy. It won't work. What if they know the plan and they have Miguel under arrest somewhere?" All these questions and concerns descended upon my mind in a tortuous gale. It was as if I were trying to talk myself out of it, almost like I was looking at myself in the mirror and my image was begging me, "Don't do it!"

As I got closer to the gate, I could see the nice officer standing and talking to people crossing through the gate. He was a decent man. He had a natural smile. "Why am I doing this to this man?" I asked myself silently. "This just isn't right." I was doing everything possible not to do what I had been so sure I would have no problem doing.

All of a sudden I thought, "My brother was right. I should have agreed to go back to La Mira."

At this point my body was drenched in perspiration. My hands were cold and clammy, and my heart felt as if it had dropped out of my chest and was rolling in front of me on the sidewalk.

I stopped, whipped around, and ran back less than a quarter of a block. I made my way between two buildings and leaned against one of the building's outer walls. My back felt wet against the dry cement of the wall. I was frightened. I wanted to run and run fast, but I couldn't move. I felt so very exhausted.

Soon I found myself in a trance, as if I were talking to my grandfather, pleading, "Abuelito, Abuelito, Abuelito, Abuelito, *ayudame*—help me!" Then I recalled something from years before:

My grandfather, a friend of his, and I were at my grandfather's farm near Playa Azul to make sure that bugs weren't eating the corn and the watermelon vines. We were there all day. Towards the end of the day, right at sundown, my grandfather's friend got bitten by a snake, a dangerous, venomous snake.

My grandfather turned to me, saying, "*Hijo*, this man is going to die if we don't get help. He's a very heavy man. We only have one donkey. It is impossible for us to carry him on the donkey and get him to help in time. So, Edgar, I'm going to ask you to do something. Now you're going to have to be strong and run to La Mira and get some help immediately."

I saw how the man was suffering. He was holding a knee up against his chest as he lay there against a tree trunk. His breathing had become heavy and slow, and his eyes were staring but unfocused.

My grandfather said, "I know that you don't like it, but you must go and get some help because I can't do it. I'll be too slow. You need to run. You can run faster than me, and you can make it and bring help."

My grandfather continued, "I know what you're going to tell me. You don't want to go because you're afraid of the cemetery."

My grandfather knew that every kid feared this road because it went through a dense forest and a crude cemetery. The soft and sandy road from his farm to town at a certain point passed through a forest. The trees surrounded the road to make a dark, dense tunnel of tall, short, and medium-sized trees. The trunks were huge with holes in them, and vines like thin masses of snakes covered the trunks. Abruptly the tunnel opened up and tombs popped up on either side of the road, like they were filled with the newly dead, pushing to get out. The whole area had all the ingredients to make it extremely scary and spooky.

He held both of my shoulders, looked me straight in the eye, and said, "*Hijo*, we have no choice. Can you do this?"

"Yes, Abuelito, I'll go."

I had tears in my eyes.

My grandfather stated, "What you're going to do now is you're going to run really, really fast until you get to the entry of the forest. As soon as you enter that forest area, I don't want you to look to the right or to the left, and I don't want you to look back. As a matter of fact, when you leave right now, you run and you never look back. Once the cemetery starts, stop running. That's when you walk. It will seem to take a long time. But don't run and don't look back. Just walk through it. Once you get to the other side, you start running again."

I said, "Yes, Abuelito."

He hugged me tight and said, "Go. Go and remember, no matter what you hear, don't look back because it will distract you and scare you more. Ignore everything. You're going to hear noises of leaves dropping. Promise me you won't look back and promise me you're not going to run through the ceme-tery—you're going to walk steadily."

"Yes, Abuelito, I promise."

I ran quickly down the road. I dashed through the tunnel of trees to the start of the cemetery. It was like a huge hole in the middle of so many trees. That's where I stopped and started walking slowly.

Walking through it, my hands were sweaty, my heart pounded, and my eyes were tearing up. I couldn't even open my mouth. My jaw was clamped shut.

Slowly I headed right into the cemetery. To the left and the right in my peripheral vision, I could detect graves. I did not dare shift my eyes. I focused, straight as an arrow, on what lay ahead of me. I kept walking and walking. There was only enough light for me to see right in front to my next footstep and a bit to my sides; beyond that was complete darkness.

I continued to walk deliberately slowly. My steps sounded out loudly. I could hear other noises too. My grandfather had told me that I would hear leaves falling. Indeed, he was right. I heard birds too, birds sounding their last chirps and caws before settling to sleep. Occasionally I felt a spurt of wind like an unwelcome slap on the back. I was tempted to look back, but I didn't because I knew what would happen.

Suddenly, I looked up above the trees, and I could see small spots of light; it was from the moon. At that, a little tranquility washed over me. I started thinking, "The moon will guide me out safely." I remembered that my grandfather once said that the moon could direct our mood and determine our future.

As I walked farther and farther, I started to become less frightened. I noticed my hands had dried, and my teeth were no longer chattering. I was able to move my jaw. My thoughts had become clearer too.

I knew that as soon as I left the cemetery, I could run again. I was tempted to start running early, but I didn't want to do that. I wanted to wait until I was completely out of the cemetery and the forest.

Once I made it through, I started running. I sprinted. I could make out the very dim torchlights of La Mira. I ran.

Finally I met a man that I didn't know. I started screaming at him that we needed help, that a man had gotten bitten by a snake on the other side of the cemetery and we needed help. I was yelling.

Some people gathered around me. Quickly two men understood what I was trying to communicate, and they got into a wagon and drove fast down the road. I could almost make them out as they disappeared into the forest.

I shook my head, bringing myself back to the present. I

moved my head from side to side, releasing myself from the trance.

I noticed my body and mind had calmed. My jaw went from tight to relaxed. My heartbeat slowed to a normal rhythm. My mind had centered. I regained control and tranquility.

I wiped my tears, cleaned my face, and headed directly out and over to the entry-exit gate, all the while keeping my gaze straight ahead, not looking to the right or left or behind me. I walked at a steady pace.

As I approached the officer from a distance, I smiled at him. He looked at me briefly as he was checking someone's document.

Once I was close to him, I asked, "How are you today?"

He responded, "Great. How about you?"

"Very well, thank you."

He then asked, "Would you get lunch for me later on today?"

I told him, "I will. I'd be happy to, sir."

Then I looked him in the eye and asked, "Is it okay with you if I go to the store over there and buy some grapes?" I did not show any emotion or anxiety.

He showed no concern as to what I had just asked.

He looked me right in the eyes. After a brief moment, he smiled. Then he gave a nod that meant yes.

I walked through the gate.

I moved slowly, not looking to the right, left, or behind me, keeping my gaze straight ahead. After a half-block I increased my pace some but maintained my straight-ahead gaze.

When I saw my brother at a distance ahead of me, I smiled and wept at the same time.

My brother walked to me.

"Good boy," he whispered.

He hugged me tightly, and I hugged him back just as tightly.

"I will never leave without you. Never, never," he told me.

We got into the car and drove away.

11

Miguel asked me, "Do you remember when you were a kid and we were in Nogales and we went to that clinic to get the medical paperwork for your visa?"

"Yes, vividly," I replied.

"Do you remember what you told me when you saw the doctors?"

"I believe I said that the doctors in their white coats and suits looked amazing and that I wanted to be one of them when I was older."

"Yes, that's what I remember you said too. So, Edgar, now that you've finished your residency and earned your surgeon credentials, I think it's time we went suit shopping for you. When you open your private practice, I want you to be dressed to the nines. As my gift to you I want to buy you some suits."

At that time, even with my hard-earned credentials and degrees, I'd only just completed my residency program and was only earning enough money to cover the essential living expenses for me, my wife, and Miguel and Marisa, our two children. Not only did I have student loans to pay off, but I'd just taken out a substantial loan to set up my own practice. Miguel knew all about my financial situation, and that's one of the reasons he wanted to treat me.

"Miguel, you've been so generous to me and to everyone around you all your life. Your generosity and your loving kindness are endless. I thank you, brother."

"I just want to do something special for you because I'm so proud of you," he responded.

So, Miguel and I went shopping for some suits.

Working in the men's clothing department was a well-dressed gentleman wearing a beautiful suit with a handkerchief in the jacket pocket. His shoes were glossy and clean. I noticed too that his nails were nicely clipped and polished and shining. I immediately recalled how César, my fourth grade teacher in La Mira, would talk to us about keeping our hands clean and our nails nicely trimmed. Every Monday, before we started class, he would stand in the doorway and, as we entered, we would have to show him our hands. I recalled that my mother would clean and trim my nails every Sunday in preparation for this Monday examination.

Miguel approached the gentleman, saying, "My name is Miguel, and this is Dr. Edgar Hernandez. He's a surgeon, and we're here because I want to buy him a couple of suits."

The gentleman responded to Miguel, asking, "Then you must be his father, Mr. Hernandez?"

I interjected, agreeing, "Yes. This is my father, Miguel Hernandez."

As I was preparing to choose some suits to try on, Miguel pulled me aside, urging, "Pick the suits that you want, and don't worry about the price. Right now, I'm all set to buy whatever you need. If you want three, we'll buy three. If you want four, we'll buy four. I saved enough money for this event because I knew it would come."

I barely managed to hold in my tears of gratitude.

After an hour of trying on suits, shirts, and ties, we left the men's department with three complete outfits.

On the way out, Miguel commented, "Edgar, we aren't done yet. There's another thing you need—a pair of shoes. You need some professional shoes." So we proceeded to the shoe department.

"Miguel, I know I don't need to say it—but you know what this reminds me of?"

"Of course—when we went to JCPenney's so many years ago and you got your first pants and shirts—and your first pair of shoes. I can still see you trying to walk for the first time wearing shoes—what a sight to behold!"

Miguel and I both grinned wide grins and chuckled at that memory.

★　　★　　★

Sitting there in the car with my brother driving, I almost felt free of turmoil, like a huge weight had been lifted from me. I looked at my brother. I looked outside. I felt the wind hit my skin since the windows were down.

"It's going take about 3.5 to 4 hours to get to Phoenix. We'll stop along the way to get some food. You can relax now, Edgar. I know it's been a big day."

It was a big day, and I was exhausted, so exhausted that my mind had slipped into overdrive with mostly happy thoughts swirling about: "I can't believe that we're going to be living together, and I'm going to be going to school in the US! Miguel even promised that he is going to take me shopping to get a brand-new pair of shoes and also some new pants. I'll start school soon. I'll have to learn more English to do well at school and to make friends."

Underneath the pleasant buzz of possibility the weight of worry slipped through at times: "What have we done to the friendly officer? Is he going to get in any trouble? What does it mean for me to be in the United States illegally? Will I even be able to go to school? Will Bernard and Margaret Lambert still like me once they meet me?"

Miguel was aware that high hopes as well as worry were traveling with us in the car, so he tried his best to console me. He started with small talk, reviewing the funny and entertaining parts of our long voyage from La Mira up to Nogales—the father and daughter at the cantina who'd recalled our father, my first experience with ice cream, the man who took us out to dinner, the young lady with the purple hat, our sister Surama.

Finally, I had to ask, "Miguel, what will it be like for me because I've entered illegally? What might happen?"

He told me he'd been at the homes of Mexican friends and without warning federal agents, sometimes wearing distinctive green uniforms and driving green cars and other times wearing regular civilian clothing and driving everyday cars, had raided the house. Those at the house who had entered illegally would flee the scene and hide. Everyone else, like Miguel, would simply show their documents to the agents. If anyone who'd entered illegally got caught, they'd be deported back to somewhere in Mexico. He said that La Migra's surprise raids could happen at restaurants, homes, on the street, at church—anywhere really.

He told me I had to be prepared to run too—to run and hide and stay hidden for hours.

"I don't like telling you this because I know how scary it sounds. I hate it that I've had to put you in this position, but until we get that final paper, this is our reality," he told me.

In Tucson, we stopped at a dazzling restaurant called Dairy Queen. We got hamburgers and chocolate milkshakes, the special ice cream and milk combination that Miguel had already described to me. The taste of the chocolaty, milky, sweet, smooth, thick food-drink was strange and delightful. "Should I eat it with a spoon or drink it through the straw?" If I drank it too quickly through the straw my head would spin from the hard blast of cold hitting my teeth, tongue, throat, and stomach. It was weird and magical.

When we were eating, Miguel started telling me about the school I would attend. "It's a small school, only about three blocks from where I work. You'll be able to walk there because we're going to be living in the second-story apartment above my workplace. Bernard and Margaret are letting us do this since the house I bought isn't ready yet, and it's going to take some time before it'll be ready."

Back in the car after what seemed a long time, I noticed more and more traffic on the road. I found the cars and trucks exquisite. Each was painted a vibrant color—bright yellow, sunshine orange, sea green, or royal blue. They seemed more colorful, shinier, and sleeker than the vehicles I'd seen in Mexico.

Miguel explained the signs on the road with the big numbers written on them. "That's the fastest a driver is allowed to go. We cannot exceed that number," he said and indicated where the number was located on the speedometer of the car too. He went on to tell me that since he had bought the car and started driving it, he had never gotten a traffic violation, and he was going to keep it that way.

After several hours I was met with an impressive view of tall buildings and wide, black, smooth, clean streets ornamented on each side with green and red plants. It was a spectacular cityscape unlike any I'd seen before. It was Phoenix.

Miguel drove down a street called Seventh Street. Then we made some turns and came upon a white, two-story building that Miguel pointed at, saying, "That sign reads, 'Silver by

Lambert—Indian Jewelry.' We're going to drive around back, and then you are going to meet the finest and most generous people in Phoenix."

At the rear of the building, we passed through a security gate to park the car. Several men exited the backdoor and were standing, ready to meet us.

Miguel told me, "These are the Navajo Indians that I work with. They are my friends."

Once we exited the car, one of the men called out to Miguel in their native language. When Miguel responded with utter ease in that same tongue, I was delighted at how good he sounded. Apparently he was telling them my name because I heard several of them saying my name. In response, I waved, smiled, and shook several hands.

Next a woman appeared out of the backdoor. She had very light skin and long hair that she wore in a high ponytail. Her eyes were a green-blue, and she wore eyeglasses that had a long chain around them. As she was walking towards me, she pulled the glasses off her face and they dropped to her chest, dangling there on the chain.

When she reached me, she said warmly, "Hi, my name is Margaret." Then she turned around and yelled, "Bernard! Come down here! Come over and meet Miguel's little brother!" She yelled several times, and Mr. Lambert took a while before he appeared.

"Bernard, come here and meet Edgar. This is Miguel's little brother."

With a soft voice, Mr. Lambert greeted me, "Hello. My name is Bernard Lambert. It is so nice to meet you. I heard a lot about you."

Miguel looked at me and winked.

Then Mr. Lambert added, "Please call me Bernie."

He was a tall, white-haired, skinny man who had a very thin, white beard.

Margaret turned to her husband, suggesting, "Let's make some hot dogs. Are you hungry, Miguel?"

Miguel admitted, "Yes, I am, thank you."

Then she turned and asked me, "Are you also hungry?"

I confirmed, "Yes, I am."

Before going inside, Margaret hugged Miguel and said, "We

missed you dearly. Haven't we, Bernie?"

Bernie agreed softly and said one of his favorite phrases, "You bet."

Once inside, Margaret took my hand and asked, "Would you like a Coca-Cola?"

I said, "Yes, thank you."

I was relieved I had taken those English classes in Nogales and had practiced as much as I'd done, so I could communicate even this little bit with the Lamberts. Initially I was concerned that I would not be able to communicate very well with them, but I felt that they understood my brief responses and were patient and sympathetic people.

Margaret explained, "Edgar, this is your home. There are living quarters upstairs. You can stay here as long as you want."

Then she asked, "Miguel, how's your house coming along?"

"Slowly," he told her. "It will not be finished for quite some time."

When he started to discuss his financial difficulties, Margaret interrupted, "Don't worry about it. Bernie and I are going to help you. We already talked about this."

In exploring the building, I came upon a large room with many tables, around thirty or forty. Each table had its own light and something that looked like a torch.

Margaret explained, "Those are the work tables. You want to see the table where Miguel works out of?"

She and Miguel took me over to his area. I saw a heavy, worn chair, a workbench with a drawer in its bottom, and a bunch of tools inside it as well as pieces of silver and turquoise.

Margaret told me, "Edgar, did you know that Miguel produces the finest Indian jewelry around here? That's not just me saying this. The Navajo Indians who work here say that Miguel is the most talented silversmith in the jewelry shop."

Then she asked, "Edgar, did you know that your brother speaks excellent Navajo? I only understand a few words, but Miguel's with them full-time, so he picks up all these words and now he's fluent in Navajo. His English is getting better and better all the time too."

Miguel added, "Yes, Margaret's right. I spend a lot of time with my Navajo colleagues. Some of them are very dear friends of mine, and they've taught me about their culture's beautiful and unique jewelry that they have been making for many, many years, passing down the skills from generation to generation. They will pass this art on to their children also. It's a talent that very few people have, and the language they speak is also beautiful. It's a noble language, and you ought to hear some of the kind words they say about people. They are wonderful people, the Navajo. They have taught me a lot—and I owe them a lot."

Margaret then began to talk logistics, "Miguel, when are you going to sign Edgar up for school? Fairly soon, I hope. If you can't take him to school, I will be more than happy to do that. I already told you that you can count on me for anything you need. I just need you to stay here and take care of business, creating pieces for these jewelry orders that we have. Right now we have plenty, and we are behind. We really needed you. I just didn't want to worry you, but we really have missed you. We need you badly."

"Thank you, Margaret. I am grateful to you. I'm so happy to be back and thank you so much for helping me with Edgar. It means a lot to me," Miguel responded.

On my part, I couldn't help but think that Margaret was incredibly kind. Miguel had already told me this, but it was impressive seeing her thoughtfulness and generosity in action.

Miguel had already told me, "The Lamberts don't have any young children. Their son is now an adult—an airline pilot—he visits sometimes and he loves taking pictures. You'll get to meet him. Know that the Lamberts are happy and anxious to have you here as part of the family."

In this first encounter with the Lamberts I found myself taking several deep breaths. I just couldn't believe that I'd made it to a comfortable home and found two such loving, supportive people. It seemed like such a blessing after so many weeks of loss, goodbyes, stress, disappointment, and anxiety. Yes, there were some great times in my last weeks in La Mira and in the journey to Phoenix too, but there were many trying times too.

My first bite of a hot dog—it was scrumptious. I loved the green, zesty relish, the yellow mustard, and the red ketchup too. Also I ate some crunchy potato pieces called "potato chips." I had never tasted anything like these American delights, and I absolutely loved them. It was as if I were in a wonderful dream.

In the kitchen I studied the stove—another dream machine.

I told my brother, "Mamá would certainly love to have something like this. Someday, I'm going to buy her a stove, so she doesn't have to be out there cutting wood to make into coals for the daily cooking. It's hard work. It's dirty work. And then she has to breathe in all that smoke. Someday, she's going to be able to push a button and have a clean fire to cook on. I'm going to make it possible for her someday."

"Come here, Edgar," Margaret called, "I want to show you where you will be sleeping. Miguel, please come too."

We walked upstairs and entered a room off the hall. Margaret told me, "This is where your bed is. That one is Miguel's and this one is yours. Sit down on it."

I sat down on a soft, spongy, springy expanse. I noticed a fluffy pillow and a bright red blanket. It was so different from the half-inch thick, circular *petate* I'd slept on at home.

Margaret sat next to me and put her arm around me. "Edgar, it's a pleasure to have you here. I look forward to getting to know you."

I responded, "Thank you, Margaret."

Then she commented, "You speak pretty good English too. I'm impressed."

I told her, "I speak only a little English. I will learn more."

"Soon, you will speak perfect English. I know it."

Looking at her, I responded, "Thank you. I hope."

Miguel stood in the doorway of the room, grinning at us.

"Miguel, Edgar speaks pretty good English. He must have had a really good teacher." She was referring to my crash-course teacher in Nogales.

"Yes," he agreed.

Miguel then looked at me to explain, "I have no secrets from Margaret. She and Bernie know everything that has gone on in my life from the first time I went over to visit you almost two years ago, to the death of our father, to my plan for bringing you here. She agreed that you should come here illegally while we wait for the last papers. She knows pretty much everything about our entire family and our lives, and soon you will get to know her well. Again, like I said before, you will find her to be an extremely generous, intelligent, and thoughtful lady."

The following morning, Miguel made me soft, fluffy discs of bread with a sweet, dark sugar sauce poured on. The food was called "pancakes," and never had I eaten such deliciousness. It was also the first time Miguel had cooked for me. From then on, I came to realize what a great cook he was—plus, he could make both American and Mexican foods.

It was the end of August and school would start soon, in early September, so Miguel announced, "We're going to a wonderful store to buy you shirts, pants, shoes, and some socks. You'll need these clothes for school."

I had never owned such items as these. Except for the shirt and pants Miguel had brought me for the fateful interview at the Consulate in Nogales, I always wore the traditional white sackcloth shirts and drawstring pants that all the kids and many men, like my grandfather, from La Mira wore. My shoes were the open-toed *huaraches*. I'd never worn socks because they weren't necessary.

Miguel and I drove in his car to a big, gorgeous store called JCPenney's. Inside it was massive, like a small village, and so bright, clean, and pleasant smelling. The floors were made of marble, and they were shiny and smooth like glass. Again, it was like a dream world. Sometimes I would close my eyes and open them quickly to test if it was real or a dream—and this glorious world flashed back to me. It was real.

In the store, we encountered metal stairs that moved themselves upwards, and again, I couldn't believe what I was seeing. I stopped and stared in wonder and confusion.

Miguel took my hand and instructed, "This is called an escalator, and it is going to carry us up to the second floor. Over there is another escalator that will carry us back down to the first floor. What you do is walk next to me. Step where I step and then stand right by me."

I loved it so much that once we reached the top, I asked, "Can I go back down on the other side and come back up on this side by myself?"

I did it three times while my brother watched with a huge grin on his face. He chuckled as I ran from one side to the other, going down and coming back up.

After my third round, Miguel promised, "Okay, let's move on and before we leave, you can have another round on the escalators again."

We walked to an area that held hundreds and hundreds of

pairs of pants. My brother chose a pair of Levi Strauss pants for me to try on.

I tried my best to walk out of the fitting room wearing the new pants, but it was difficult because the pants he'd chosen were huge—both very long and very wide at the waist.

"Miguel, these are really big." I felt bad saying it, like I was complaining about something beautiful.

"You are correct, Edgar, they are big. But, if we buy them in your correct size, by next year, you're not going to be able to wear them anymore because you'll outgrow them. However, if we buy them big right now, you'll grow right into them. We'll just give you a firm belt, and then we'll roll them up three or four times, and you'll look fantastic."

Once I understood, I agreed, saying, "That sounds good to me."

Miguel bought me two pairs of Levi's, two shirts, and some blue underwear, which I had never worn before either.

"It's now time for us to take a look at shoes for you."

Everything was very exciting. The beautiful clothing smelled so wonderful and felt so solid and durable. Again, it wasn't a dream. It was reality. I had come to a world that I could never have imagined. I had expected that the United States would be wonderful and beautiful, but I had never imagined it to be this gorgeous.

We approached the shoe department, and a tall lady with blue eyes greeted us, asking, "Is there something I can help you with?"

"Yes. We are here because Edgar is getting his first pair of shoes," Miguel explained.

"Well, this is a big day for Edgar then. Let's start with socks. We need to get you a pair of socks to wear when you try on shoes."

Miguel agreed, "Yes, he'll need socks."

She returned with socks, saying, "Here are three pairs. Go ahead and put this pair on."

I sat down and took off my *huaraches*. I pulled a sock up over one foot and then did the same on the other foot.

"How do they fit?" she asked.

"They fit good—I think."

"Now let's get you some shoes. Which shoes do you want?"

I pointed to a pair of very handsome brown leather shoes that I learned were called wingtip shoes.

She brought back three pairs in different sizes. I tried them on until we found the size that seemed best. We couldn't go by how they felt because I didn't even know how to gauge that.

"How do they fit?" Miguel asked.

"They feel very uncomfortable. They feel really tight like my feet are suffocating."

"What you are going to do is start walking in them over the next few days. Then you'll break them in and they'll also break your feet in—you'll get used to each other. Then it'll feel a lot better."

"My sandals felt a lot more comfortable," I added.

"That may be the case, but you can't wear them to school. You have to have shoes to go to school. They'll become normal—I promise."

With the shoes and socks on, and then the shoes all laced up, I stood, took about six steps, and then toppled to the floor. The beautiful, shiny floor made for a very slick and tricky surface to start learning to walk in shoes on!

"Oh dear. Are you okay, darling?" the saleslady called out as she and Miguel rushed over to pick me up and dust me off.

"I'm okay," I replied, feeling embarrassed.

Miguel reminded her, "He's fine. He just needs a little practice walking in his first pair of shoes."

And getting "a little practice" is exactly what I did. I kept my shoes on for three days straight. I didn't take them off once. I slept with them on because I figured that the more I wore them, the faster I would get used to them, so when school started, I would be really comfortable in them and have no trouble walking. Really, once school started I didn't want to be distracted and miserable because I wasn't used to wearing shoes.

During the night, I would wake up and walk to the toilet or to get a glass of water or I'd just walk up and down the stairs a few times—in order to practice walking in the shoes. I loved looking at them and noticing their shiny brownish-yellow leather that felt so soft and smooth. They were absolutely beautiful.

I remember waking up in the night and then my brother woke up too. He asked me, "Why aren't you sleeping?"

I said to him, "I'm enjoying myself so much, and I'm so hap-

Edgar H. Hernandez   139

py to be here. I don't know that I could ever leave this place."

I truly felt that I belonged in the United States of America, that it was my destiny and this was my life.

Miguel told me in a loud whisper, "Remember what I told you? We're going to make it right. I need to earn some money right now, and we need to wait for that final document to get to Uruapan and then get certified. Really, Edgar, you and I are the luckiest two people in the world. You know why?"

I replied, "Yes, Miguel, I know why. Because of Mr. and Mrs. Lambert."

Miguel smiled and added, "You know something, I think you and Margaret are going to get along real well. I can see how happy Margaret is—and Bernie too—having you here. Even though he doesn't express it, I know he feels the same. Bernie's just a quiet man, but he has a heart of gold. I know him real well."

12

I knew there were people inside the cinder block house, but they refused to answer the door. I gave up knocking, and instead spoke to them in Spanish as clearly and kindly as possible through the door.

"*Buenas tardes.* My name is Edgar Hernandez. I do not work for La Migra or ICE or the government. I am a student doctor working with other medical staff. We want to provide you with medical care if you would like it. I came to the USA from Mexico. I too know how scary it is to live here without papers, and I promise I am only here to give medical help. I am not involved with deportation. Let me work with you and your children, please."

For the past few summers in between semesters of medical school, I'd worked alongside my fellow medical students and doctors in clinics that targeted migrant communities. Most of these migrants were undocumented agricultural workers traveling all over the USA according to harvest seasons. Our aims were to provide them and their children with medical care and to teach them how they could access good health care, no matter their legal status.

However, as was the case currently, many families simply didn't trust us when we came knocking on their doors to present our services. It didn't matter to them whether the person at the door was clearly not Hispanic or whether it was a native Spanish speaker, like me. Some families simply wouldn't mix with anyone outside their community of seasonal workers.

Luckily, this wasn't always the case. We had many opportunities to teach hygienic dental and medical practices to families and to examine and vaccinate their children, and overall it was very rewarding. The families who opened their doors to us typically had very limited English skills, and it was their children who spoke English and worked as the translators for their parents. This reminded me of when I was a youngster working with people in Nogales to help them get their visas—I was their child translator.

And I neither blamed nor got frustrated with the families who refused to open their doors to us because I remembered quite vividly my time living in Phoenix without papers. Immigration raids—and the ever-present possibility of a raid—had taught me, at that time in my life, to exist in a constant state of anxiety and suspicion, so I understood what they were going through.

★   ★   ★

Wearing my new shirt, pants, shoes, and socks, I walked with Miguel to school. It was my first day.

As we walked down a hall, I noticed the floors were brown and very shiny, as if they'd been polished with the same polish I used on my shoes.

We met the principal, Mr. McCormick, a tall gentleman with gray hair. He was polite and kind. He told my brother that it would be good for me to start in the fifth grade, so I could catch up and refine my English language skills.

He spoke to me softly and slowly, and I responded as best as I could.

Miguel told him I had learned some English while in Nogales and that I was a good student and would soon catch up with the rest of the class.

Mr. McCormick walked us over to a classroom, so I could meet my first American teacher, Mrs. Tudor.

We entered a lovely room where I saw a large chalkboard and rows of elegant wooden desks with children sitting at them. It seemed there was no shortage of chairs in this classroom.

Mr. McCormick announced to the class, "Boys and girls, this is Edgar. He is from Mexico. He does not speak very much English, so we want all of you to help him and make him feel welcome. This now is his new home, and you all will become good friends and classmates. I expect all of you to help him, so he can become a good student like all of you."

He looked at the students again and asked, "Will you all do this for me and for your teacher?"

All the students responded, "Yes, sir."

After that, Miguel looked at me and asked, "What are you waiting for? Go hug your new teacher."

I approached the teacher and gave her a hug. All the students laughed, and I turned to smile at them, thinking to myself, "I think I'm going to like this class."

Many of my classmates were helpful, and I managed to make friends and pick up on my studies quickly. When I did not understand something, they made every attempt to be absolutely sure that I could understand what was going on. They became part of my life, and I saw them not just as my classmates, but also as family. It was just as my parents had told me, "Remember that your classmates are part of your family and your teacher is your second parent."

I was very lucky to have Mrs. Tudor as my teacher. She was an outstanding instructor who had only one goal in mind—to make sure that the fifth graders excelled and were totally prepared to succeed in the sixth grade.

After three months, I was able to communicate in English really well. Towards the fourth month there were parent-teacher meetings in the evening after school. Because Miguel was sick with the flu, Margaret came with me.

When Margaret and I entered the hallway that led to the auditorium, I could tell that the other kids were taking note of us. With their eyes on me and Margaret, I reached out for Margaret's hand. We held hands till we took a seat. She looked down at me and I looked up at her and we both smiled. She made me feel really good. She made me feel like I was a part of her life. I also felt that we were meant for each other, a real team, a mother-and-son combo of sorts.

Mr. McCormick took the microphone and welcomed the parents and students. He praised the students for our hard work and let us know how proud he was of us. He also praised the teachers.

Mr. McCormick repeatedly emphasized the importance of education. Regularly he told us that we were the future of our country and that soon all the older people around us would be dependent on us. He emphasized the importance of our teachers and how through their good teaching, they were shaping us, students, into intelligent adults, fruitful citizens, and strong leaders.

He also spoke of integrity, saying, "A person that has integrity speaks and acts honestly and with high moral standards. I challenge the students and the adults in the audience to live with integrity."

After his opening address, it was time for individual parent-teacher meetings. At our scheduled time, Margaret and I met with Mrs. Tudor.

When she saw us, she inquired, "Where's Miguel?"

"He's sick at home and drinking a lot of fluids and eating chicken soup," Margaret told her.

Mrs. Tudor then asked, "And who might you be?"

"I am Margaret. Here's a letter from Miguel explaining that I've been given authority to represent him in his absence. We got it certified, so it is official."

After Margaret's relationship to me was established, we proceeded with the meeting.

Mrs. Tudor explained, "I probably don't need to tell you, but Edgar is an outstanding student. In my opinion, he is the hardest-working student that I have in my class—lucky for him because he needs to work harder than the rest of the students, so he can master the English language and succeed in the coming years in school."

Mrs. Tudor then handed Margaret a folded piece of paper. Margaret opened it, looked at me, looked at Mrs. Tudor, smiled, and then winked at me. Apparently my report card met her high expectations.

After Margaret assured Mrs. Tudor that Miguel would know everything about the meeting, we exited the classroom.

Margaret and I walked down the hall, hand in hand. A few kids waved at me, and I returned the waves with my free hand.

Once outside, Margaret asked, "How would you like a root beer float?" That was her favorite.

"I would love one," I told her.

In just a four-month period, Margaret and I had bonded so well that I felt it would be impossible for me to be separated from her. She was like having my grandfather, godfather, and mother all rolled into one. Margaret was a real stickler for perfection and demanded hard work, responsibility, and discipline.

As my godfather had urged, she would always tell me, "Never waste time."

I went with her everywhere in her gray Studebaker. On our outings she always wore her dark hair up in a ponytail tied with an elegant ribbon that matched the outfit she was wearing. She had smooth skin dotted with many freckles. She always wore bright red lipstick and carried a very large purse.

It seemed as if I had known her for years and years. When I got sick, Margaret would bring me juices, and she fed me matzo ball chicken soup. She was nurturing, supportive, and had high expectations for me, all at the same time.

Margaret always made sure that I got all my homework done. After I completed my homework, she would review it with me, asking me one item after the other. I would answer as accurately as possible. Margaret could tell right away when my answer was insufficient or confusing. Lucky for me that was a rarity because I knew how important it was to her that I be precise. I think she accomplished her goal of teaching me discipline and accuracy because even Mrs. Tudor took note of my strong study habits.

Margaret always told me, "Prepare for your day the night before you go to bed. Prepare your clothing. Clean your shoes. If you prepare everything for the following day, you'll become disciplined, and people will always look at you as being competent."

I was like her son, and she was like my mother. She always wanted me to be at her side, and I always wanted to be at her side.

In Mexico, we celebrated the birth of Jesus on January 6. It was called the Epiphany or *Día de Los Santos Reyes*, Day of the Holy Kings. This happened the twelfth day after Christmas when the three kings found baby Jesus and brought him gifts. On the morning of January 6, my siblings and I would find our *huaraches* filled with small gifts, like a wooden toy called a *valero*, little dolls, or fruit, that the three kings had put there overnight. Our family would enjoy a *rosca de reyes*, which is bread that had fruits in it and was shaped like a wreath.

From the Lamberts, I learned some other ways of celebrating. First, there was a nine-branched candlestick called a menorah. Margaret would light a candle a night for eight nights. She also lit small oil lamps that burned fresh olive oil, which emitted wafts of delightful fragrance throughout the house.

I also experience my first Christmas. Margaret and I went

together to choose a Christmas tree, similar to those striking pines I'd first encountered in Morelia, only smaller and fatter. We brought the tree back to the shop, and Margaret brought out some boxes of ornaments for it. Together we looped long, shiny ropes in circles onto the tree. Then we placed colorful balls of blue, gold, silver, pink, red, and green onto the branches of the tree. At its top we placed a small angel doll. Also—there were fat lights on a rope that we looped around the tree. These little lights blazed with bright colors once we plugged the end into the wall.

I'd never seen anything like this dazzling tree wearing its very handsome holiday attire. I would stare it up and down, smelling the fresh, crisp pine scent and letting its sparkle and shine transport me to a place of tremendous happiness. Again, it seemed I was living a fantasy, this beautiful American life.

I want to add that Miguel insisted we keep the tree up in the shop until January 6, *Día de Los Santos Reyes*, as a way to honor the Mexican tradition and merge it with the American way of celebrating Christmas. Margaret agreed with him, so that's what we did.

I also learned about Santa Claus and about Christmas presents—special gifts that were covered in thick, picturesque paper showing snow scenes or designs of red, green, gold, and silver, and then tied with curling, colorful ribbons and mighty bows that complemented the color of the wrapping paper. There were gifts for all the employees and for me. Many of the Navajo jewelry craftsmen gave me gifts too. We listened to Christmas songs together, like Burl Ives singing "Rudolph the Red Nosed Reindeer," and ate delicious foods and candies. It seemed crazy to tear apart the beautiful paper-and-ribbon creations, but that's what we did.

Margaret explained to me that the night before Christmas Day was called Christmas Eve and it was a time to spend with family. That's when families had a special meal together, and that's what Miguel and I did with the Lamberts. Also their grown son Michael visited them for this holiday meal, and that's when I first met him.

With Gene Autry singing "Down Santa Claus Lane" on the radio, Margaret prepared turkey, stuffing, mashed potatoes, and cranberry sauce—my favorite. Also, she baked an assortment of muffins and cupcakes. She was famous for her chocolate cupcakes. But my favorite were the vanilla ones—and, yes, I learned what vanilla was!

I remember Bernard would always cut a muffin in half, plop a big spoonful of cranberry sauce on one half, put it back together, and then eat it like a small sandwich with his turkey. Michael loved the muffins too.

It was an amazing and different type of Christmas than the way of celebrating I'd grown up with in La Mira. I really missed my sisters and brother, and wished they could be with me in Phoenix to experience an American Christmas.

Margaret knew me so well that she sensed this longing. She hugged me and whispered, "Pray for your sisters and brother. Pray that they're well and healthy and that the three wise men visit them on January 6 and they get gifts too."

Soon after the start of the New Year, Miguel and I were visiting some friends of his, fellow Mexicans. Wearing sweaters and light jackets we could still enjoy the outdoor weather of Phoenix in early-January, but once the sun went down, we knew we'd have to go inside. We were having a lovely meal of beans, rice, salsa, and corn tortillas, talking, laughing, and enjoying the coziness and joy carried over from the Christmas and New Year's holidays.

When I heard the patio gate open, I scooted my chair over to allow the newly arriving guests—two well-dressed men—a place in the party.

Before I could settle back into the chair, men, women, and kids shot up from their seats and began charging for the door of the house or over the fence. Food, plates, forks, and knives fell to the ground as people scattered.

"¡Correr! ¡Ir! ¡Tienes que irte ahora! Get out of here and hide!" Miguel ordered me.

"It's La Migra, so run and hide. We'll find each other later on. Don't ask questions," he repeated.

I took off through the backdoor of the house and out the front, sprinting, sprinting. I could hear the two men behind me, yelling, "Hold back! Hold back!"

There was a car parked by the side of the road. I ran to its far side, dropped down to lie flat on the ground, and scooted myself under it.

I could hear the two men, calling, "*¡Papeles! Muéstranos tus papeles.* Show us your papers."

I heard them say this about ten times. Apparently they'd moved to the front yard of the house, and I could hear Miguel speaking to them.

They wanted to know what Miguel was doing there and what information he could give on the other people at the house. My brother told them he was only visiting acquaintances, and he only knew them by first name.

My body was trembling. I had to put all my energy and concentration towards not crying, not making a sound, not moving.

I waited at least three hours underneath the car. I didn't move once.

At one point, I had figured it was safe to get out from underneath, but then I feared if I emerged too early, I would get caught: "Maybe they are hiding and waiting for the runners to feel safe and return. Then they'll capture me and I'll get sent somewhere and Miguel will have no idea where I am and I won't know either." I was in torment.

One moment everything was great—this new life with shoes and socks and school and English and a Christmas tree and Margaret and Bernard and enjoying a meal with Mexican friends in Arizona—and then I was being hunted.

Three hours later, I scooted out from underneath the car and made my way home through back alleys and in the shadows. It was late and dark when I reached home.

Miguel was outside, pacing.

When I showed myself, he ran to me and held me in a big hug.

"Those were immigration officers looking to haul away people with no legal documents," Miguel explained.

"People like me, right?" I asked, already knowing the answer.

"Unfortunately, yes," he replied in a voice barely above a whisper.

"Where's Margaret?" I inquired.

"The Lamberts went out of town for three days, remember?"

Miguel had warned me from day one that these raids happened. We knew it would happen to us; it was just a matter of when.

Miguel said, "We must stay together, and we must have composure. We have about eight months, at the most, until your document gets certified in Uruapan—we can make it. We must."

I was still so frightened that I didn't know what to say. I just wanted to put that horrible scene out of my mind.

When the Lamberts returned, Margaret could sense something had happened. I didn't have the heart to bring it up to her, but she actually came to me, asking, "When were you going to tell me about what happened to you?"

"Did Miguel tell you about it?"

"No, he didn't want to talk about it. George Nalje found me and told me because he's worried about you and Miguel. You two are like family to everyone here."

Margaret concluded, "You need to stay by my side. If I had taken you with me, it would never have happened. I really feel bad about it. Nothing will happen to you as long as I'm here by your side. I'll tell Miguel to stay away from certain areas. He needs to stop visiting friends that have no documents."

Miguel stayed quiet for three days and then came to me, saying, "I want to tell you that I'm going to work twice as much as I'm doing right now so that I can save more money faster. Then we'll have more options for getting your last document faster."

"Miguel, what happened to those people? Those children?" I asked.

"I don't know exactly, Edgar," he admitted with tears forming in his eyes. "And I am truly sorry you had to experience such an ordeal."

As time went on I witnessed more raids and saw people I knew get hauled away before my eyes. I realized that despite her good intentions, Margaret wouldn't be able to help me.

Margaret even went to the immigration office and got all the requisites for immigration. She told us that she had asked them several follow-up questions such that they had asked her if she had any illegal immigrants working for her. "I told them I only employ Native Americans and that they were welcome to come over to the store and check that out themselves." She knew she'd made a gamble by saying that and acknowledged she may have made a mistake.

Four weeks later Miguel and I went to a popular Mexican restaurant. We'd just taken our seats when we heard crashing, rattling, breaking, and stampeding sounds from the kitchen. It was like a bomb had detonated. Cooks, dishwashers, waiters, and waitresses escaped from the kitchen and with them waves of people from the dining area joined to form a massive herd stampeding towards the restaurant's front door.

"You know what to do. Run and hide. Run fast and hide and don't look back. You understand? Just run," Miguel urged.

And I was already on my feet, a part of the stampede.

I noticed a man in a green outfit had his eye on me, so I ran and ran. I could see people scampering all over the place, swarming to different areas, rushing across the street, behind homes, down alleys, onto buses, over fences and walls.

I jumped a small fence two doors down from the restaurant and made my way into a neighborhood. There were at least six other runners doing the same. I passed several houses before making my way behind one where I found a small crevice between a wall and a water heater. Standing straight up, I could just fit in this small, shadowy alcove.

And so I found myself quiet, trembling, and breathing in sharp gasps. My jaw was tight. My leg muscles shook with fatigue. I didn't know whether I'd faint standing or collapse onto my knees in tears. It was agony.

But I didn't make a sound. I closed my eyes and pretended I was at the ocean with my grandfather. I waited and waited—ten, fifteen, twenty minutes passed.

Then I heard soft padding. Footsteps. The footsteps were getting closer and closer and closer.

I dared to open my eyes.

I looked up and found a man standing before me, staring at me right in the eyes. He was wearing a light green jacket with a special patch on its sleeve.

He looked at me, and I looked at him. I held his gaze without blinking.

Time seemed to stop.

Without a word, he turned and walked away.

I stumbled out of the crevice and fell to my knees. I stayed there on the ground, waiting for my body and mind to calm. I couldn't move. I could hardly breathe. I felt ill.

After many minutes, I managed to stand and make my way back home to find Miguel standing outside, pacing, in worried wait for me.

"*Estaba muy preocupado. Lo siento.* I am so sorry," he repeated as he held me tightly.

He continued, lamenting, "I never wanted to do this. It seemed like the right decision at the time, but now it seems so wrong. It's my fault, and I am so sorry. *Lo siento, mi hijo.*"

I responded, "Miguel, no—it's okay. I want to be here with you. I'm learning a lot, and, no matter what, I don't think there is anything that has been lost by me being here. And I know we'll make it right. This won't be forever."

One Saturday morning Miguel explained, "Edgar, I finished making a pendant necklace for one of my longtime clients. She's a really nice woman. We're going to walk to her restaurant to deliver the piece to her."

After walking for thirty minutes, we arrived at the restaurant. As we approached the door, I noticed a sign in the window: "No niggers or spics allowed."

"Miguel, what's going on with the sign?" I asked, feeling nervous.

"Edgar, don't pay attention to it. Ignore it. Like I said, I've known Emma for years, and she's a wonderful person."

With that he pushed the door open, and we entered the small mom-and-pop diner.

As soon as we walked in, we heard a loud call from across the room, "Miguel, did you bring my stuff? Do you have my necklace? I can't wait! Show it please!"

A fast-talking, bubbly lady with a huge smile on her face jetted across the room to greet us. It was Emma.

Miguel gave her a hug and then pulled out a small paper sack from his inside coat pocket. Next he reached into the sack and pulled out an exquisite pendant necklace. Emma turned around so that Miguel could put it on her neck. Once it was on, she sprinted away, calling back to us, "I've got to go take a look at it in the mirror."

We heard joyful screeching from the bathroom, "I love it! This is beautiful! Miguel, you're a genius! This is exactly what I've been wanting! Ernest, come over here and look at the necklace that Miguel made for me."

We saw her husband go to look at it. "Oh, it's okay," he commented. He returned and said with a wink, "I don't think I could have done it better myself."

Once Emma settled down, she reappeared to ask, "Miguel, who is this handsome young man you've brought with you?"

"Emma, meet Edgar. He's my younger brother."

"Is that so? In honor of Miguel's amazing craftsmanship, I want the both of you to have a seat and enjoy a burger and milkshake on the house. Please. Now tell me what kind you want," Emma offered.

Miguel and I enjoyed a wonderful lunch together at the diner. There were other people in the restaurant, families, couples, and individuals, and no one treated us like we were unwelcomed.

In the middle of our meal, Miguel observed, "Edgar, you see what I mean? Emma and Ernest are nice people. We aren't going to let that sign interfere with our relationship with them. I don't know what it's about, and I'm not going to worry about it. The USA is a country of opportunities. You'll have so many opportunities—you'll see."

Before we left, Miguel thanked Emma and Ernest warmly. In her highly animated way, Emma responded, "Miguel, you're a beautiful man, and I don't care if my husband hears me. You're a beautiful man with a big heart."

Miguel laughed and gave her a hug.

That night, when Miguel was watching the news, he turned to me, pointing at the TV, and said, "You see that man? There's an angel for you."

On the TV I saw a dark-skinned man with a slight mustache. He was wearing a suit and surrounded by many people.

"Who's that, Miguel?" I asked.

Miguel explained, "That's the Reverend Martin Luther King, Jr. He's working to get equal rights for black Americans—and all Americans. He's been arrested several times. But even still, he doesn't call for violence. He's all about peace and love. He even thanked the people when they released him from jail. This man loves everybody. He's a big inspiration to me."

As the weeks and months went by, I was progressing in school, and my English was getting better and better. Every day after school, Margaret had me put everything in writing that I'd done that day. She figured the writing would allow me to express myself in English better and to write and spell more accurately.

Every afternoon I would spend about ten minutes writing these descriptions and then Margaret would review the writing with me. After some weeks of this routine, Mrs. Tudor noticed that both my writing and speaking had dramatically improved.

In addition to homework and improving my speaking and writing, I also worked in the jewelry shop after school. When I arrived home, after I ate a snack, I would sweep the entire shop, all the floors and underneath every table. I would collect everything I'd swept up in a glass jar because in my cleaning, I swept up tiny silver and gold filings along with dust and dirt. Each jeweler and silversmith had many instruments and tools, and, as they would file, shavings and small bits from the precious metals would come off and fall to the floor.

When the two containers were completely full of debris, I would take them into a room and separate out the precious metal shavings from the dirt. After several weeks when there was a substantial amount of these shavings, Margaret would sell them.

After sweeping, my job was to clean the store's secured room. The Lamberts kept all the precious metals, gold, silver, precious stones, and completed jewelry pieces in a large vault in a secured room. My job was to make sure that all of these valuable items were in the right place and labeled correctly. Ongoing orders and incoming orders were also organized in the room. We kept everything tidy and systematized.

Margaret also taught me to appropriate the needed amount of precious metals required for specific jobs. For example, if there were to be thirty bracelets made out of silver, I would appropriate a certain amount of silver for those bracelets based on weight and what the silversmith requested. This work happened in the secure room too.

Only the Lamberts and I had access to this room. None of the workers, not even Miguel, ever entered the room.

When personal buyers and vendors came to place orders, pick up jewelry, or sell items, they interacted with Margaret.

No one and nothing came into or went out of the jewelry store without Margaret's knowing about it. No clients dealt with anyone other than Margaret. When I was out of school and available, I worked as Margaret's "right hand man," as she explained it.

One time when I was working with Margaret, a vendor was there to sell Margaret an item. I'd been going back and forth, in and out of the secured room, when the vendor turned to Margaret and asked, "What's the deal with the kid going in and out of the vault?"

"What do you mean?" was her reply.

"Aren't you worried about losing anything?"

Margaret stopped what she was doing and looked him straight in the eye. Next she stated, "First of all, it is none of your business. It's of no concern to you how I run this place. Second of all, Edgar is my most trusted son."

Since he'd been working with Margaret for years, the vendor retorted, "Your son is an adult, and you don't have any other children."

Margaret paused for a few seconds and eventually replied, "Now I do. And don't you ever say anything like that again."

He became quite embarrassed and apologetic.

Margaret then instructed me, "Edgar, get this man a cold drink of water while we finish this transaction."

I returned with a big glass of cold water.

"Thank you, Edgar," he said as he took the glass from my hand. It seemed that he wanted to say something else to me, but he stopped himself.

Miguel and I were at Pitman Foods, a specialty grocery store that had the largest array of fruits, vegetables, spices, and cooking and baking supplies of any grocery in Phoenix. They even sold coconut popsicles and an array of ice creams. It was a very popular store with customers from all different backgrounds because it offered a huge selection of items for making both American and international foods.

We were there, searching for a certain *chilé*, when boxes and bags went flying. Customers and employees dropped what they were doing and fled to the door. It wasn't a siege or a fire—it was an immigration raid. As this was a busy store, a huge bottleneck of people formed at the door, fighting to get out. And I was right there with them.

Though many got detained right there at the door, I managed to push my way out, ducking under the arms and legs of green-suited officers, and I dashed down an alleyway. Then I mashed myself under a gate, crossed another street, and scooted my way through some shrubs to the back of a house where I encountered a dog on a long chain. It immediately started barking. I hesitated, wondering if it would be a benefit or a liability to stay with the barking dog.

A short chain-link fence separated the house from the next, so I climbed over it and kept moving. I found a house that sat on top of large cement blocks, almost like it was on stilts. I got down on my hands and knees, and crawled into the dark, damp crawlspace underneath. Two cats bolted out past me. I continued dog-walking it deeper and deeper underneath. I made my way past pipes, tubes, and more cement support columns. It was tight and mostly dark but with occasional lines of light coming in from the outside.

I had to keep my head low, so as not to hit it. I didn't want to go too deeply in because I feared scorpions and snakes. But I knew I shouldn't stay too close to the periphery because that made me vulnerable to being seen.

I felt my heart pounding. My breath was short and rapid. "This is it. This is the time. I'll never see Margaret and Miguel again. Mrs. Tudor and my classmates will find out I'm illegal, and then they'll feel angry and betrayed!" my mind shouted.

I heard sounds from the outside. Louder and louder and more firm—footsteps. Then they stopped. After several seconds I heard them again. Then they stopped.

I froze. My hands sat stiff and firm in the cool dirt. My knees and feet also rested in a kind of paralysis. My head stayed low but cocked, so I could make out potential noises.

When I turned my head, my gaze shifted to a beam of light, and there before me, I made out a face staring straight at me. A man, also on his hands and knees, with his eyes directly on me, was positioned a few yards from me underneath the house. He was wearing the distinctive green uniform.

A gruesome, cruel episode of déjà vu was playing out before me. Horror and nausea washed over me. I stayed frozen.

The man was pretty much in the same position as I was.

Both on our hands and knees, we faced one another. We stared at each other. Time seemed to stop in this eyes-locked stance. Occasionally noises from both the outside and also from inside the house made their way to us.

Without warning, the fear left me. Extreme exhaustion took its place. I became so tired that I no longer cared. "I give up," a voice inside my head announced. "This is the end—so be it. He'll capture me and they'll throw me out of the country—and that's fine," the voice in my mind declared.

It was interesting, the way my feelings changed in an instant, from fright to not caring about anything whatsoever. I'd accepted the outcome.

All the while, the face continued to watch me. I even detected a small smile, as if trying to coax me into trusting.

Then the man reversed his crawl, carefully moving backwards and out from underneath the house. The sounds of his footsteps grew fainter and fainter. He was gone.

I burst out crying. I cried hard for only a minute and then made my exit from the dank, dark underneath. I left the backyard, jumped another fence, and made my way home.

This was the second time I'd been granted a pass to go free. Why? What did it mean? What should I do?

Over the months since that first raid, there had been days and even weeks when I hadn't thought of raids and deportation. I could immerse myself in school and chores and relationships. But other times, when I was out with Margaret or my brother or when I was at school or the jewelry shop, I'd look around and plan my getaway in case a raid suddenly occurred. I'd become paranoid and stifled. It was a burden and a horror knowing that in a span of a few minutes my life could be turned completely around.

When I arrived home, the mood was sour. Margaret was very upset, and Miguel distraught. He hugged me, saying, "I'm sorry."

Margaret came to me and lamented, "This can't go on. You must leave. You must go and get this fixed, and I will help you with everything that is needed."

I agreed. It was time to start over because I couldn't handle another raid. I just couldn't do it again.

We made a plan that Miguel and I would return to Nogales

in three days' time.

After a sleepless night, I went to school the next day. I didn't know what to say, but I knew I would not lie to Mrs. Tudor. I had to tell her the truth—that I was leaving and why—though I knew it would be difficult and I'd feel ashamed.

When I saw Mrs. Tudor, my eyes were slightly teary, and I felt a very empty sensation throughout my body and soul. I was about to say something when she said, "I know something is bad, Edgar. We'll talk after school."

I had no appetite. I only ate a couple of bites of my lunch, which was very unusual for me. A couple of my classmates thought that I was sick.

The dreaded meeting took place at 4 pm in the teachers' lounge. Mrs. Tudor sat down and lit a cigarette. All the teachers were permitted to smoke in the lounge. Though Mrs. Tudor wore perfume, probably to camouflage the smell of smoke, it did not help. I'd known since first meeting her that she was a smoker.

Mrs. Tudor was quite old. When she carried her purse on her left forearm, I could see wrinkled skin hanging from her arm. She had drooping skin underneath her chin and jaw. She tried to hide her wrinkles with makeup, but it did not help much. The makeup exaggerated the wrinkles. Her eyes were beautiful, and her feelings towards me were genuine and sincere. I greatly respected her and considered her an elegant lady. However, I worried about her and the smoking because of my father and his terrible death. If only she would quit.

Mrs. Tudor cleared her throat as I sat in front of her. "What's on your mind, Edgar?" she questioned. "I can tell something bad is going on."

I told her, "It has been a wonderful few months, being here with you as my teacher and having all these classmates help me and support me. They have helped me learn a lot. I have come to appreciate all of you, especially you, Mrs. Tudor, for all the things you have taught me."

"This sounds like a departure speech," she observed. "Is that the case? Is Miguel okay?"

"Mrs. Tudor, I came here illegally. I have no documents. Several times now I have come very close to being deported. It's been difficult, so Miguel decided that it's time for me to return to Nogales, so I can get my legal documents. We don't know how long it will take. All I know is that I want to get my legal documents and come back to the United States as soon as possible. I just wanted you to know that I will not be here on Monday. Please let my classmates know why I left the country and tell them the truth. They don't deserve to be lied to."

"Do you really want me to tell them the truth?" she asked.

"Yes. I would like for you to tell them that I came here illegally and we're going back to Nogales to make it right. Hopefully, we can come back safely, and we'll meet again."

"You know, this is very big of you and big of Miguel. You are in a very tough situation, and I don't envy you one bit. It's also honorable of you to be able to tell me this. You didn't have to do that. I don't know whether I'll see you again. Truly, you did not even have to tell me anything. I know it is very difficult for you to share this, but I want you to know how much I appreciate your candor."

She continued, "It's not every day most people encounter the events that you, as a young individual, have had to deal with. And now you've chosen to share your situation. Thank you, Edgar.

"Miguel is a good and honest man, and he's had to make some difficult decisions for you. The fact that you're going back to straighten it out is good. Once you return, you will never be deported, and you'll no longer have to be afraid."

"Yes, Mrs. Tudor. That's how I see it too," I concurred.

"I gather that there are many people living here in the United States, hiding as you have been doing. Some people have been living here for years and have been in hiding longer than you. There's also a lot of people working hard to get their legal papers. We hope that everybody does it and does it soon."

Mrs. Tudor stood up, gave me a hug, and wished me luck. She said she would explain everything to my classmates and the principal. She assured me that they would not judge me harshly.

Even still, I told her that Miguel and I hoped that they would not be too upset at us.

In May 1960, after spending seven months in the United States, I was set to return to Nogales. I was ten years old.

Margaret approved of my return to Nogales, but she was also broken-hearted. She could hardly speak in those three days before my departure.

Miguel's fellow jewelry craftsmen knew we had to leave and why. They put together $200 for us. It was an immense amount of money. I've never forgotten their kindness and generosity.

Miguel had $1,500, which he hoped would be enough to get all the expenses paid and the immigration process completed. Early in the morning, we got in the car and began driving, exiting Phoenix in the reverse order from my arrival. It was bittersweet driving along the wide and glorious Seventh Street, in the opposite direction—back to Mexico rather than into the US—but I knew it was right. I felt positive and confident about what we were doing.

13

I absolutely loved my time as chief resident in the pediatric surgery rotation because I loved with a passion all my pediatric patients—children and babies.

I'd been monitoring baby Jonathan for the past five days. Since birth, five days earlier, he'd been on a respirator because he had poorly underdeveloped lungs, secondary to the fact that his intestines had moved up inside his chest through a congenital defect, or hole, in his diaphragm, which, in turn, did not allow his lungs to fully develop and expand. Therefore, from birth baby Jonathan's biggest problem was the inability to ventilate his lungs. I was experienced enough to know that when the babies were born with congenital defects, it was not uncommon that they died of complications. However, it didn't make it any easier for the parents, nurses, or me.

Upon arriving in the morning to the neonatal unit, I learned that baby Jonathan had died. It was not good news. I'd become quite attached to Jonathan and to his parents. We'd see each other at least two times a day to confer. I knew that the young couple had been trying for some time to have a baby. And now I needed to speak to them—to tell them the sad news. The question was—what do you say to parents that just lost a lovely baby?

The attachment that the mother and father had developed to Jonathan was something to see. They'd been at Jonathan's bedside almost nonstop since he'd been born. The couple was kind, gentle, and quiet. They had a full understanding that the chances of their child making it were quite small. Even still, they didn't hold back their love. They loved Jonathan whole-heartedly.

It is the job of the physician to talk to parents in these circumstances, inform them of the death of their baby, and console them, but how can you console someone that just lost a small baby? I did the best I could.

I delivered to them the news in the gentlest manner possible, and the couple received it—quietly, painfully, sadly.

When he could speak, the father told me, "Dr. Hernandez, thank you and thank everybody for the care you gave our baby. We knew from the outset that the prognosis was not very good."

With tears streaming from her eyes the mother managed to say, "Dr. Hernandez, I'm young enough. I can have another baby, I hope."

Her husband added, "Yes, honey, we'll have another baby, but right now let's just comfort each other."

I hugged the couple and made every effort not to get overcome by my own melancholy over the death of their baby. You see—my ears rang with the song of the crying violin. Anytime I was confronted with the death of a child, the wailing chords of Santos Ortiz's violin pursued me to distraction and sometimes to despair. It seemed unlikely that my first real memory—the funeral of the boy who died of a scorpion bite and the despairing music of my town's eccentric that I'd witnessed when I was about 4.5 years old—would dog me into adulthood, but that's what happened.

Just as with this couple, most parents who lose their babies take it very hard but also hope for another, which is understandable. We all need hope. They reminded me of a wonderful Mexican couple whom I'd first met when I was a boy. This couple also yearned for a child of their own—and they got one, just not in the way they'd expected.

*   *   *

"I know you don't need more bad news," Miguel began, "but there's something I've got to tell you—Aurelio died five days ago."

"No—oh no. What happened?" I asked, shaken and bewildered.

"He always had some kind of medical condition. It involved his blood vessels. I think it got really bad, and it killed him."

Miguel went on, "Aurelio had no family, no children, only a sister who died several years ago. His death is very sad and a big loss for all the people he helped with immigration. Another man that I don't know named Juan Robles has taken over the business. Brenda, the secretary, is still there, and she has documents for us."

So, I wouldn't be seeing Aurelio, a man who I'd grown to understand had a big heart for assisting people. Yes, it was a loss, and I could tell that it was a different Nogales that I was returning to.

I'd also thought of the American border officer, the one whom I'd deceived. While I was relieved to be returning to Nogales, I felt afraid and anxious when I considered this man. I determined that just as I'd told Mrs. Tudor the truth, if this man was still working in Nogales, I would tell him the truth and I'd ask for his forgiveness.

We arrived at the checkpoint in Nogales, a very familiar place to me. The entry and exit gates had changed somewhat; they were more modern and looked more robust. There were no more chain-link fences. Actually, there were no gates either, only tall cage-looking sort of closets where the attending officials were housed. A door would open and the officer would emerge from the cage-closet space to speak to people, both pedestrians and drivers. I found it more modern and fancy.

After getting a room in the same hotel we'd stayed in last time, Miguel and I made our way to Aurelio's office to see Brenda. We talked some with her about Aurelio's death, and then she introduced us to the man who had taken over the business, a short, stocky lawyer named Juan Robles.

Mr. Robles let us know that he was a man of education who came from a wealthy Mexican family. When he spoke of immigration, it seemed he resented Mexicans trying to immigrate to the United States. He also said that Aurelio had given too much advice that didn't make sense, something Miguel and I both disagreed with.

Mr. Robles went on to tell us, "Here's all the documents Aurelio left for you. You owe the office $15 for processing fees and for the time spent collecting your documents. You'll find my fees are to be paid on an hourly basis, which differs from Aurelio's payment system."

Needless to say, Mr. Robles didn't impart a similar level of concern that Aurelio had shown us.

Miguel paid the bill, and we took the documents back to the hotel room. There we reviewed them, item per item—all seemed to be in order. We even had our father's death certificate, which had arrived five weeks prior, based on the date of the envelope.

We immediately headed over to the Consulate. At this point, we felt confident in our knowledge of the immigration process. We knew where to go and what to do because we'd done it before. Now we had all the documents that they'd told us to get.

We took a number from the counter and found seats. Again, we found ourselves in the very big, very busy open room. Kids were running around, and people nervously sat, waiting their turns, wondering about their futures. I just hoped and prayed that they had their documents in order and would pass legally into the US. I didn't want any of them to have to experience the terror of raids.

I noted that our number was seven, we'd driven down Seventh Street, and I'd spent seven months in Phoenix—did these sevens signify good luck? I didn't know, but I was grabbing for anything that suggested we'd find success on this day.

I saw the lovely blonde-haired, blue-eyed lady that had reviewed our documents last time. She was moving from one place to another in a hurried manner. I hoped very much we would be working with her again. I knew she would help us if she could.

My brother observed, "There she is again. Let's go to the counter to see if we can work with her because she is familiar with our case."

At the counter sat a tall, well-groomed gentleman. He had a small mustache and wore a blue uniform with patches and decorations on the shoulders. "Can I help you?" he asked.

"When it is our turn, I was wondering if we could see that young lady there because she took care of us last time. She's knows our case."

"I can't make that arrangement. You just have to wait your turn, and you'll get a chance to meet one of the officers here— maybe her, maybe someone else—whoever is free. It really shouldn't matter because they all do the same work. Take a seat, and we'll call you as soon as we can."

It was disappointing that he wouldn't allow us to work with

her. I thought it would have been a nice gesture, but we were all just numbers to him, so we would have to wait our turn and work with whoever was open—just like everyone else. Overall Miguel and I understood that this was fair.

As we were returning to our seat, two young kids ran in front of us and almost tripped my brother. The place had become even more crowded in the twenty minutes we'd been waiting.

"Number 7—it's your turn. Number 7 please."

Miguel and I showed our number and walked through an entryway and down a long, straight hall. The woman with the blonde hair and blue eyes was in the hallway.

"Good afternoon, do you remember me?" I asked.

She replied, "Maybe, but I can't be sure." After that she slowly walked away and looked back at me twice as she proceeded down the hall.

They placed us in a room where we waited anxiously. I was hoping that it would not take very long and that soon we could re-cross the border back into the US, so I could return to school and catch up with any lessons I'd missed.

An officer, a young man, entered the room, greeting us and asking that we be patient while he reviewed our documents. He was very polite and quite social. He made small talk with us, asking about the weather and how we liked the city of Nogales. We answered all his questions politely and gave him the additional documents that the officer had asked for on the previous visit.

With all the documents in a carefully sequenced stack in front of him, he started reviewing each one. As he looked at each item, he sort of talked to himself, reading parts aloud and making checks. This is how he reviewed all twenty-five documents. It took him forty-five minutes, and we answered his questions as they arose.

After that he closed the folder and put a signature on the outside, something that we found promising.

He explained, "Edgar needs to go get a TB test. Also I'll need four photographs of him. Please return with these things in three days. At that time, you'll be able to meet with my senior office to do a second review. That's when they'll make a final decision on your application."

We had a doctor conduct the tuberculosis test. The doctor found no problems. We returned to the Consulate three days later with those results and the photographs.

Because my application had been filed and was already in progress from the meeting three days prior, we didn't have to wait with a number. Instead, we could head into a room to meet with the more senior-level official.

A gray-haired man entered, immediately announcing, "You passed the TB test. Let me see the photos."

He never looked us in the eye. He never said anything else.

From here, he opened my file and began examining the twenty-five documents in it, starting with the birth certificate.

After a few seconds, he asked, "Why does your last name, Hernandez-Hernandez, on your birth certificate not reflect your father's last name, Hernandez-Cabrera? It doesn't make sense."

Miguel was equally perplexed but for different reasons. "We saw an officer several months ago and another yesterday—both of them made no mention of this, so we thought everything was fine in that regard."

The senior officer stated, "You need to get a birth certificate correction."

Miguel retorted, "We have documents signed by Edgar's mother. This means that we have her consent, so consent really shouldn't be an issue."

"You are right," the gray-haired man responded, "But I'm not saying consent is the problem. The problem is how to differentiate Edgar Hernandez from another Edgar Hernandez. If Edgar's last name was corrected to Cabrera, it could prevent potential fraud and confusion. It would be most clear and easy for the Mexican and American governments if his last name were listed correctly, on his birth certificate and the visa. This is standard procedure, and you must comply with it to get a visa."

"Can we just go ahead and process the application, and I'll file to get it corrected at a later time so that we will not have to wait so long?" my brother pleaded. "The priest who wrote the birth certificate was in his eighties when Edgar was born, and it is likely he simply made an error."

"But that's not all that's missing. We also need documents from Edgar's school. The documents you've given here don't account for what Edgar has been doing this current school year," the man informed us.

Needless to say, Miguel and I were devastated. Once again, we faced a real problem—and a new problem.

Miguel realized he had to concede and then figure out how to best proceed. My brother asked, "Would an addendum to the birth certificate be appropriate or not?"

"Yes, an addendum signed by the city president and by the boy's mother—I think that will suffice. We must have an official letter explaining the error and giving the correction. Also we need to have a letter from the principal where he's been going to school this school year. It is essential that we have that. We'll go ahead and keep the application on file until you produce the required documents. We'll leave some of these segments blank until you produce the requested items."

Miguel and I were stunned. Shocked. I didn't say anything. Both of us were speechless and utterly disappointed.

We trudged out, ragged and defeated.

It was a very long walk back to the hotel. We paid no attention to the people around us or the vehicles that zoomed by us. We were in our own zone of stunned defeat.

I wondered if this setback was a sign that I should stop and turn back. I told my brother, "Please let me go back home to La Mira. You've done all you can. I've had the happiest months of my life while I was in Phoenix. I learned a lot, and maybe the English I speak now will be of some benefit to me in the future. I feel very confident that I can have a good life."

My brother responded, "No way. We're not going to give up on this. We're too far in, and we won't give up. How many of those hundred-plus people in that room do you think will be successful? And for those who find success, do you think it's easy for them? Don't you think that many of those families in there are going through obstacles worse than ours? Maybe some of them will never even have a chance. But we have a good chance. Let's go ahead and sleep on it, and then in the morning, we can stop by and see Mr. Robles to get his advice."

The next morning with heavy hearts we went to see Juan Robles.

His response to our situation: "That's the law and you have live with it."

"Yes, we already realize this. We are wondering if you have any advice or suggestions for going about fulfilling these two requirements," Miguel explained.

"You mean you don't want to entertain the alternative—and have the boy go back illegally?" Mr. Robles offered sarcastically.

"What should we do? How should we go about it?" Miguel asked again.

Mr. Robles responded, "You do exactly what everyone else does. You wait and you comply and then you'll get a signature and then you can go across."

He then added, "I don't understand why all these people are flocking to go to the United States. Mexico is a great country. Why can't you make it here? I'm a lawyer. My family is all lawyers, and we're making very good livings."

My brother responded, "You are a lucky man from a fortunate family, but many other Mexicans are not as fortunate as you are. So many of us don't have many options to live well. We're looking for a better way of life, not just for ourselves but for our families. This is what I want for my brother, and I'm willing to sacrifice whatever it takes so that we get him legally immigrated. I made him a promise many months ago that I would never leave him, I would never leave without him, and I would always have him by my side—and I will never break that promise. I also said to him that we would do it right. We're going to proceed and do whatever it takes, so if you want to help us with some guidance, then fine. If you don't want to, then don't."

Miguel's fierce words managed to resuscitate me, giving me that fighting spirit I'd been lacking. My brother became stronger too. Also Mr. Robles experienced a dramatic shift in demeanor.

"Can you get a letter from Edgar's teacher in La Mira that covers Edgar's schooling all the way up to the present even though Edgar was going to school out of that area in these past seven months?"

"I think so," my brother said, "I think we can send him a letter and explain everything to him. Maybe he will help us, but he's a very honest man, and I don't think he would lie. I hate putting him in this position, so we'll have to see what he has to say."

Mr. Robles expected the addendum to my birth certificate would take some time. He really felt that this correction, from a legal standpoint, wasn't necessary. Also he didn't understand why the signature from my mother was needed, considering she'd already given Miguel parental rights over me. But if the officer made these requirements, they wouldn't change them, and we'd have to comply.

Miguel turned to me, explaining, "Because this will take several months, in all likelihood, Edgar, you are going to have to stay here in Nogales while I return to Phoenix and work. I'll visit you regularly. I'm not abandoning you at all. We are going to have to find a good person or family for you to stay with. Does this make sense?"

"Miguel, I understand. I'm not afraid," I told him.

"Mr. Robles, I was thinking of asking Eliseo Perez, the jewelry store owner, if Edgar could stay with him for a few months. Do you think that's a good idea?"

"No, stay away from that guy. He's a drunk and irresponsible. He runs a good business as a jeweler, but come sundown he turns to drink. He's been in jail at least a dozen times this year. I know for a fact because I've helped get him out."

Miguel looked at Mr. Robles and asked, "Would you show some kindness and let Edgar stay with you? I will pay you."

"Miguel, I don't think it would be a good idea. I'm not married, and I don't have children because I'm not ready to be a family man. I don't want that kind of responsibility right now."

We weren't surprised at his response. He seemed like a ladies man. He dressed well and frequently combed his hair. He had two mirrors in his office that I assumed he used to regularly evaluate his appearance.

My brother asked Brenda, but she also declined.

At least we can say that they were honest. My brother appreciated their responses and thanked them, as he always did, with sincere kindness.

Once outside the office, Miguel looked me in the eye and announced, "We need to talk about what we're going to do. My idea is you'll stay here somehow. Then I can go back and work and come here periodically to see you. No matter what, I'm not going to take you illegally back to the US, and you're not going to go back to La Mira either. You'll stay here until we get all of the proper documents, and then we will show the American immigration officers that we are responsible people and we intend to comply with whatever documents they need."

My brother added, "You may be twenty years old by the

time you cross, but if that's what it takes, then I'll stick with you."

Truly, Miguel was making me really confident that we could handle these obstacles and that we wouldn't be giving up.

That same day, Miguel wrote a letter to César explaining what we needed from him. He told him all the events that had occurred since I'd left La Mira. It was a lengthy letter. He asked César for a rapid response and emphasized the urgency of the situation. We went to the post office where Miguel mailed the letter.

After that, we went to a restaurant called Elvira's to tackle the issue of where I would stay and with whom.

"Miguel, I'm not scared at all. I'm not even scared to stay here in Nogales alone. After all we've been through in Phoenix, for some reason, I feel safe here in Nogales. It doesn't seem like a huge question mark."

"Edgar, I appreciate your bravery. And you make a good point. But personally—where and who you'll stay with concern me. And I'm not talking in terms of money. I want you safe, comfortable, and happy. I have to feel comfortable with who you stay with. We need to find a kind person to help us. Someone with a good heart. Someone that can understand everything that has happened to us. We'll find somebody. I believe we will find someone."

We had a good lunch at Elvira's. Our waitress was also named Elvira, but she had no relation to the owner. She was nice, well groomed, with clean nails and smooth-looking hands. She had beautiful dark skin, black hair, and pretty eyes with thick eyebrows and long eyelashes.

My brother suddenly asked me, "What do you think of our waitress? Do you think we should ask her to sit with us and talk about you staying with her for a while? It's not busy right now, so maybe she has time." He went on to joke, "And with our luck, we might end up getting shot by her husband or sent to jail just for asking for her help."

I could tell he was in good humor. I laughed. We both laughed. A couple of people sitting nearby glanced at us, wondering what we were laughing about.

At that time, it was okay to have some humor. Miguel felt secure at his job and in his relationship with the Lamberts, so he knew that they would support him if we had to wait it out for even a year. We even figured that we could get lucky, and the paperwork could get approved in six months.

When the waitress asked if we needed anything else and if we were satisfied with the food and the service, my brother responded, "More than enough."

Next Miguel asked, "Is it okay for me to talk to you about something?"

With a puzzled look on her face, she turned to us.

Miguel continued, "Granted, we are total strangers. However, we need your help. My brother, Edgar, could not get all the documents to immigrate to the US, and I need to leave him here in Nogales because I live and work in Phoenix. Would you consider letting Edgar stay with you?"

As soon as he posed the question, she was taken aback, waving her hands back and forth as if she didn't want to have anything to do with continuing the conversation.

Miguel kept on speaking, "It will only be for a short amount of time, and we'll try not to be a burden to you."

"How long?" she ventured to inquire.

"Several months to, perhaps, a year,"

"A year? That's impossible," she told him.

She looked at me and then back at Miguel. She seemed to have calmed some and continued to listen to what my brother was saying.

He conveyed to her that he knew he was asking for something big—and that it was hard for him on his part to have to ask. He explained everything about our situation, even my seven-month stay in the US illegally and the fact that we had to make it right.

She said to Miguel, "I don't know what to say. It's a great responsibility to take this child with me, and I really need to talk to my husband."

My brother told her, "I'm an honest man. I have a very good job. I promise you that you will be compensated. I would come back every three weeks like clockwork to visit all of you."

"I'd like to go ahead and talk to my husband. I have my break soon, and I'll return with him after the break."

Fifteen minutes later, we saw her with her husband. He was a short man with a little mustache and curly hair. They didn't come near us; they stayed over by the counter and talked for a while.

Finally, they approached us. The man inspected us thoroughly from top to bottom and then stuck out his hand, saying, "My name is Javier."

Miguel shook his hand, responding, "I'm Miguel. This is my brother, Edgar."

"How long is this going to take?" Javier asked.

"A few months to, perhaps, a year," my brother answered. "I just don't know exactly. We have an attorney here by the name of Juan Robles who can attest to our honesty and good intentions."

Javier noted, "We need to talk about this more—and in private."

My brother agreed, "Please take your time. We have all the time that you need, and we don't want you to feel that you have to give us an answer right now. You can wait and we can come back and meet you here tomorrow or we can meet where you work or wherever you like. We just need your help, and we need your help desperately."

My brother continued, "As I told your wife, I have a good job in the United States, and here are letters attesting to my financial and personal integrity. The letters are from our attempt to get Edgar a visa. This letter is from my employer."

Javier replied, "I can't read English."

"I can tell you in all honesty that this letter says that I have a secure job, that I own my own car, and that I have a clean record with the Phoenix police department, so you never have to worry about anything like that."

My brother took them outside to see his car. He showed them the title and registration. They talked for quite some time.

After talking for a while, Miguel returned and suggested to me, "Why don't you smile at them, okay? Let them know that you're a nice kid and you're very polite."

I looked over to where they were standing and smiled a couple of times. They regarded us with suspicion and some curiosity too. I continued to smile at them.

Then they approached us and said to my brother, "You say you'll return here every three weeks?"

Miguel confirmed, "Yes, sir, I will be here. I will give you

$100 now, and then I will pay you $20 a month. I will bring food from Phoenix too."

Elvira turned to Javier, urging, "We should help them. Besides, we have no children. He is a small child and won't take up very much room in our tiny apartment."

Miguel suggested, "Can we have breakfast, lunch, and dinner together for two days straight so that we can become acquainted with each other and get more comfortable with this possibility? I would very much like to do that. I think it would be good for all of us."

Javier and Elvira agreed.

Over those two days, we hit it off really well. Elvira and Javier seemed like really nice people. Elvira was warm and kind, and Javier had a laugh that was contagious. He laughed like a chipmunk.

Miguel looked very much at ease. He felt confident about the arrangement.

Javier commented to Miguel, "Edgar speaks excellent English."

Miguel added, "He can write and read in English too. He does very well."

Javier observed, "He could be very helpful. I work at a hotel and we get many American tourists that come to do business here. It would be nice to have someone that can read, write, and speak fluently in English."

"Javier, whatever you want me to do, just let me know. I would love to do anything to help you out," I offered.

Javier looked at me, and I smiled. We all felt pretty good about everything. So it was set—I would stay with Elvira and Javier.

Miguel drove away in his Ford Fairlane, and I walked with Javier and Elvira to their small apartment. Right after its entrance to the left of the front door, a stove was nestled in an alcove. There was a mini-refrigerator, about 24 by 24 inches. A curtain separated the kitchen area and the bedroom. Connected to the bedroom was a little closet about the size of a small kitchen table. That would be my sleeping quarters.

Elvira explained, "You will sleep in here. It's not a real mattress, but it's very spongy and comfortable, and it's warm in here."

I said to them both, "I am very lucky to have both of you helping me. Some day, I'll make it up to you. My brother's a very honest man. He's a man of his word. He will be here every third Thursday, and he will compensate you for everything you do for me."

Elvira gave me a hug and assured me, "You have no reason to worry. We both work, we don't have any children, and I think it will be great to have you here."

I thought to myself, "I am so blessed to have a third mother."

I kept very busy. I worked at the hotel with Javier, running errands and assisting the hotel administration. I took clothes to the cleaners and shoes to get repaired or polished. I made sure people's clothing was nicely ironed and their suits had no wrinkles. I picked up meals.

At the hotel I met people from Mexico City—engineers, business people that worked with textiles or home-building products, and other professionals. It was a huge event for me to see all these people coming into the hotel with their beautiful luggage and handsome suits. I saw Americans too. It was a very active hotel.

I tried looking for the English teacher that had taught me in my first stay in Nogales, but he had taken a job in Hermosillo. I ended up finding another English teacher named Gloria. She taught English to children of fairly well-off parents. The parents hoped that if their children learned English, they could travel to the United States and someday attend Arizona State University or the University of Arizona or another university there.

I ended up working for Gloria twice a week. My job was to show the pupils how to conduct brief conversations in English. We practiced English in a less formal and more conversational setting. I enjoyed working with the young children. They were a lot of fun and were very interested in learning. I felt extremely lucky to have the opportunity to work with them.

Probably the majority of the time that I was in Nogales, I informally assisted people who were trying to immigrate. From the meetings first with Aurelio and then with Juan Robles and my two attempts, I'd become very comfortable with the immigration process. I knew all the general requirements. I could locate all the departments, agencies, health centers, and other businesses that people needed to visit to meet the various paperwork requirements. I knew where to go for the professional photos and where to go for the blood tests, skin tests, and vaccinations. I knew the most efficient and economical notaries. I also knew the reliable lawyers.

There were numerous items that needed to be done in the immigration process, and I could lead people to the experts who could help them. So, through word of mouth, individuals and families sought me out. People would say, "Go over to the hotel, and you'll find a kid named Edgar. He knows the process and the people—doctors, accountants, lawyers, clinics, agencies— he can show you around. He speaks really good English too."

Someone even told Javier that they trusted me more to lead them to the experts than they trusted the adult professionals because some professionals tried to defraud people or charge a lot of money.

It was true that I helped many people save money. I steered people away from so-called experts who would have overcharged for very simple tasks or who purposefully took a lot of time on tasks in order to make more money off of people who didn't know any better. It gave me great joy to help people just like me—people seeking better lives for themselves and their families in the US.

Sometimes the people I helped would even give me a little money. When this happened, I passed that money on to Elvira and Javier. I treated them like my parents. I wanted them to have whatever I made. I felt that I owed them that much. They were humble people. They didn't want to take any money from me, but I told them I wanted to share everything with them because they'd opened their home to me.

My favorite people to assist were families with children. I loved working with children. I wanted to protect them. I wanted to make sure that everything went well with them. I remember one couple that had two little boys, twins. They told me that for 3.5 years they had been saving money, preparing documents, and preparing themselves for immigration. They'd even sold their small home. The man was a teacher. He was hoping that he could find a better life for his children in the US. I worked with them a lot over several months until they successfully immigrated.

I assisted people from very different backgrounds. Some

people were educated; some people were very poor. Some people seemed to have plenty of money. Other people had no education at all—they could neither read nor write. Though some folks were extremely poor or uneducated, they really wanted to immigrate and help their families and loved ones go across later.

I found people's desires to immigrate so noble. They were not selfish. They wanted to share everything that they were doing. They figured, if they crossed the border, they would make it a chain and bring other relatives across. I thought it was the most wonderful thing, hearing them explain their dreams to me. This is what ignited me. I would wake up in the morning very enthusiastic about assisting these people.

It was very important to me that people steer clear of immigrating illegally with *polleros*. Basically, *polleros* would charge people a hefty fee, several hundred dollars per person, or more, and they would lead people across on back roads and trails through the desert and scrublands. They gave no guarantees, and they took no responsibility if there were problems. People would die of thirst, fall off cliffs, or even get caught by immigration police, and the *polleros* with them would simply deny responsibility, saying something like, "Hey, I don't know these people. They asked me for a ride, so I gave them a ride."

I came to see *polleros* as more terrible than La Migra because at least La Migra had a sense of ethics and responsibility. La Migra had specific laws they were supposed to follow. *Polleros* were lawless and represented only themselves. They provided a service for greed alone. The risks resided only with the immigrants because the *polleros* took no risks and faced no consequences themselves.

I remember when a family of four became so disillusioned with the immigration requirements that they opted to pay *polleros* to take them across illegally. The *polleros* put the husband, wife, and one child in the trunk of a car. The other child wouldn't fit, so they sandwiched him inside a mattress and packed many items around the mattress. Prior to crossing the border, they got out of the line of vehicles and returned to the warehouse where they unpacked the items and opened up the sealed mattress. The child had turned a dark ash gray. The color of death. Apparently, he had suffocated.

Another time I remember seeing a young girl first in the

large room at the American Consulate and then later she had joined a group that was to cross illegally with *polleros*. Apparently her family opted to pay the *polleros* because they thought it would be easier and faster. I heard screaming from behind a building, and when I went to scope out the situation, I saw two *polleros* raping this young girl. I was hidden myself, so I started shouting, making enough noise to worry the rapists. They ended up getting in a car and speeding away while other people came to help the girl.

After witnessing firsthand these two travesties at the hands of *polleros*, all of whom, I should add, got away with no repercussions, I became more adamant than ever that the people I assisted not give up on pursuing the legal process. I emphasized the dangers of paying *polleros*. If I felt that the adults were not taking my advice seriously, I would repeat my appeal that they be patient. Most of the time, I had the feeling the adults agreed with me and accepted my recommendations; however, with some adults, I realized they considered me a child and didn't think I knew what I was talking about.

As time went on, Elvira, Javier, and I made it a point to have breakfast together every Saturday, so we could talk about our week and share stories. Javier was a fabulous storyteller. He loved telling stories about people that would come to the hotel. He told us about an engineer who had lost the use of his legs, so he was in a wheelchair. Apparently this man's upper body was incredibly strong. The man had very large, broad shoulders and thick arms. His hands were huge, and his fingers were massive. The man had amazing dexterity, maneuvering himself and his wheelchair in and out of his car. It was a car made especially for him. Javier found the car very interesting because it could be driven completely with the hands; no leg or footwork was required. The engineer told Javier that the car had cost him a fortune.

Javier told us about wedding receptions that were held at the hotel. He described the fancy dress and radiant joy of the married couples. He described their extended families from grandparents to aunts and uncles to little children. Javier was a person that paid attention to details, and Elvira and I loved listening to the stories of all the people that he'd seen coming to the hotel.

Then, of course, he had to tell Elvira stories about me. He explained how I'd gone to the cleaners to pick up four suits. At the cleaners I found myself deep in conversation with a guy when I was retrieving the suits off a rack. I put them on my back while I was conversing. When I reached the hotel, I handed them over to Javier, who asked, "What's this?" That's when I realized I'd picked up the wrong items—three dresses. Javier just laughed and laughed and laughed. I was embarrassed. I ran all the way back to the cleaners to get the suits before they closed. When I got there, the manager was standing there, waiting for me with the four suits. He had a big smile on his face. While I felt very embarrassed about this story, I knew Javier told it to Elvira in good humor.

I also had some stories of my own; however, many of my stories about people trying to immigrate were not so funny. One thing that I did tell Elvira and Javier was that I truly felt that the majority of people that were trying to immigrate had every good intention of becoming good citizens of the United States. They wanted to go to college, to become teachers, lawyers, or architects. They earnestly sought to improve their lives for their own sakes as well as that of their families'.

Every three weeks, Miguel came to Nogales to see me. He typically brought small gifts from Margaret, like t-shirts and, once, a jacket. Margaret also sent hot dogs, hot dog buns, mustard, ketchup, and relish.

Miguel brought pasta, spaghetti sauce, hamburger meat, and cheese that he cooked to make a meal for Elvira, Javier, and me. I went to the bakery to buy fresh bread. Miguel put a little bit of butter and garlic in a pan and toast the pieces of bread in it. Elvira could make incredible desserts, and she always made something amazing, like *pastel de tres leches*, for our special spaghetti dinners. Elvira and Javier changed into their best clothes for these meals. Javier tucked a large pillowcase into the neck of his shirt to serve as a giant napkin and protect his nice shirt from getting splashed by sauce.

At one of these dinners, several weeks into my time in Nogales, Miguel turned to me and asked, "You look very happy. How are you keeping busy?"

Before I had a chance to respond, Elvira answered, "You're not going to believe all the wonderful things that Edgar is doing. At first he was helping at the hotel doing errands for Javier and just getting to know the city. On top of that, he got a job teaching English with a teacher here in Nogales, and he also has been actively helping people immigrate.

"Edgar has been able to help a lot of people that normally would have already been taken by some of the swindlers here in Nogales. And those darn *polleros*—they ruin people's lives, yet people continue to hire them as a path to getting across. Edgar has told us one story after the other. But he's also been able to help many people so that they don't turn to *polleros*. We're so proud of him—and we want you to be very proud of him too because he really helps people, especially families with little children. He feels that he has to help them to be able to protect the children from any hardships and from any harm."

Blushing, I explained, "I'm a kid, and I want to help other kids too."

With slightly teary eyes, Javier chimed in, "Miguel, we should be thanking you for allowing us to have Edgar become a part of our lives here. For years, my wife and I have been working really hard, barely making it. Now with Edgar we have a spark in our lives, and we find ourselves enjoying things a lot more than before. Before, it was going to work and coming home. Now we come home and we laugh, we go to the movies, we go get ice cream, and we go out and have dinner. We really have been enjoying ourselves, and Edgar has been key in it."

Miguel embraced him, stating, "Thank you, that makes me feel good. I never doubted that you and Elvira would be able to look upon him as his parents and not just as acquaintances."

Miguel turned to me, and we hugged. I missed him so much. I missed Margaret. I missed school. I missed everything in Phoenix. The only things I did not miss were the immigration raids.

"I'm impressed by all the stuff that you're doing here, Edgar. Maybe, you'll be a teacher someday," Miguel commented to me.

"No. I've already decided for a while now that I want to be a doctor, like Papá, only different. That's really what I want. And when I take people to the clinics to get their TB tests and vaccinations and I see the doctors wearing their white coats, stethoscopes, ties, and tie clasps, I become even more determined. I will be a doctor someday. I think I'll be able to help even more people as a doctor than a teacher but in different ways."

"Edgar, I think that anything you put your mind to, you can do. You've already proven that yourself," Miguel assured me.

Elvira and Javier nodded their heads in agreement.

Miguel proceeded to give us an update. He'd received a letter from César who explained that he was doubtful he'd be able to send any documents because there was a whole new administration running the schools. He would try his best to send records as well as a letter that he'd sign and get notarized. The next morning Miguel was going to talk to the people at the immigration department to ask them if this would suffice.

Regarding the addendum to my birth certificate—it was all still in process. Miguel was told to expect it to take another three to four months.

I asked, "What if César can't get those records for us? Or what if his letter isn't acceptable to the Consulate?"

"I actually have a plan," Miguel confided, "It's going to take a little bit of maneuvering, but I think we may be able to get something worked out."

About the expected months of waiting—I really didn't mind. Yes, I desperately missed Miguel and Margaret and Phoenix, but I had patience—and I felt like I was doing important work in Nogales. Really, I was having the time of my life, and as Javier had explained, we were living together as a family, not as acquaintances.

14

After performing both cancerous and noncancerous breast surgeries in my private practice, I got more and more referrals to the point that even though I was a general surgeon, I came to specialize in breast surgeries, typically those involving cancer.

It is not uncommon for me to work with patients who are in denial of their breast cancer such that the mass in their breast has grown very large, has started fungating, meaning a cauliflower-like substance has begun growing outside of the breast, and the skin around the mass is bleeding, dying, or already has died. I have also seen a mass in the breast becomes very, very large, and clearly there is a problem, but a patient in denial has put off doing anything about it until it has gotten even larger.

For patients in denial—and really any patient—pessimism doesn't help. If a doctor shows tremendous doubt or disappointment because the patient let the cancer progress to dangerous degrees, the patient ends up feeling defeated and tends to respond very poorly to the prescribed treatment. Instead of pessimism, these patients need reassurance.

So, for patients like these, I talk to them truthfully and at the same time, I try to offer reassurance and support. I am careful to never, ever put them down or make them feel foolish.

More than once, I have said something along the lines of—"You have an obvious advanced cancer. It's gotten away at this time, but there's a possibility of taking care of you in the following way." Then I'll describe a neoadjuvant chemotherapy treatment plan, which means treating the cancer first with chemo and considering surgery later. Starting with surgery in a large, advanced cancer is not feasible because such a cancer is usually attached to the chest. That's why I start with chemo to stop the cancer from growing, destroy it, and make it disappear from the breast, and then I can perform surgery later.

Like so many things in life, it is unpredictable how cancers maneuver themselves and how they behave. Some cancers that doctors are truly certain will respond to chemotherapy do not, and others do.

What I know is that I will never offer pessimism and doubt to my patients. I give them my expertise, my experience, and lots of reassurance and compassion.

I know how scary it is to sit in an office before an authority figure who seems to hold your future in their hands. It's happened to me before, but the circumstances were quite different.

Whether a patient has been proactive or in denial doesn't matter. I give the person my all because, as I see it, that's my duty.

★   ★   ★

As the months progressed, my English was getting better and better. I was also becoming much more efficient at helping people apply for immigration to the point that I asked Javier if I could sit down with people in a small corner there in the hotel as an established office of sorts.

"Go ahead and do it, it's not a problem," Javier told me.

I had about one family per day come in and see me at the hotel. We talked, and I got to know them. Then I would show them the list, explaining, "See the list? Typically there are twenty-five required documents as laid out on this list. However, depending on your specific situation, you may need more or even a few less. We'll have to see. You need to make sure that each document has its own folder, and you need to arrange the folders in numerical order. You don't want to hand the immigration officer a stack of papers. It's not good. It frustrates them. You want to impress them with your orderliness. Also the folders will keep the documents clean and free of wrinkles. And don't eat food around the documents either."

I think I drove some people crazy with how disciplined I was about everything that needed to be done. I think the discipline was something that I learned from Margaret and from my godfather.

Next I would take the people directly to get photographs, x-rays, TB tests, and blood studies. I'd take them to the best notary in Nogales. One by one I would take them to the places where they could get items from that list of twenty-five.

However, as the months progressed, an area where I, personally, lacked discipline hovered above me in a cloud of anxiety. I'd promised myself that I would speak to the kind border officer whom I had deceived so many months previously, but I found myself reluctant to do so. I avoided going near the area where he worked. Every time I walked that street, I would go south—away from him—never near his gate or close to the restaurant. I was too embarrassed to have him see me, but I'd promised myself, "One of these days, I'm going to go over and talk to him."

Around approximately the eighth month into my stay in Nogales, I mustered the courage and discipline to speak to the border officer. At this time, it had been more than a year since I'd passed through the gate illegally. In that year, I'd spent time in the United States and in Nogales.

I didn't tell Miguel I was going to speak to the man. I didn't tell Javier or Elvira either.

First I went to the restaurant next to where the immigration officer was posted. I hadn't been to the restaurant even one time since I'd returned to Nogales. Once inside, I recognized some of the waiters. One even recognized me.

"Hey, I know you," he said to me.

"I know you too," I told him. "I was here about a year ago. I used to eat bean tacos here."

"Yeah, you're the bean taco kid," he recalled. "You used to pick up food for some of the American officers too."

"Yes, I did," I told him.

As I conversed with the waiter, I regularly peered out the restaurant's windows to see if I could locate the border entry officer. I was feeling nervous, so I decided to order some bean tacos and talk with the waiter some more.

"Things have changed a lot from a year ago. The gates are different," I commented.

"Yep, they came in and fixed the street. They got rid of the chain-link fence, and now there's just an officer on each side of the drive."

I asked, "Do you remember that officer that used to work there?"

"It's still the same officers from a year ago. The officers never changed. It's the same ones since you were here before."

I decided to search for the border officer to see if he was currently on duty, so I finished my food and wished the waiter well.

Immediately upon exiting the restaurant, my heart started pounding. My legs felt slow and jelly-like. I felt my jaw tightening and my teeth chattering a bit. Everything in my body was telling me not to look for the officer. I said to myself, "He can't arrest me, he can't hurt me, so what am I afraid of?"

I stopped and took some deep breaths. I resolved that I would find him to tell him the truth and to apologize—and that was that. With this newfound determination, I managed to regain my composure. I headed towards the gate.

From a distance, I spotted him. He was wearing a fairly new uniform and a cap that looked military-like. He looked crisp and professional.

Upon seeing him, I started feeling good about my decision to speak to him. After he looked at the documents of two people, it was my turn.

He looked at me, and I looked at him.

He asked, "So, how are you? *¿Cómo estás tu?* Come on in and have a seat. I've got some cold drinks."

"Thank you very much," I told him when he handed me a drink.

"Your English is great," he commented.

I laughed, and he laughed. But we didn't say anything.

Then after a moment, he asked, "What are you doing here?"

"I'd like to talk to you. Is there a time that you and I can talk? I hate disturbing you while you are working."

"I'll be ready to have lunch in about an hour."

"I'm just going to go run a couple of errands, and then I'll be back. We can meet at the restaurant," I told him.

He looked at me and then asked, "You are coming back, aren't you?"

I laughed again, a little louder than before, and he laughed also. Here we were—laughing about that thing that had happened. I realized that this man was an incredible person. I couldn't wait to sit down and talk to him over lunch.

I went to the hotel to find Javier.

At the hotel, Javier called out, "*Hijo*, what are you doing?"

"I just came over to pick up those documents that were supposed to be notarized and dropped back here for the family I'm supposed to meet later on."

"Yeah, they're here. They were dropped off this morning by the notary. They left an invoice for you too. I told them I would go ahead and pay it, and then you can repay me. But they said it's not a problem. They said that you can go ahead and pay them later on because they have other documents for you. Looks like you have a pretty good relationship with the accountant and notary. Typically they're strict about getting paid, but I guess they're not worried about you."

"They never have to worry about me because I always pay on time."

Javier said, "Good boy. That's what I like."

Then I asked, "Do you remember the story of when I crossed the border and I told you that I lied to the very nice immigration officer? I said, I am going to Safeway to get some grapes, but I never came back?"

"Yes, I remember. What about it?" Javier asked.

"I went over to visit the officer this morning."

"You did?" Javier responded quizzically.

"Yes, I did. I went over to visit him."

"What did he say?" Javier asked.

"He didn't say anything. He just laughed, and I just laughed. We both laughed. When I left, we were still laughing. So I'm going to go back and meet him for lunch soon."

"Good boy. I'm so proud of you. You're becoming a man before my eyes."

A while later, I walked back to the restaurant to await the border entry officer. When he entered, he had a smile on his face. As he sat down next to me, he asked, "As I recall, your name is Edgar. Am I correct?"

"Yes, Edgar Hernandez. What about you—what's your name?"

"I'm Larry. Larry Murphy."

I told him, "I've been here for about eight months, and I had every intention to come and see you. But, I had fears about facing you, and then finally I decided it was time. I want you to know how badly I feel because I lied to you."

"There's only one thing I want you to promise," Mr. Murphy responded, "Promise that outside your parents and people that you have confidence with, you won't talk about what happened."

I told him, "Anytime I talked about it, I never mentioned your name. For one thing, I didn't even know your name. And now that I know your name, I still won't use it."

"I knew you weren't coming back," he revealed.

"You did?" I asked, surprised.

He continued, "I knew it. I know everything about people here. And I don't know why I let you cross. I still, to this day, don't know why I did it. I thought about it all that day, 'What did I just do?' I went home, and I talked to my wife. I said, 'Can you believe what I did today?' The first thing she said, 'Don't you be talking about that. You could get fired.' But I told her that you would never talk about me in particular. I knew you wouldn't. I told her I just didn't think you'd do that."

I replied, "I never did. I only described you as a nice officer, and that's
about it."

"Well, thank you. So, why are you here?"

"I spent seven months in the United States, and those seven months were the best months of my life. I went to school and had a wonderful teacher and great classmates. There's a kind lady who became like a mother to me. But there were some issues that occurred that made me come back to immigrate legally. I escaped several raids. God only knows why but there were two inspectors at two different times that could have snatched me, deported me, and separated me from my brother—but they let me go. Now I'm back in Nogales because I want to be a legal resident of the United States. My brother always regretted my illegal crossing into the US and we want to make it right."

Mr. Murphy replied, "I maintain that it was wrong of me to let you cross illegally. And what you're doing now—you're doing what very few people do. You returned to correct the situation, and to me that cancels out the initial wrongdoing. I knew you had something special going because you befriended me so fast. You were learning English quickly too, and I knew you were not going to go across and be alone."

"Yes, it's my half-brother Miguel. He lives in Phoenix. He already has his green card and comes here regularly, checking in on me and bringing money, so I can continue to live here while I wait for the final paperwork."

"Well, Edgar, I think that we should feel good about everything, and I hope that you get your papers in line. I'd like for you to find me when everything is complete. We have a new American Consul here. I don't know him, but I hear he's very good and very nice."

"Thank you for everything," I told Mr. Murphy. "I don't know what else to say."

He responded, "Let's just laugh about it, and you come by and visit me again."

Watching him leave the restaurant, I thought to myself, "What a nice, decent man. When I grow up, I want to become an adult like him—and like Miguel, Javier, my godfather, and, of course, my grandfather. Ah, my grandfather, the love of my life—I miss him so much."

Nine months into my stay in Nogales, when we still hadn't heard back from César, Miguel decided to pursue his alternate plan for getting the school records. Gloria, the English teacher whom I was assisting, connected Miguel to a local school principal.

Miguel and the principal seemed to get along well right from the start. After the initial greetings, I left the room, so the two of them could discuss business. The plan was that the principal would manufacture documents as if I had been a student at his school in Nogales for the past year. Miguel would pay him for the work. Again, this wasn't honest, but under the circumstances we were desperate.

After ten months my brother announced, "We're ready. We finally have all the documents."

It was a very rainy Thursday when our appointment at the Consulate was scheduled.

On the afternoon of the day before the appointment, I decided to visit my immigration officer friend, Larry Murphy, to share the news.

"Mr. Murphy, I've got all the required documents, and tomorrow I'll have the interview," I told him.

He was delighted. He said, "Good for you, Edgar. I'm very proud of you. Once you cross the border and you go back to

Phoenix, you'll probably never see me again. I would certainly like to think that you would come by and see me sometime."

"I'll certainly try, Mr. Murphy."

He looked at me with a kind smile and gave me a thumbs up for reassurance and success.

Before I left, I told him, "I know I said this to you already, but I want to say it again: I am truly sorry about what happened last year. I never meant to harm you."

He looked at me again and didn't say anything. He just gave me a smile and a slight nod similar to the one he'd given me more than a year prior that indicated I could step across the border.

The rain fell hard and then stopped for a few hours and then started again. When the rain came, it was very, very heavy to the point that water flooded many of the streets. It continued on like this, even on Thursday, the day of the appointment.

Of course, I was looking forward to the appointment, but at the same time I felt a strange anxiety. I felt a kind of emptiness on the inside, a sort of hollowness. I worried about the meeting somehow failing, but also I thought about all I'd leave behind if it were a success. Leaving Elvira and Javier would be tough on me as well as on them. I frequently visited Elvira while she was working at the restaurant, and when I entered, she met me, almost like she was greeting her son coming back from school. She smiled warmly, and her eyes opened wide with happiness.

She always had iced tea for me, and she sat with me for a few minutes. I told her what I was doing that day. It was like I was talking to my own mother or to Margaret or to my grandfather. I felt very comfortable with her. She loved hugs and would hug me and tell me how proud she was of how I was doing. "What mother wouldn't want to have you as her son? You are no problem to anybody; on the contrary, you are therapy for someone like me!" she'd exclaim with delight.

Javier had told me, "You know every time you go to the restaurant to visit Elvira, people think that you're her son, and it makes her extremely happy. These have been some of the happiest months of her life."

With an umbrella in hand, Miguel met me at the lobby of the hotel, so we could review the documents again before the appointment. We had the addendum from the birth certificate that clearly stated that my father was Miguel Hernandez Cabrera and that legally I should be named Edgar Hernandez Hernandez. The principal did a really good job placing my reports in the customary manner, making them appear convincing.

Miguel and I then left directly to the Consulate.

There were five other people waiting at the Consul's office when we arrived. Miguel and I both knew that nobody was allowed to wait in that office until they had passed all the rigorous requirements of the process. We knew that everybody was there for only one reason—to get a signature from the American Consul to go across. Everybody was a little dressed up. I know I was. I wore a brand-new shirt, brand-new pants, and my shoes were really shiny. They were the brown shoes that my brother had bought me at JCPenney's. My brother was well dressed, clean-shaven, and he smelled good.

As we waited our turn, I thought I recognized a couple emerge from a meeting with the Consul. I realized that in fact I didn't know them. I knew it would make me feel really good if, while waiting my turn, I ran into people whom I'd assisted who'd made it to the end of the process and had found success. However, I didn't see anyone whom I recognized.

When it was our turn, Miguel and I walked into an office to meet a tall gentleman with a flat top. To shake hands, he extended his arm straight out, like he had no elbow. I found it an awkward manner of shaking hands. I soon noticed that the way the man moved in general was awkward, which increased the tense feelings inside of me. I could tell too that Miguel was on edge.

We all sat down and the Consul started looking through the documents, one sheet of paper after another. He would look at the front, the back, and then put it on the right side of the desk where he would smooth his hands across it, almost like he was trying to iron the paper or flatten it out. He did this to each document.

After twenty minutes of detailed examination, he stacked the papers, put his hand on top of the pile, looked up at us, and stated, "I can't let him go across."

He was a man of few words. He looked tough in terms of his physical appearance, and his manner was stern.

I saw Miguel turn from pink to gray to white.

I sat with my feet dangling off the chair. I did not know what to say or do, other than to keep still and listen. I knew something was about to be discussed that I did not want to hear.

Miguel managed to ask, "But why, your honor? The papers are all perfect. They are complete. We were here several months ago, and we were told that we needed to have these two final items. Now with everything complete, you're telling us that Edgar cannot go across. We have done everything right, your honor. Please. Is there anything else that we need? What is it that we need? What can we do?"

My brother's voice trembled.

The Consul had a very large, gray-blue desk with a gray-blue matching chair. There were certificates on the wall behind him. This man had many certificates—college and university degrees, military diplomas, plaques given in his honor, and even a law degree. The wall signified an impressive and educated man. It seemed like he was a man of discipline and accuracy and firm about what he determined.

He leaned back in his chair. He removed his thick, dark glasses and put them on top of his desk. Then he quickly put them back on and leaned forward to state, "I can't let you take him across because you're his half-brother. His mother is down south with the other children. His father has died, and I don't know what your intentions are with him by taking him to the United States."

Then he looked Miguel straight in the eye and tapped his fingers on top of the documents. "When I put my signature on a document to allow anyone to go across to the United States, I become responsible for them. I am ultimately responsible for every individual that crosses the border, and this young child is not going across because I don't know whether you're going to make him a slave or you're going to beat him or what."

Miguel responded by saying, "Your honor, I have the most noble purpose in caring for my half-brother—"

The Consul interrupted, asking, "Why aren't you caring for the rest of the children in the family too? Why only him?"

"It's a matter of finances, a matter of capabilities, sir. After bringing Edgar to Phoenix, the greatest hope of my life is to bring the rest of his siblings and his mother across as soon as I become more financially stable. You see, your honor—I have a home that I own. I own my own car, and I am saving money—"

The Consul stopped my brother right away, "I know that. I know everything about you. You have an excellent boss. The letters that I have here are impeccable. I see many applicants come through here, but I have yet to see an endorsement better than yours. So, there's nothing wrong with the documents. I just can't let him go across because you're his half-brother."

I saw my brother calm himself down. Then he asked, "Your honor, may I talk to you in private?"

"Yes, but make it quick," the Consul responded.

Miguel turned to me, "Why don't you step out, so I can talk privately?"

Once outside, the secretary asked, "Are you done?"

"No, my brother's still there."

"You speak English well," she commented.

"I have been practicing," I told her.

I sat and waited. The ticking of the clock seemed to get louder and louder, but at the same time, time seemed to stand still.

I came up with two scenarios for what could happen. Scenario one: I could find Elvira and Javier and ask them if I could continue living with them. If they agreed, I could go to school and run errands to make money. Then I could try to get my visa every year until they would accept me.

Scenario two: I could forget this dream of becoming an American doctor and return to my family in La Mira and pursue a life there.

In looking around the room and observing the other people waiting their turn, I found a measure of tranquility. I saw that I wasn't the only one with hopes and dreams—we were all in pursuit of something. I prayed to God that their outcome would be more positive than mine. I spent time hoping for the best for them. I smiled a couple of times at them, but I didn't say a word.

After a while, the door opened. My brother came out, the Consul stood in the doorway, and I stood and approached them. The Consul gave another awkward, straight-armed handshake to Miguel, saying, "Good luck to you, Miguel." He turned to me and said, "Good luck to you, Edgar." Then he went back in and closed the door.

Miguel stated, "Let's go."

Outside the rain had stopped somewhat.

"Why don't we go across the street and buy a couple of pastries, and then we can head on home?"

"Which home?" I quietly asked.

"Phoenix," he stated with a half-smile.

I told Miguel that I needed to go to the hotel and to the restaurant to say goodbye to Javier and Elvira, so we agreed to meet in thirty minutes outside the restaurant.

At the hotel, Javier told me, "I was sure you'd already left because it's gotten late. I thought your meeting must've ended a while ago."

"Nope, it just ended, and I wanted to say goodbye again and let you know that I will come back to visit you."

Tears started to fall from my eyes, and Javier reassured me, "Don't cry, you should be happy. We are celebrating your success—you deserve it."

He gave me a hug and said, "Go over and say bye to Elvira. You'll make her day by stopping in once more to see her. Last night she was taking it pretty hard."

When I walked into the restaurant, I saw Elvira taking orders from a customer. When she noticed me, she paused in her work and then continued.

After she placed the order with the kitchen, she came over to see me, asking, "Everything okay?" She was concerned.

"Everything's fine. We're going across soon. I just wanted to see you again to say goodbye."

She hugged me and asked, "Will you be coming back sometime?"

"Of course," I promised.

She gave me another hug and asked, "Can I ask you one big favor? I was afraid to ask you yesterday, but I'll ask you now."

"Yes, Elvira. Anything," I replied.

"Will you please say to me, '*Adios* Mamá'? It would please me plenty to hear you say that."

So I said to her with a big smile, "*Adios* Mamá."

She gave me a kiss, and I kissed her back.

Outside the restaurant my brother was waiting for me, leaning against his Ford Fairlane. It was shiny and cleaned by the rain. We were set to go across the border.

I was tempted to stop and see my officer friend at the gate, but I knew I could visit him when I returned to Nogales later to see Javier and Elvira.

We got in a line of vehicles set to exit Mexico and enter the USA. When our turn came, the border entry officer emerged from the phone-booth-like outpost. He had a cap, shiny badge, and blue uniform.

My brother rolled the window down.

"Papers," the officer stated.

My brother handed over a folder of documents.

The officer took the folder and headed back to his phone-booth-like station. Ten minutes later he reemerged and approached the car. He stooped down to peer in at us. Looking towards me in the passenger's seat, he asked, "You're Edgar Hernandez?"

I replied, "Yes, sir."

"Congratulations, you are now a legal resident of the United States of America."

At those words chills traveled the length of my body. A feeling of total success engulfed me and simultaneously a weighty burden seemed to melt from my shoulders. A mighty hope and sense of possibility descended upon me. I wished the same glorious feelings to all the many applicants that were enduring the rigorous process of immigration. It was a feeling of pride and relief and a welcomed sense of responsibility for what it meant to be a legal member of the United States of America.

The border entry officer then handed over the folder of documents to us and told us to continue on. We drove away.

I stayed quiet, but also happy.

We stopped again in Tucson for burgers, milkshakes, and French fries—this time as carryout. About fifteen miles past Tucson at a line of trees Miguel parked the car. We got out and sat down on an old 1.5-foot wide tree trunk to eat in the shade.

My brother explained to me what came to pass. "I ended up cutting a deal with the Consul. I had to promise not to discuss the deal with anyone other than you. We can't even tell Margaret. You understand?"

"Yes, I understand. Tell me."

"When I asked you to step out, I didn't know exactly what I was going to say. All I knew was that I had to do something and I had to do it quick. I told him that you were my life and

I could not leave without you. I also told him the truth. I told him that you and I had broken the law and that I took you across illegally, that we had already crossed the border. I explained that I enrolled you in a school in Phoenix, not as the documents from the Nogales principal indicated, so I let him know those were false. I told him that we came back to Nogales to do it right and that you spent another 10.5 months in Nogales staying with a couple that we happened to meet and that weren't even your blood relatives.

"After I told him this, he didn't say one word to me—for at least a whole minute. He actually put his glasses on and took them off four different times. I waited until finally he said, 'Tell me more.'

"So I told him that I didn't mean to offend him, that I had no right to contradict his authority because he was a man of great respect and education and experience—but I couldn't leave Nogales without you. I could hardly get these words out I was so uncomfortable and nervous about challenging that gentleman. I couldn't stop squirming in my seat I was so nervous trying to speak to him.

"I told him I'd give him my green card if he'd issue you a green card and allow you to return to the US with me. I begged him to let me live as an illegal in the US if it meant that you could be there legally. I promised him that we would return in a year, so he could see you and also read letters from your school to learn how you are doing. If he approved of the life you were living in the US, then he could return the green card to me.

"I tried to make sure he understood how deeply I respected him and his position and at the same time how serious I was about bringing you to the US with the best intentions. I hoped that the extreme step of me giving up my green card would prove to him how sincere I was in my intentions.

"The whole time he was sitting way back in his chair, listening to me. Eventually he stated, 'You understand that this just isn't right. It's just not right. However, what you have done is something that I'd like to see more of, and I do see it but never like this.' Then in a matter of two seconds, he leaned forward in his chair, reached out and took my green card, put it in his drawer, stood up, and said good-bye. That was it.

"I promised him that I would not disappoint you and I

would not disappoint him. Then I left."

I was speechless.

Miguel stayed silent too.

Then I thought to ask, "Miguel, without your green card why did the border entry officer let you through?"

"Edgar, I wondered the same thing. I noticed that there was a handwritten note in the folder. It had your name on it and something about your 'companion,' and it was signed by the Consul. We must have waited ten minutes for the officer to look at your documents. I figured he called the Consul from that little booth, and I was given a special pass. Once the officer returned and it was apparent he was letting us through, I felt so relieved that I just wanted to go. That's why I didn't ask for details."

As we were getting in the car, I noticed Miguel was suddenly smiling and chuckling to himself, so I asked, "What is it? Why are you suddenly laughing, Miguel?"

"Edgar, I couldn't help but laugh at the irony—you were in the US illegally, so you spent the last ten months getting together your papers. You are reentering with legal status—but now I'm the one who's here illegally! Who would've thought?"

Upon entering Phoenix we drove down Seventh Street— just like before, except Miguel seemed to be driving even more carefully, if that was possible, than he typically did.

"Can we drive past the school?" I asked.

And we did. Miguel stopped the car. I stood outside the school and took a deep breath. I could smell the cafeteria. I could smell the halls. I could smell the detergents that they put on the floors. I could smell everything. What joy.

When we arrived at the jewelry shop, we drove to the back. Nobody was there. Margaret's Studebaker was not there.

We walked inside and headed upstairs to the little apartment. I went to the bedroom and sat on my bed. It was covered in that big red blanket. There was a Coca-Cola waiting for me on the bedside table along with a note, reading, "Welcome home. We missed you. —M and B."

PART THREE

15

Earning an MD, obtaining a specialty license in the area of surgery, and renewing these certifications regularly over the years meant that I spent many years going to school and hundreds of hours preparing for exams and taking exams.

After four years in college, there was medical school, which lasted another four years. After that, there were five years spent doing surgery residency. Regularly my fellow students and I had to take grueling examinations that determined whether we would pass to the next stages of our training—or not.

Then there were the state board exams, which I had to pass to earn my license to practice medicine. Because I aimed to specialize in surgery, I also had to take another series of exams called the surgical boards. And after every few years I had to take exams again—to renew these licenses.

In 1961, when I returned to Phoenix as a legal resident of the United States of America, I laid the strong foundation for test preparation, which became necessary for the studying and test taking I would do over the course of my studies and thirty-plus-year career as a surgeon.

At eleven years old and with the help of Margaret I laid a foundation of discipline and highly focused study to prepare for a test that would impact my near future. It was the first of many such major tests that I'd be taking—in high school, college, medical school, residency, and beyond. And it all started in elementary school.

*   *   *

On Monday morning I got myself ready to go to school. Admittedly, I was nervous about returning. I didn't really know what to say to the teachers and my fellow students. My old classmates were well into the second half of their sixth grade year, and I was afraid I might have to repeat the fifth grade because I'd left a few months shy of completing it.

I wanted to enter the sixth grade, so I'd be with my old classmates and so I wouldn't have to repeat, but there were only a few months left of the sixth grade year, so I knew it was very possible the school wouldn't allow it.

When Miguel took me to school, it was almost like I was having my first day once again. Like the first time, we went directly to Mr. McCormick's office. We greeted him. He shook my hand and Miguel's hand all the while making me feel welcomed.

"I'm so happy to have you back, Edgar. We never forgot about you," Mr. McCormick stated.

He continued, "Your teacher, classmates, and I were impressed and humbled by your honest explanation of why you had to leave last year. Your classmates are always asking about you, and I think they'll be very happy to see you. Mrs. Tudor will be happy too. Welcome back."

Mr. McCormick then laid out the plan for how they'd figure out which class to place me in. I would meet with the sixth grade teacher to talk and take some examinations. If I did well on the tests, I would enter the sixth grade class, finish up the sixth grade school year, and move on to the seventh grade. If I didn't do well on the tests, I'd go into the fifth grade.

"Normally we would have you go to a different institution for these examinations, but we're going to go ahead and have you do them internally. I talked to the teachers and they want to do that for you," Mr. McCormick confided.

Miguel and I thanked Mr. McCormick. Miguel shook his hand and warmly expressed his gratitude for everything he had done for me.

After school I had a joyful reunion with Mrs. Tudor. She also introduced me to the sixth grade teacher, Mrs. Crawford. They gave me several books and booklets that they wanted me to read and study. A week later I would return to take the placement examinations.

I was delighted with the plan. I took the books, went home, and laid out a study plan with Margaret.

"You already know what to do, Edgar. You don't come out of the apartment. You stay and you study for hours every day. Every afternoon, I'll quiz you."

With Margaret's help I studied. I became confident that I had a good grasp of the math, history, science, reading, and spelling lessons. I felt very good about it.

I met with Mrs. Tudor and Mrs. Crawford a week later. I took the examinations and passed. They both felt very comfortable that I could enter the sixth grade, finish it in just a few months, and proceed with my classmates to the seventh grade. I was ecstatic—and relieved. Margaret was proud of me too.

"I never doubted that you'd do it," Margaret told me. "Edgar, you can do anything that you decide to do. You told me that you want to become a surgeon, and I know you'll do that too."

Along with her total belief in me Margaret also had very high expectations for me. I had the same high expectations for myself, and perhaps even greater, because I knew I'd be returning to the American Consul in Nogales in a year's time, and I wanted to impress him with excellent reports from my teachers to ensure that Miguel would get his green card back.

Since we'd returned, Miguel was living like a fugitive. He did not want to put himself in a situation where he'd be asked for papers—which he no longer had. He refused to use his car—even though he had an Arizona driver's license—because he knew that driving put him at risk of getting stopped. He wanted to avoid any extra risk. So the rare times he did leave the workshop, he walked. When we needed food, he walked to the grocery store and walked home, overloaded with bags. He was also too afraid to go to the bank to cash his paychecks, so he requested that Margaret pay him in cash for a while. I knew it was going to be a long, stressful year until we could return to Nogales and get that green card back.

On my end I wanted to ensure that there was no way the American Consul wouldn't return the green card. Margaret never accepted any grades under 98, and I managed to succeed such that most of my grades were in the 100-plus range. However, I wanted more than excellent grades and exemplary conduct. I also sought to get perfect attendance. To do this I went to school even if I had a temperature of 101 or 102.

Every Monday morning, my school had a brief flag-raising ceremony during which we'd raise the flag and say the Pledge of Allegiance. Every Friday the flag was taken down. After I gained legal status, I felt great pride and satisfaction in participating in this ceremony. I was a part of the great USA.

My life had other wonderful routines too. Similar to my first stay in Phoenix, I continued working in the jewelry shop, cleaning and organizing, every day after school. I did my schoolwork, and Margaret helped me review and study. Miguel cooked dinner. He could cook anything, and his enchiladas were, by far, the best.

In addition to crafting jewelry and cooking meals, Miguel stayed busy renovating the home he'd bought. He had specific plans for fixing it up because, just as he'd told the Consul, he had plans to bring my mother and siblings from Mexico to Phoenix, and we'd live together in the house—someday. Of course, he was doing this without the use of a car, which made it difficult. I could sense his general anxiety about living and working as an illegal, but he didn't like to talk about it with me. He simply wanted to make it through the year without a problem—and he wanted me to thrive at school.

"Edgar, your mother has sent you a letter. I want you to sit with me when you read it," Miguel told me somberly when I got back to the little apartment after doing chores in the jewelry shop.

In the letter my mother told me that she'd gotten news that my godfather, Edgar Schwartz, had died. He'd fallen off some scaffolding at a building site and died immediately from the fall. My mother had no more information beyond that. Whether he was in Germany or somewhere else in the world when it happened, she didn't know. We had no information either about my godfather's burial or how his wife was coping. My mother was shaken, and I felt a pit open in my insides. I felt sick and sad and confused—my godfather was too young, strong, smart, and careful for such a death to befall him. I was incredulous. Bewildered. I even felt guilty, wondering, "If I'd returned to Germany with him, then maybe this wouldn't have happened to him."

I wept bitter tears.

Miguel sat with me at the table and held my hand.

My sixth grade year ended and seventh grade began. Over the course of these school years, I collected report cards and additional letters of recommendation from my sixth and seventh grade teachers. Just as I'd been so adamant with the families whom I'd assisted in Nogales about the careful maintenance of the paperwork, I organized my papers in separate folders in a logical sequence. Every document was clean and wrinkle-free, so when it was time to share them with the Consul, he'd be impressed.

At exactly a year to the day of our last appointment, Miguel made an appointment for us to visit the American Consul in Nogales.

Before leaving Phoenix, Miguel had to service his car because it hadn't been driven over the past year though he'd started the engine and let it run in idle for a few minutes each week just to make sure it was still working. We put air in the tires, cleaned the interior and exterior, and changed the oil. Miguel drove right at the speed limit, like he always did, but somehow it seemed we were moving more cautiously than before, on this now familiar drive from Phoenix to Nogales.

We arrived the day before our appointment, so we could visit Elvira and Javier. When we walked into the restaurant, Elvira was all smiles. Waves of happiness radiated from her being. Elvira embraced me and cried tears of joy.

"My biggest regret is that you'll be leaving again so soon, and I won't see you for a while," she lamented.

"Elvira, I promise we'll come back and visit as soon as we can," I told her.

Next we went over to the hotel to see Javier. When we arrived, he was in the middle of registering a guest. "Excuse me one moment, sir," he told the guest and hurried over to give us hugs.

"Edgar, you look great! You've grown; you're almost a man now. And me—I'm a bit older, and I have some gray hair, but I'm still alive and active. I'm sure you saw Elvira and noticed how great she looks."

We enjoyed a wonderful spaghetti dinner that night, reminiscent of old times with Javier tucking a pillowcase into his shirt, Elvira's sensational *pastel de tres leches*, and lots of stories and laughter.

The next morning before our meeting, I went alone to meet with my friend, Larry Murphy, the border entry officer.

"Mr. Murphy, I happen to be in Nogales, and I wanted to say hi," I greeted him.

He gave me a handshake and a warm smile, saying, "I hope everything is okay with you. I figured you got the visa when I didn't see you. Tell me how you are doing."

"I'm doing really well. I'm in the seventh grade at a school in Phoenix. I love it."

"So, Edgar, what's your big life dream? Now that you are in America, what are you going to do with the opportunity?" he asked.

"My father did dental work and medical work in the town where I grew up and seeing him work was a big inspiration. But I want to do more than he did—I want to become a real doctor. I want to attend an American medical school and become a surgeon. That's my goal."

I noticed he was regarding me curiously as I shared this dream. After a few seconds of silence, he told me, "I've always had a feeling about you. You make things happen—for yourself and other people. I know you are going to do it—become a surgeon. I believe in you."

His supportive words landed straight in my heart. I found myself standing taller and seeing farther. I thanked him and wished him well.

"Keep in touch if you can," he told me.

Next I walked to the American Consulate where I met Miguel.

While there had been many surprises and a lot of distress when we'd gone to the Consulate in the past, Miguel and I had no worries this time.

Miguel even commented, "Strange to say, but it feels good being here." I agreed.

Miguel went on to add, "I said it to the Consul a year ago, but I want to repeat it to you again today, Edgar. I'm going to get your mother here and the rest of our brothers and sisters. It will take me a few years to get together the money, and I want the house to be ready for them—but it's going to happen."

I believed him. When Miguel made a promise, I never doubted he would keep it.

We entered the lobby where the secretary greeted us, "Miguel, you look wonderful, and, Edgar, you've grown. You've gained some weight, and you've got some color in your cheeks. I'm so happy to see you. It's not every day that people come back to say hello, and we do appreciate you coming over."

We were taken aback that she remembered us. It was a positive start to the coming meeting.

"He's waiting for you. Please go on in," she told us.

The Consul greeted us warmly. His handshake had stayed the same—a very straight arm and no bending at the elbow.

I placed my neatly organized binder of documents on top of his desk and took a seat.

The Consul sat at his desk, leaned back in his chair, took his glasses off, and regarded Miguel and me.

He wiped his forehead. Then he moved to wipe his eyes, which made me notice his eyes were slightly teary. He leaned forward, opened the drawer, pulled out my brother's green card, and handed it over to Miguel.

At that he stood up, saying, "Good luck to you, Miguel, and good luck to you, Edgar."

"But what about the documents?" I inquired. "I brought letters from my teachers and report cards covering the last twelve months."

"Come over here. Come to my side here," the Consul stated.

To me the Consul was a gentleman of such authority and honor—as well as sternness—that it didn't seem appropriate that I stand right next to him. It seemed too informal. Too casual. So, though he'd told me to walk around his desk and stand next to him, I couldn't bring myself to move.

When he repeated, "Come here. Come stand right next to me, son," with the repetition of the command I managed to push my body past his desk to stand next to him.

Much to my surprise, he put an arm around me.

Next, he stated, "Son, these papers you brought here have a lot of meaning to you and me. These papers are for you to keep because you'll need them more than I do. You see, son, when young people in this life mature, they come to a crossroads. At that crossroads, you have the choice of turning in one direction that will lead you to doomsday, failure, and disaster, where you mean very little to society—where you become a burden to society. And then there's the other direction. You go in that other direction and you find success. You actually mean something to society, and you become someone that does something to be proud of. So, Edgar, when you reach these crossroads in your life and you don't know what you want to do, that's when you can read these letters. Then you'll know exactly what road you need to take."

I was breathless at these words.

The Consul himself seemed to have tears in his eyes, as he continued, imparting this significant message, "Some events that have taken place in your life could have been done better or could have been done differently. There were some errors that could have led to disaster. But, at the end of the day, what counts for all of us is that we made corrections so that we can do right. Don't ever forget that honesty is always good for the soul."

"Thank you very much, sir," I responded.

"Thank you," Miguel added.

When I walked out of there, I told Miguel that that gentleman had given me the never-ending American dream.

We left the office and prepared for the drive back to Phoenix. At the entry-exit gate, the officer approached us. We rolled the window down. "Documents please," the officer stated.

My brother pulled out his green card. I pulled out my green card. The officer reached in through the window, took the green cards, looked at them for about five seconds, and handed them back to us.

"You may pass."

16

It was my sixth time speaking before one of Mrs. Cane's eighth grade classes. Each time I came to speak, Mrs. Cane, who had been my eighth grade teacher about nine years earlier, prompted, "Edgar, please tell these young students how it is that you came to this country because I imagine that some of them have a similar story."

So, I shared my immigration story. Next, I told them my goals in life—to become a surgeon and work with patients in the area—and how I was currently in college at Arizona State University, finishing my pre-med classes, and about to apply to medical schools.

They asked me many questions about ASU and the college experience: *How much does it cost? What about your study habits? Are the teachers like Mrs. Cane? What's your daily schedule like? Do you have to work? Do you have classes every day? What happens if you don't understand something—are there teachers or tutors who will help you?*

I answered the questions as straightforwardly as I could. My goal was to be honest and at the same time encouraging. I told them that as soon as I'd left high school, from that point on, I had been going to college year-round. I told them it was paying off because I was getting my requirements out of the way, I was learning a lot, and I was preparing myself for a very rigorous career in medicine. Soon, I would apply to medical schools—and simply applying was another rigorous task in itself. The eighth graders appreciated everything that I told them.

I ended my talk by stating, "When I was in the eighth grade with Mrs. Cane, she taught us her philosophy of unity and helping one another and setting big life goals. She taught me and my classmates the beauty of discipline, honesty, and responsibility.

Her teachings never left me. That's why I came back to speak to you all because she made such an impact on me. I want to inspire you as she inspired me. I remember being in your place, sitting and listening to her former students come in and talk about what they were doing to achieve their life dreams—in physics, finance, the arts, sports, the sciences. They showed me that I could do it. And I want to show you that you can do it. It's all about discipline, honesty, and responsibility—all things that you can master, starting now."

★   ★   ★

It was my eighth grade year, and I was fortunate to be assigned to one of the greatest teachers ever—Francis Cane. She was ex-military, and she acted like a military teacher. She was extremely popular. Her former students in high school, college, graduate school, and beyond regularly stopped by the classroom to greet her. Her students adored her. They respected her.

Mrs. Cane's philosophy was that there was no such thing as an average or below-average student. She wanted to make sure that all of us in the class were given an equal opportunity to learn, and a key part of this was teamwork. The students collectively had the responsibility to help those among us that were struggling, for whatever reason. If we were all willing to pitch in, then nobody in our class would fail or receive an inferior education. Mrs. Cane's philosophy and the way she created a strong sense of family in our classroom reminded me so much of my beloved teacher César.

Mrs. Cane used the word "teamwork" as if we were preparing for a game against a competing outfit. And her philosophy worked. We were amazed at how well our classmates that had been lagging and had had poor grades and attitudes in previous years performed with Mrs. Cane. It seemed like whomever she touched turned into an excellent student.

In essence, she could awaken the most reluctant or unconfident students and make them outstanding. She always said she just had to make sure that all students first felt good and loved themselves so that they had confidence in themselves. After that learning was easy.

Mrs. Cane was a person of the highest character, and she represented the true sense of the word integrity. She disapproved of laziness, complainers, gossipers, and tattletales. She disliked it if a student came to her and complained about another student. She warned us, "That is not the way you treat your classmates. Never, never do I want to hear any of you complaining to me about any of your classmates. Not one of you. I will not tolerate it."

There was never a time when she lacked enthusiasm. She demonstrated enthusiasm to us every day of the school year. Even when she was sick with the flu, had a cough, or was sneezing, she never missed work. She wanted to show us what hard work was all about, explaining, "You can't let the small things in life get you down. A cough or a sneeze shouldn't sway you from your commitments." She proved it to us herself, and we knew how strong this lady was.

She was not young either. Mrs. Cane was already in her late fifties when she was our teacher. She carried a wooden cane with a rubber sleeve on its curved handle. She had been teaching for many years. Before that, when she was a young adult, she was in the military.

Every year, Mrs. Cane received the "outstanding teacher" award. She was a very special person. The other teachers and school administrators applauded the recognition that our school gained due to the excellence of Francis Cane. She was adored by everyone.

Frequently her former students who were now in the high school located just a few blocks from our school would informally drop in the classroom to say hello. Mrs. Cane welcomed them and introduced them to the class. She was never put out by these unexpected visits.

As soon as they entered, Mrs. Cane would say, "Okay, ladies and gentlemen, I want you to meet one of my distinguished students who's now a sophomore in high school. She is here to visit with us for a few minutes. I want you all to say hello." Then she would put the student on the spot, asking, "What do you have to say to my students about high school? Are you enjoying high school or not?"

She was very blunt when asking questions. Not only that, she was famous for putting students on the spot. She explained to us that by doing that, students would develop the discipline to become quick thinkers and be able to make decisions and respond to questions in the best manner possible in a matter of seconds. She argued that it was good preparation for life.

She would tell us, "Soon, you will graduate from my class and go on to high school, and I'd be willing to bet you a penny that most of you will come back to say hello. It is among the most important moments of my life when my students come back and say hello."

Mrs. Cane's scholar days were the most memorable part of that school year. On these days, she invited certain former students who were already in college, graduate school, or pursuing their careers to speak to the class. They described their study paths and career choices. They answered our questions. And they all emphasized hard work—"If you are willing to work hard, you can achieve your goals."

On one scholar day Mrs. Cane invited a young attorney who had been in her class many years previously. This man was extremely humble and very well mannered. He told us, "When I was in fifth, sixth, and seventh grades, I was an average student. But in eighth grade with Mrs. Cane, everything changed. The encouragement I received from my classmates and Mrs. Cane sparked a new feeling of confidence inside me. I realized I could make something out of my life. I learned to become more disciplined and responsible. I changed the direction of my life in the eighth grade."

When he was sharing this, my classmates and I found ourselves looking around at each other, as if saying with our eyes, "Aren't we so lucky to be here?"

While many students may have entered Mrs. Cane's class without thinking of their futures at all, quite soon all of her students were talking about their future careers and dreams. Students who had only had the vague goal of finishing high school, getting a job, making a few dollars, and, perhaps, marrying, transformed their goals to something more lofty. They began talking about going to college to become a teacher, a lawyer, an architect, or a scientist. They wanted to make a positive difference in their communities and the world.

Because I'd already realized my goal years earlier—to become a surgeon—I was thrilled to find myself surrounded by classmates who were also thinking in terms of the big picture. It seemed all of us were thinking about the long term and about bettering the world. I wasn't alone in my dreaming and planning big—I was part of a group of peers in which it was the norm. I found it ideal.

She not only opened up our minds to what we could do in the future, but we also learned the importance of generosity, kindness, and sharing. That's what the constant teamwork taught us.

Mrs. Cane encouraged us to talk to her directly when we were concerned about something she said or did. She told us, "You need to come sit by me and talk to me. I don't want to hear you talking outside the class that you're concerned about something or that you're not happy about something from class or from me. You need to be a young lady or a young gentleman and sit by me. You need to look me in the eye and talk because that's the way you're going to make it when you start your careers."

All of us students occasionally tried to play a little trick on Mrs. Cane. We'd hide her cane. Once we were preparing for an outing. We were going to take a bus and visit a museum. We were all in line, getting ready to walk out of the room, when Mrs. Cane declared, "We're not leaving until I have my cane in my right hand, and that cane better be touching my skin in a few seconds' time; otherwise, all of you will have to take a seat because we won't be going anywhere!"

Everybody began scrambling to get the cane.

Mrs. Cane turned around and announced, "I've turned around. I don't want to know who hid the cane from me. I don't care. I just want my cane back."

We were all talking, asking, "Who has the cane? Where is the cane?" Finally, it was found hidden underneath her desk. Somebody retrieved it and placed it in her hand.

After we walked out and were on the bus that's all we talked about—how respectfully she'd conducted herself with us. How she cared for us. She was not a teacher that held grudges with students. She showed equal love and affection for all students.

I arrived home from school to find Miguel waiting for me. Normally, he was in the shop working at this time, so I was surprised.

"I've got a letter. I want you to read it," Miguel told me somberly.

The letter was from my mother informing me that my grandfather had died. She explained that he had been working on his farm as he usually did, going to work early in the morning, working all day, and returning home at sundown. As he was packing to return home, according to another man that was there, he started feeling dizzy and complained about having paralysis in one arm. Then he collapsed to the ground, and he passed away. It was a sudden and immediate death.

My mother wrote that she didn't want me to return to Mexico for the funeral. I would miss too much school, and it would be expensive.

My grandfather had been a huge part of my life. He'd set the foundation in me to be curious, loving, and respectful in regard to the natural world and to others. He always encouraged me and believed in my capacity to do anything I wanted in life even when I was a little child. He was a great philosopher although he'd never had a first grade education.

I was taken aback and very upset about his death and about how I wouldn't be there for his burial.

The one comfort was remembering that he would always say to me that I needed to become an educated person. It would pay off for me in the long run, and I could be a huge service to my brothers and sisters.

With these words in mind I dug in and applied myself with all my heart to all that Mrs. Cane was teaching us.

Eighth grade graduation was very sad and very special for all of us in Mrs. Cane's class. At graduation Mrs. Cane told me, "Edgar, I will never forget you. In all the years I've been teaching, I've never had a student ask as many questions as you. On a weekly basis, you ask more questions than most students ask in three months' time."

I told her, "Mrs. Cane, my teacher down in Mexico and my grandfather used to tell me the same thing—except they said I asked too many questions. My mother warned me to be careful not to annoy people with my constant questioning."

"Every one of the questions you ask is important, Edgar, so continue to ask questions. It will make you a better student," she urged.

Another reason this graduation was so special for me was that Miguel, Margaret, Olivia, and Pedro all attended.

Olivia was my half-sister. She was quite older than me and two years older than Miguel. Pedro was my brother, and he was about ten years older than me. They'd immigrated into the USA in 1956, a year after Miguel and several years before me.

Though Pedro and Olivia both lived in Arizona, they lived far from Phoenix, so Miguel and I rarely saw them. They both worked in the home of a kind family taking care of two of the family members who had been paralyzed since childhood from polio. Olivia and Pedro worked very hard, doing a lot of the manual labor to care for these two individuals. They worked days, nights, and on weekends.

They lived in a small shed on the family's property. They weren't paid much for their work, and they also had to pay rent to live in the shed, all of which meant that they had very little money.

Miguel's plan was for them to move into his house once he finished fixing it up. They could then get other jobs, and because they wouldn't have to pay rent, they'd be able to save money. With the three of them working and saving, the plan was that eventually Pedro would be able to return to La Mira to retrieve my mother, sisters, and brother, bring them to Nogales, assist them with the immigration process, and then bring them to the house in Phoenix where we would all live together. The goal was for all of this to happen in two years' time.

On their parts, my mother and siblings were eager to immigrate to the USA to live with us. Since I'd left La Mira, my mother had remarried a nice man. Though her husband did not want to leave Mexico, my mother planned to leave with the children, and, according to her letters, he agreed to it. They even had two sons, Jose Angel and Salvador, so I had two younger half-brothers whom I'd not yet met. At some point, if they wanted, we wanted to help Jose Angel and Salvador to immigrate to live with us too.

Margaret and Olivia sat next to one another at my graduation, and it was on this day that the two of them came to know one another. After spending the afternoon together Olivia learned to appreciate all the things that Margaret had done for me, and she expressed to Margaret in broken English how grateful she was for the kindness with which Margaret cared for me.

Margaret responded, "It's been the easiest thing I've ever done. Edgar is an important part of my life."

Miguel chimed in, "Olivia, did you know that Margaret has gone to more of Edgar's parent-teacher meetings than I have? She knows Edgar's teachers well, and she is responsible for making him into an excellent student. You have to see the grades that Edgar brings home and the comments that his teachers say about him."

That brought tears to Olivia's eyes. She hugged Margaret and became devoted to her from then on out.

That summer Miguel finished renovating the house, and we moved out of the second-story space above the jewelry shop and into our own small house. This move was consequential for many reasons. For one thing, Miguel had lived above the shop for about a decade, the whole time he'd been in the USA. That space had also been my home for the four years I'd been in the USA. So, for the first time, we were to have a home of our own. More importantly, it signaled that the plan to reunite our family in the two-year timeframe was progressing accordingly.

The move did not mean that Miguel would be able to work less and enjoy free time. He had to continue working seven days a week as he'd been doing for years because he wanted to accumulate the money to pay for the immigration processes for my mother and siblings.

Several weeks after Miguel and I moved into the house, Olivia and Pedro came to live with us. They got jobs and began saving to contribute to the fund for bringing the rest of the family to Phoenix.

Miguel had promised us many years earlier that he would reunite the family in Phoenix, and he stood by that promise, enduring years of relentless work to earn and save the money required. Olivia and Pedro stood by Miguel and his promise. With their help, the reunion was going to happen.

Though Margaret was pleased, on the one hand, that Miguel had finished the house and that our plan for reuniting the family was in action, on the other hand, she was deeply saddened, lamenting, "Miguel, I worry that I'll hardly see Edgar."

Margaret's worry proved unfounded because I worked all summer long in the shop. Margaret always worked in the shop from the early morning until late at night, so we were as inseparable as ever. When school started, I continued working with her every day after school. I'd arrive and Margaret would have a hot dog and potato chips waiting for me before I started working. We stayed close.

17

The patient, a heavyset man with glasses, a beard, and thinning hair, had come to the ER with complaints about pain in his abdomen. The man's x-ray showed that he had a hole in his bowel, so he'd need to go into surgery immediately. The situation was dire.

I could see him sitting with his wife. It was apparent he was in agony.

I quickly approached him, extended my arm, and began, "I'm Dr. Hernandez. I'm the surgeon on call today. I have reviewed your studies. I'm afraid to tell you, sir, that you need to have an operation—immediately."

He ignored my extended arm and, instead, responded, "How long you been doing this?"

I was taken aback.

The man asked again, "You ever done this before?"

"Yes, many times, sir," I assured him.

"Where'd you go to medical school? You speak with an accent. You foreign trained?"

"I went to medical school in Utah and did my surgical residency right here in the Phoenix area," I replied.

"But you talk with an accent. How could you do your schooling here if you talk with an accent?" he pushed.

"I wasn't born in this country, sir. I immigrated here when I was ten years old. Since then I've lived in Phoenix except for the years I was in medical school in Utah," I answered.

"I don't know about this. Are there any other surgeons here that speak really good English?" he went on to ask.

I responded, "Oh, I'm sure there are, sir. However, I would love to take care of you. I promise to take care of you like you're my own flesh and blood."

He stared at me, evidently surprised by my comment.

Finally, he decided, "Is that so? Well, not so fast. We'll talk to the nurse and see if we can get another surgeon. We'll let you know."

I informed him, "Please be aware that delaying your surgery is very dangerous. With the hole in your intestine, poisons have released in your abdomen. Your temperature's high, and your pulse is high; plus, you have a white blood cell count that's elevated. I hope that you will make a decision soon."

I explained the situation to the ER doctor. He responded, "That's crazy. This man needs to be operated on."

Twenty minutes later, the nurse who'd been speaking to him reported to me that the man wanted to call another surgeon. We knew of another surgeon who might agree to the operation and decided to call him.

Shortly thereafter my beeper sounded. It was Miguel, notifying me that he wanted me to call him.

I called Miguel and explained the situation. I admitted that I wasn't happy and wasn't even sure that I wanted to work with the patient if, for some reason, he decided to go with me.

Miguel listened and then offered, "Remember one thing, Edgar. You're a surgeon and even though the patient is getting personal, ignore him. Be the trained professional that you are. In fact, I think you should return to him and repeat that he's very sick right now and that you promise to take very good care of him."

"Miguel, I told him that already—but it didn't convince him," I explained.

"Do it again—and tell him more. Explain that you trained under Dr. Harry Hale, one of the finest surgeons in the USA. He probably doesn't know Dr. Hale, but it doesn't matter. Say it. Try," urged Miguel.

And so I did.

The man ended up agreeing to work with me. I performed the surgery, and it went well. Over the five days he was in the hospital recovering, I met with him each day. I gave him a handshake and noticed how he warmed up to me more and more with each passing day.

Before he was discharged, his wife embraced me and thanked me.

I ended up getting many referral patients from this man and his wife. They ended up being two of my biggest fans.

While this wasn't the first time I had to overcome my pride and win over someone who doubted me based on my accent and ethnicity, I still felt the sting of their prejudice. It was frustrating and hurtful. But, as happened in similar instances earlier in my life, with the wise words of a loved one giving me that extra bit of support, I managed to keep my eyes on the prize and put in the work to win the person over to trust me and believe in my capabilities.

★　　★　　★

In the first week of my freshman year, I met with the high school guidance counselor, Mr. Hayes, to get his recommendations on the classes, extracurricular activities, and anything else I should consider during high school to prepare me for college and an eventual career in medicine. High school guidance counselors were a big deal not only because they advised students but also because they had leverage to help particular students get into certain colleges. For this reason, I knew my relationship with Mr. Hayes would be important.

I remember telling Margaret, "I'm going to be meeting the high school counselor to discuss classes that I want to—"

Margaret excitedly interjected, "Edgar, make sure that when you talk to this gentleman, you tell him you want to go into medicine and you want to take classes that pertain to medicine because I don't think you should waste your time with other nonsense classes."

This was classic Margaret. She did not mince words. She spoke her mind, and I liked it.

I replied, "Margaret, I agree with you, and that's exactly what I'm going to do."

When I met with Mr. Hayes and explained my long-term goal, he responded, "Now, son, that's a big goal for such a young man. Something to keep in mind is that simply graduating from high school will be challenging enough. So graduating and going on to college—well—that in itself is big, and that doesn't include medical school. Tell me—what is it that your parents do?"

"I live with my older brother. He's like my father. He is an expert craftsman and silversmith."

Mr. Hayes nodded his head, saying, "Yes, a man who works with his hands. Now there's demand for skilled jobs like that, jobs that require specific knowledge—think sheet metal work, mechanics, refrigeration—these are the kinds of skills pretty much everyone can master. They don't require high-level science or math, and they pretty much guarantee that you'll get a good paying job that you can buy a house and raise a family on. I've steered a lot of kids into these jobs, and the ones that listened have found success."

"Sir, I thank you for considering this for me, but that's not what I want. Since I was a young boy, I decided I wanted to be a doctor, and in the past few years I refined that to a surgeon. I would appreciate your counsel on how I should structure my high school classes to put me in a good position when I apply to colleges, keeping in mind that my ultimate goal is to become a surgeon," I explained.

"I realize you've set your heart on this dream, but talk to your brother about it. If you aim for a technical skill, you can achieve that know-how in a few months to a year—and it's a guaranteed job. A medical degree could take ten to fifteen years to earn. Can you afford to be studying for that many years? And the classes are very difficult. Plus, there are so many tests. You could spend ten years pursuing the degree, and if you fail one test, then it's all for nothing. I want you to take some time to consider the reality of becoming a doctor. Talk to your brother—tell him what I've said. Then get back to me," Mr. Hayes urged.

Needless to say I was disappointed with this first meeting. Miguel had been supporting my dream to become a surgeon for years now, so I didn't think it would be helpful to talk to him, as Mr. Hayes had suggested. I visited Mrs. Cane to get her advice.

"Edgar, look at me. He will soon fall in love with your vision, and he will soon recognize what an excellent student you are. He will rapidly change his mind about you. Don't give up on your dream and don't give up on Mr. Hayes helping you," Mrs. Cane insisted.

I trusted Mrs. Cane's recommendations and decided to prove to Mr. Hayes that I was serious. And after a semester I managed to earn Mr. Hayes's trust and support. I set my course in high school taking math and science courses as recommended by Mr. Hayes. I was extremely studious. I didn't do any sports. I would go to school, do my work, return to the jewelry store and do my homework, and then work at the shop for several hours into the evening. Margaret paid me for the work, and I contributed the earnings to the running of the household with Miguel, Pedro, and Olivia. While my schedule remained steady over the four years of high school, my high school experience was, in fact, far from easy.

It was the 1960s, and there was great political and social unrest. The Vietnam War had started, and male students at my school were getting drafted all the time to serve. One of my teachers advised me, "Most of the students in your class will be drafted. You, I'm confident, will be spared because of your grades and because of your hard work in school. Also you have a goal as to what you want to do with your future, and you are working towards it with dedication. Keep up the good work, and, I guarantee, the draft people will never touch you."

However, it wasn't the draft that I was most concerned with—riots, assaults, and gang violence were the immediate threats.

On our campus there were numerous marches organized for various causes, including peace, improved schools, better jobs, and equality. Students who were gang members would take advantage of these gatherings to jump other students—and then total chaos would ensue. The organized marches sometimes turned into riots that could go on for a few hours until the administration, who didn't want to draw attention from the outside to the fact that the school was suffering from a serious disturbance, reluctantly called the police. The attacks were sometimes so nasty that ambulances were called. It was a scary scene.

In the course of a regular school day—riots aside—the number one fear of every student and teacher was getting assaulted by vigilante students who typically were members of gangs. Light attacks included getting kicked, punched, or slapped, possessions or money getting stolen, or the hurling of verbal abuse.

I witnessed at least a half a dozen assaults and beatings of teachers. These occurred in the classroom. A student or students, usually gang members, would hit a teacher in the head, push the teacher in the chest, or stand over the teacher and berate them to the point of total humiliation. This happened time and time again. Those teachers would leave the school and get replaced by other teachers—and it would happen all over again. At one time, I had five different teachers in one year for the same class.

The rest of us in the class witnessed the assaults occurring but felt helpless to stop them because we were afraid for our own safety. Gangs retaliated violently against anyone who interfered with gang members in any way.

My method for keeping safe was maintaining a very low profile. I arrived at school very early, before anyone else was around, and went to the library to study. Then I went to classes and ate lunch quickly. After school I returned to the library to study some more, and then I went to the jewelry store to work. I never participated in any marches because they would likely become violent. Because gangs resided in the neighborhood where our house was, I worried about getting attacked when walking to and from school, so I had to be careful there too.

Trying to keep a low profile didn't always work. Before I stopped eating lunch in the high school cafeteria, I remember standing in line with two friends. We were waiting on hamburgers when another student came up behind us and kicked one of my friends to the ground. Then he pulled me back and punched me in the chest. He was after our lunch money.

I found it ironic that I was living with a similar anxiety about getting ambushed as I'd had when I was living illegally in Phoenix. I never thought that once I got my legal residency, my life in the USA would suddenly be easy—but I certainly hadn't expected that I would have reason to worry about surprise attacks. And really, these ambushes were worse than those of La Migra. Anyone could be in a gang. They didn't wear green uniforms like La Migra, so they weren't obviously identifiable. Gang members were also very violent, breaking bones, gashing skin, burning buildings. They inflicted both physical and psychological wounds.

Many of my classmates who were intelligent, hard-working students gave up and quit school. It was too violent and stressful. I too reached that intersection where I had to decide to endure or give up. Towards the end of my freshman year, I found three guys from my neighborhood, Bobby, Sam, and Frankie, who were also in the ninth grade, waiting for me after school. I'd been studying in the library since school had ended, so I knew they must have been waiting for me on purpose.

"Edgar, we want to talk with you. We'll walk you home," Frankie informed me.

"I'm not going home. I have to go to my job, and I can't be late," I explained.

"Okay. We'll walk with you. We just want to talk," Sam told me.

"We got an idea for makin' some cash, and we need your help. You can make a little too," Frankie started.

"You know that restaurant, Prime Rib? They gotta lotta nice supplies in their backroom—coffee, chocolate, sugar, canned fruit, liquor, stuff like that," Bobby explained.

These guys had found out that Miguel was friends with a waiter at Prime Rib. So, they wanted me to go to the restaurant right before closing to visit Miguel's waiter friend. During the short visit, I was supposed to somehow get to the backdoor and unlock it. Later that night I would meet these boys, and we would steal supplies together.

"When you work with us, we can make your life so good. But when you don't work with us, your life can get pretty bad," Bobby warned.

Of course, I wasn't interested in helping them steal, but I also didn't want to get hurt. Somehow I managed to communicate that I wasn't interested in their plan, and then I got away from them without getting assaulted. But I knew it wasn't over with them. It was just the beginning.

As I made my way to the jewelry shop, I was in shock that I hadn't gotten hurt, but I feared future repercussions. Plus, I was late—and I knew Miguel and Margaret would notice and wouldn't be happy.

"Why, Edgar, you must be twenty minutes late to work to-day. What in the world is going on?" Margaret asked me when I walked in the shop.

"I . . . I left one of my books at school, so I had to walk back and get it. Then I saw a teacher and talked for a few minutes," I lied so as not to cause Margaret to worry.

A few hours later at home, Miguel stated, "Margaret told me

that she's worried about you. She thinks something is going on. Can you tell me what's happening?"

I ended up telling Miguel about the three boys and what they'd proposed to me. "And those guys have bad reputations too. One spent time in a juvenile home. Another threatened a teacher. So maybe they didn't do anything to me today, but I worry that later on, they'll try to get even," I admitted.

Miguel tended to look at people and situations in the most positive way. He always gave them the benefit of the doubt. In response to what I'd told him, Miguel advised, "Remember, they did not assault you today. You told them you weren't going to do it, and they didn't assault you. That's something. All you can do is treat them with respect, stand your ground, but also show no fear. That's what you already did and what you'll have to do again if it comes down to it."

The next morning I left for school even earlier than usual and headed directly to the library. I went to my classes, and during lunch, I returned to the library. There was a small courtyard accessible via the library where I ate my lunch. This was the first day of my practice of eating lunch in the library area rather than the cafeteria. After school, I changed up my patterns. Sometimes I would stay and study in the library; other times I would go directly to the jewelry shop. I changed up my walking routes, entrance and exit ways, and timing too.

Miguel went to Prime Rib to warn his waiter friend about the situation. The restaurant management took him seriously and made arrangements to secure the doors and windows.

Weeks went by and all was fine because I remained careful.

On a Saturday afternoon as I was exiting a store in the neighborhood, Bobby, Sam, and Frankie happened to be walking by on the sidewalk. I started to walk the other way, but one of them managed to punch me in the back. Physically, it wasn't serious, but the psychological impact was huge. I felt very unsafe and intimidated.

I tried hard to concentrate on school and work. I became even more vigilant and hyper-aware, peering through windows or around corners before walking outside or in a new direction. Margaret was very concerned, and she decided to pick me up after school each day. She made sure she was already there, waiting for me in her car so that I would not have to wait for her and expose myself. I wasn't sure whether this would make things worse for me, but I decided to do it because the alternative of walking to the shop after school was very scary.

One time I saw the three boys at school and actually approached them. Why I did this, I had no idea. I went directly to them and made small talk, like we were all friends. For some reason in this moment I had no fear, and I didn't show any anger towards them. And they accepted my conversation.

One day as I was having lunch in the courtyard of the library, Frankie, the youngest of the three, showed up and sat next to me.

"What's going on?" he began.

"Nothing big. Just about to eat some food. What about you?" I responded.

"I'm fine. A little hungry. Didn't eat since lunch yesterday," he confessed quietly.

"I got this sandwich," I told him. "I'm actually not that hungry. Why don't you eat it?" I offered.

"Thanks," he said, taking the sandwich.

I really wasn't sure what was going on. I worried it was a setup and the other two would show up to beat me up or humiliate me. I wasn't sure. But I didn't run away. I sat next to Frankie and made small talk with him.

"So, I been talking to my mom and she asked me what I wanted to do with my life. And you know what I told her? I said I wanted to be a fireman or a police officer . . . maybe even a teacher," Frankie told me in a low voice.

"I think about that too—what I want to do with my life. I decided I want to be a surgeon, so I can help a lot of people. And that's how I see firemen, police officers, and teachers—they help a lot of people too."

So our small talk morphed into a more substantive conversation. I could tell he was sharing things he had never told anyone our age before.

"You wanna go to a baseball game on Saturday?" he asked.

"Sure," I told him.

When I arrived at the shop after school, I was beaming.

"You look like a different person. Tell me, Edgar, something good happened. What is it?" Margaret asked.

I told her about Frankie.

Margaret responded with enthusiasm, saying, "I think you should go to a game with this young man. This is really good, Edgar. I'm proud of you. I worry about you every day. Do you understand?"

She almost made me cry.

She added, "I'm not as trusting as Miguel. Miguel seems to trust everybody, and it's turned out well for him. I think he could win over anyone in the world. There's no one that would harm him. He says that some day you'll be like him. I think you'll be like him too.

"I'll tell you what I'll do. I will go ahead and take both of you. We'll go and pick Frankie up, and we'll go to the game. Then afterwards we'll stop and get some hot dogs or a hamburger and a milkshake. You can tell him that Margaret invites him as well," Margaret suggested.

Frankie and I went to that Saturday baseball game and enjoyed a fun day out together. We never ended up becoming close friends, but I never had any trouble again from him, Sam, or Bobby. Even still, high school did not suddenly become worry-free. Riots, gangs, and violence terrorized me and my fellow students right to the day I graduated.

When Frankie, Sam, and Bobby proposed their plan to me to steal from that restaurant, it was one of those crossroads that the American Consul had been referring to. One direction led to disaster and doom; the other, to success. I could have gone with the boys and done the plan. Then maybe I wouldn't have felt so threatened in my own neighborhood or in high school because I'd have a group of guys backing me, a gang of sorts. But it also would have meant I'd be required to steal, lie, and do violence to others, which equated to failure and disaster. Turning them down took me in another direction. I wasn't protected at school or in my neighborhood. I stayed stressed out and afraid, both at school and out in my neighborhood. But, at the same time, I stayed true and close to my family, I lived and worked honestly, and I continued pursuing my big life dream, which would eventually lead to success—to becoming someone and doing something to be proud of.

I didn't need to refer to those letters and reports from my elementary school teachers in order to choose which direction to move in. Their encouraging words were imprinted in my brain, never to be erased. In fact, it was my grandfather, my godfather, and César who first stamped my heart and soul with the burning desire to do the right thing, both for myself, my family, and society as a whole.

18

My dear mother died in 2014 at the age of 93. Though she'd experienced four strokes in the last ten years of her life, it wasn't until the two months before her death that she became totally incapacitated. This meant she functioned well, both mentally and physically, for most of her life and her old age. This was exactly what my siblings and I wanted for her—our dear mother who, for decades, had sacrificed her own needs for the sake of her babies.

In the weeks before her death, I couldn't get her life out of my mind. While I was seeing patients, operating on patients, and managing my practice, in all that time, a movie of my mother's life played before me. I could hear her voice and see her as she cooked breakfast, lunch, and dinner, shaping tortillas by hand. I saw her moving throughout the small adobe house of my childhood with two babies strapped to her body—one on her chest and the other on her back. I saw her waving the fumes of smoke as she was making the fire to cook our meals on. And she never complained.

Starting in 1990, when she was in her late seventies, my mother lived in her own home that I'd set up for her with all the accommodations for an aging person. My wonderful older sister Surama and younger sister Asunción lived and cared for our mother in that home. And it was in her familiar and comfortable home that my mother died at the age of 93.

One of my happiest and most satisfying memories was when Miguel, Pedro, and Olivia brought her and my younger siblings to the USA. So, I should note that that home where my mother, Surama, and Asunción were living was only a few streets away from the Arizona home where my wife, our children, and I were living. My mother, Surama, and all my siblings made it to the USA. We managed to reunite as a family in Phoenix—we've been blessed on so many levels.

★   ★   ★

In the six-plus years I'd been away from my mother, I always kept in touch, writing her letters and sending her money orders. I wrote her about everything that was going on in my life. My mother had never learned to read or write at school, so I figured that one of my siblings read my letters to her and helped her write letters to me. Sometimes I noticed parts of letters written in an unpracticed, delicate script that I figured my mother must have written herself. She told me she'd been teaching herself to read and write, and eventually she learned to read and write in Spanish quite well.

In her letters she would confide that when she felt worried about me, she would tell herself, "As long as I know Miguel is with you, I have no need to worry." She knew that Margaret was like another mother to me in the United States and that I also had another mother named Elvira. She always wrote about them as if she knew them, and that's because she trusted and loved them so much.

Each time she received a money order from me she would always write me, asking that I thank Margaret for making me the fine son that I was. My mother loved Margaret dearly.

After two years of hard work on Miguel, Olivia, and Pedro's parts as well as receiving a loan from Margaret, finally we were ready for my mother and siblings to come to Phoenix. As planned, Pedro traveled to La Mira to bring my mother, Lupe, Asuncion, Reyna, and Manuel to Nogales.

Miguel met them in Nogales to walk them through the immigration process. He'd actually started their paperwork a few weeks before they arrived to save time and money. From the years it took to achieve my immigration, Miguel had met a lot of people at the Consulate and the people there were very accommodating in helping with my family's immigration. The same serious but kind American Consul headed the agency too. The process was very smooth and even less expensive than when I'd immigrated.

Six weeks after Pedro had left to fetch them, my mother and siblings arrived in Phoenix. It was a glorious day when they arrived at our little house. We were finally together.

I ran to my mother and hugged her, and I couldn't stop crying. I cried and I cried. I couldn't help myself. It had been over six years since I'd seen her. Then my sisters hugged me, and they were also crying. Manny joined in the hugging and crying too until finally, Miguel put his arms around all of us kids. He told them, "Come on into your home. Let me show you around."

Once inside, Miguel pointed out the floor of orange-and-white checkered linoleum tiles that spread throughout the house. There were three large bedrooms. The five of us kids would sleep in one, Miguel would have another, and my mother would have her own. There were two bathrooms, one that had a bathtub and the other a shower. There was a small kitchen and a living room area. It was a tiny, humble home that felt like a palace to all of us.

That evening we sat down to eat a celebratory meal together. Before eating, Miguel spoke. He started with a small prayer for unity—unity in the world and continued unity in our family. Then he spoke about the power of faith—faith in God, in fellow human beings, and in hard work—and how it had led to the achievement of bringing our family together. He praised and thanked the American Consul, immigration officers, and one person after another. He must have named thirty people, including Margaret and Bernard. It took him a long time to thank everybody.

The rest of us sat there, in awe of the wisdom with which he spoke. His message overflowed with gratitude and sincerity. He talked about integrity, the integrity of the immigration officers and the integrity of the American Consul. He was so eloquent.

I noted to myself, "He speaks from the heart. He speaks out his mind. He speaks like an angel. Someday, I would like to be able to speak like him."

After his moving introductory words, we enjoyed enchiladas and ice cream.

Miguel made sure to ask my mother, "What do you think of the stove?"

In response Mamá burst out crying.

"You'll never have to put another log on the fire. You've done it for so many years, and you cooked thousands and thousands of meals for these children. Thank God for that. And now, you'll never have to put a log on the fire," Miguel told her.

With tears streaming from her face, my mother thanked God for the wonderful gift of life and for bringing us back together.

In that moment the yoke of toil and suffering slid off my mother's shoulders to reveal a younger woman full of love and hope. No more gathering wood and making wood into coals. No more smoke. Now she could put a match to the stove, it would light up, and she could cook meals in a matter of minutes. I saw nothing but smiles on my mother's freckled face.

Then the conversation turned to my two younger half-brothers, Jose Angel and Salvador. These were my mother's sons with the man she married after my father died and I left.

"In a few years' time after we've saved more money, we'll bring them to Phoenix if they want to come here," Miguel promised my mother.

The first thing my siblings wanted to do was learn English. My siblings all decided it was very important to speak English well to be able to go on to college and to get good jobs. Some of them wanted to become professionals. Some of them wanted to work immediately after high school. Miguel and I emphasized getting a good education to ultimately get a good job.

We also wanted Mamá to learn English. My mom felt shy whenever I reminded her that she needed to learn English too.

"I predict that the way you'll learn English is from Manuel. He's the youngest, so he'll be reading comic books and other books for younger kids. You'll hear him reading aloud or speaking simple words or sentences, and through him you'll end up learning English. Don't be afraid because you can do it," I encouraged her.

"I'm not so sure about that," Mamá said in response.

"Trust me. When you hear him talk, you will learn."

Lupe, Asunción, Reyna, and Manuel picked up English incredibly quickly. They became fluent in their first year in Phoenix. They earned excellent grades and reports from all of their teachers.

Our greatest difficulty was finances. Miguel was in debt because of all the money he'd put into the home, and he owed Margaret money for the loan. My sisters were worried because there just wasn't enough money to buy adequate clothing. They pretty much wore the same clothes every week. They washed these clothes on Saturday and Sunday and then wore them again the next week.

Miguel noticed this and urged, "We have to stick together. We'll work hard and save and save, and then we can buy new clothes and new shoes when the time comes. The main thing is that we are together."

The main thing for Miguel really was that we were together, whether we were poor or not. He felt that as long as we had some food on the table, it was enough because being together was so important and special. He always looked at life with optimism.

My mother's life changed completely when she moved to United States. The way of life, the way to take care of a home, the way to cook, the way to take care of the children, the way to shop for food, the way to move about the neighborhood and city—it required drastic changes. Using an electric iron versus the iron she was used to—one that was heated on coals—was so different. She'd always hand washed clothes in a *pila* outside the house, and now she had a washer and dryer. Her life changed greatly and changed for the better.

She coped with the transition beautifully. She made friends easily. She was happy with her new life in the United States. She was shy, yet friendly at the same time. She cautiously started communicating in English. Neighbors would seek her out because she was a fantastic cook. I remember arriving home one day to find a group of several women at our house. "Edgar, I want you to meet these wonderful ladies. They came over because they want me to show them how to make enchiladas from scratch," my mother told me. When people talked with her, they were absolutely amazed that she could do so much with so little.

My mother's greatest concern was safety. She worried about my safety in high school, and she worried about all of our safety in the neighborhood due to the gangs and robberies. We often couldn't leave our home alone because we'd get robbed. Houses were broken into. It was frequent, common, broken-record-like news to hear someone say, "So-and-so got robbed. Their windows were broken, so they've got to repair the windows. Also they must repair the doors." So, my mother became afraid for us. She prayed for each of us when we left the house, asking God to bless us and protect us.

Miguel and my mother were never harmed or intimidated. Miguel could go to any place in the neighborhood, and no one would harm him. I don't know why, but he never had any problems with anybody. Thank God for that.

When my mother met Margaret, she said, "I knew somehow that an angel would be looking after Edgar."

Margaret asked, "Do you remember the money orders that Edgar would send you?"

"Yes, I do," my mother replied.

Margaret told her, "I remember them too because Edgar used to ask me to fill out the forms to send the orders to you. He always would make sure that I got the spelling of your name correct or else you wouldn't be able to cash them in the small town where you lived. I remember them very well because I was very careful not to make an error in the way your name was spelled. I soon learned how to spell and say your name . . . I want you to know that it's been a great joy in my life to have had these years with your son. Thank you for sharing him."

My mother insisted, "No, it is me who thanks you for taking such good care of him."

19

It was 1993 and Michael Carbajal and Chiquita Gonzalez were battling it out. Michael went down in the second round and again in the fifth. Incredibly Michael managed to stand before the end of the count.

After the bell rang, in a daze Michael made it to our corner. He was bleeding profusely from his right eyebrow, and it was apparent that he was shaken.

Through his glazed-over eyes, Michael looked at me, begging, "Doc, don't let the ring doctor stop the fight. I can beat Chiquita. Please. Please. Give the go-ahead."

Danny, Michael's brother and manager, looked to me, asking, "Edgar, what do you think? He's beat up pretty bad. And obviously dizzy."

I gave Michael moist ammonia to smell, and he shook his head a few times. He drank a sip of water, and I could tell right away that he'd perked up.

"Michael, are you with me?" I asked.

"Yes, Doc. I feel great," he responded with greater lucidity.

Danny urged, "Then go get him, brother, because this is your only chance. He's going to come after you really hard right now, so understand one thing—you need to avoid him for at least a few seconds until you get back into the rhythm."

Bleeding from his eyebrow Michael managed to explode a punch onto Chiquita's chin. When Chiquita turned his head in response to the blow, Michael wailed him again, sending him flying into the canvas. Chiquita was down for the count.

Michael became the world's Junior Flyweight Champion that year and also the Champion Fighter of the Year.

It seemed almost coincidental—or serendipitous—that I was Michael Carbajal's ringside private physician. Five years beforehand, in 1988, I'd answered my phone, saying, "Yes, this is Edgar Hernandez. And who's calling?"

"Edgar, it's Danny Carbajal. We went to school together back in the day. You remember me?"

"Of course, I remember you. How did you find me?"

"From the newspapers. I read those articles about the surgical missions in Mexico that you've been doing. And that's why I'm calling you. I was wondering if you could be my brother Michael's private physician. You see—he's about to have his first professional fight in New Jersey, and we'd love to have you on our team."

And that's how I became part of the support team for Michael Carbajal, aka Manitas de Piedra [Little Hands of Stone]. I was in his corner for his first professional boxing fight in New Jersey in 1988 when he knocked out Will Grigsby, aka Steel Wool Willie. And I was there for many more of his boxing fights.

Considering how Danny Carbajal and I had last seen each other decades earlier one afternoon in our eleventh grade year of high school, the irony of his brother's fighting success wasn't lost on us.

★   ★   ★

I knew the basement where the lockers were located was a vulnerable place, so I was careful about when I went there and for how long I stayed. School had already ended, and I'd spent forty minutes studying in the library. I decided it was probably safe to zip down to retrieve some books from my locker and transfer notebooks and books into my locker.

When I closed my locker door and turned, there were four students standing in a line blocking my path.

"You ain't leavin' here till you give us yo' money," one demanded.

Before I could respond, one of them slammed me on the head with a textbook and sent me shooting backwards against the lockers and down on the ground. I landed on my back.

"You don't need to hurt me. I'll give you the money. Just give me a chance," I managed to utter.

I pulled two dollars out of my pocket, and as one of the guys was taking it from me, he smashed me in the face with his knee.

Another guy was pulling his leg back, ready to strike me in the ribs, when a loud voice called out, "Stop! Leave him alone!" It was Danny Carbajal, a kid I'd been going to school with since the sixth grade.

Danny sprinted forward to pull one of the assailants away. Then another person approached to help me. The four guys fled.

Danny crouched down to talk to me, "You okay?"

"Yeah," I garbled with blood streaming from my mouth and head.

"No, you aren't. Let's take you to the admin. You might have to go to the hospital," he determined.

I ended up going to a medical clinic where I got several sutures in my head. Miguel was notified. When he came to get me, he was very upset. Then at home my sisters and brother and mother were very distressed too.

And that's the last time I saw Danny Carbajal, at least for several decades.

I knew he came from a big family, and like mine, they were poor. He was smart, dedicated to his family, and a fast learner. I figured he dropped out of high school to support his family. Though I never saw him again at high school, I never forgot him. He'd saved my life.

Not the teachers, the administration, or the students knew how to address the upheaval going on at school. Even the best teachers, who'd been teaching there for years, were at a loss.

One of those amazing teachers was Mr. Hraski, my biology teacher. Mr. Hraski was a flat-topped gentleman who smelled of cigarette smoke. His eloquent and intense teaching buttressed my desire to become a doctor. In his class we dissected frogs and rabbits, so I got to use some of the surgical tools I'd seen my father use so many years earlier. Plus, I was doing my first slicing and incisions—something I planned on spending my lifetime doing. We watched inspiring documentary films about innovations and changes in science, physics, and biology. There were films about Albert Einstein. We saw films featuring the engineers that worked with Einstein too.

Mr. Hraski said to us, "All those scientists and engineers that surrounded Albert Einstein were once high school students just like you. It was through hard work, dedication, and curiosity that they got so far in life. And you can do the same. Every one of you in this class can become a great scientist, writer, doctor, economist, civil engineer—whatever you desire—if you are willing to put in the hard work and dedication and nurture your curiosity about the world. You have what it takes."

Mr. Hraski's insightful teaching and supportive words gave me the courage to share with more and more people my life goal—becoming a surgeon. Mr. Hraski and teachers like him fueled my desire to work hard and persist—even in the face of violence and fear, which I'd experienced firsthand. I knew my dream could come true.

A student asked Mr. Hraski, "What are we going to do about the worsening gangs in our school? They're fighting against each other, hurting each other—and they hurt us."

Mr. Hraski admitted that he didn't have an answer and that it was upsetting to him too. "The teachers and staff have tried a number of things, and it hasn't worked. The only thing I can say to each of you is—do not drop out of school, even if you are targeted—and I know some of you have been assaulted. Do not give up on your studies. Graduate from high school, and go to college. It is very hard now, but persisting with your education will lead to a life with lots of options. You can even gain the qualifications to be in a policy-making position where you can draw on this troubling high school experience to offer workable solutions to students and communities in the future," he offered.

It also seemed that anyone who discussed the violence or tried to do something about it became targeted themselves. The gangs went after students or adults whom they deemed some kind of threat, so this further discouraged people from talking and added to a collective sense of isolation and victimization. It was a very difficult time, and one without easy or apparent answers.

When I was a senior, Margaret became quite ill. She developed a constant cough, had fever and chills, and was losing weight. Towards the end of my senior year, Margaret was hospitalized with pneumonia. Seeing her small, frail body in the hospital bed made her great weight loss quite apparent. Her skin was hanging from her chin. Her face was very droopy.

In the same week that I'd be graduating from high school, Margaret was admitted to the hospital for a third time. Miguel told me that Margaret wanted to talk to me, and he was afraid that she was dying. I visited her with great sadness in my heart.

I talked to her for almost an hour, telling her that I was starting Arizona State University immediately in the summer semester. "I'm going to be in school a long time, so I want to start immediately to stay ahead. I've even spoken to a counselor at ASU about my plan to become a doctor. She told me that it's really tough to get into medical school and that only a few people qualify—and I already knew this, but it still scared me some. It also motivated me to start college immediately."

In her typical no-nonsense manner, Margaret told me, "Edgar, I have every confidence that you'll go on to medical school and become a surgeon. I'm not worried about it at all. You will achieve your dream. And the first two years of your college will be on me. Your tuition will be covered for the first two years. After that, you're on your own. Bernard and I are continuing our money donations to private organizations, as we've been doing for years now."

She continued, "The reason I'm telling you this is because I've been told that I have some type of malignancy in my body, and it's incurable. They offered me surgery, but they told me that I would never survive because the malignancy was spreading. I know I'm going to die soon. I accept that."

Next Margaret launched into a tirade against the "sidewalk vendors and amateurs that are ruining Indian jewelry with their cheap imitation knock-offs." Apparently their business was losing longtime buyers who were opting for low-quality, synthetic turquoise pieces. She lamented the devastating changes both to their own jewelry business and to the art of crafting beautiful Navajo pieces. She seemed more upset about this than about her pneumonia. I figured that her anxiety in this area was only worsening the effects of the pneumonia and spurring on the dangerous weight loss.

My high school graduation was bittersweet—"bitter" because of Margaret's sickness but "sweet" because I graduated with distinction and within the month started classes at ASU.

With the help of an ASU counselor, I mapped out the premed course requirements for all the semesters of college. Margaret had given me so much in our years together and had taught me how to prepare myself thoroughly to succeed in my studies. So, I felt prepared for the long years of study—both in college and beyond—that were ahead of me.

20

"... really hurts ... hard to breathe ..." the man whimpered.

He'd been stabbed in the chest, and the knife remained there, its handle sticking out.

The nurse and intern went ahead and put in intravenous lines to help the man. I noticed the intern had decided to pull the knife out.

"Stop immediately! Do not remove that knife," I ordered. "Give him something to ease the pain, but do not remove the knife."

I called the operating room and told them we needed to take a patient into surgery immediately. We typed and crossed him, and then got blood ready for him.

"Give us the patient's name, Dr. Hernandez," the operating room asked.

I looked at the chart—Lonny Ramirez—I froze. Then I peered closely at the man's face. It was Lonny Ramirez, one of the students in the gang of four who had jumped me by my locker so many years ago in high school. Lonny was the one who'd hit me on the top of my head with a textbook, landing a blow that sent me flying backwards and to the ground.

My heart sank at the memory. Fear from the past encounter washed over me—and then anger at the unfairness and cruelty of the deed—but only for a moment. I had to get back my composure.

"Lonny Ramirez—that's the patient's name," I reported to the operating room.

Then Lonny Ramirez uttered, " . . . know you, Doc . . . remember you from high school . . . please take care of me . . . This time, I didn't do nothing wrong . . . not my fault."

I assured him, "I know you didn't do anything wrong.

Don't worry, we're here to take care of you. I'm a surgeon, I'm not a police officer. If it makes you feel any better, the cops are outside, and they pretty much told me that the perpetrator and the people that caused your stabbing have been arrested. The rest of your family is safe."

He grabbed my hand tight and said, "I remember your name is Edgar . . . but I'm calling you Dr. Hernandez . . . you earned the title."

In the operating room, I managed to remove the knife. It had been penetrating a vessel in the middle of his right upper lung. I repaired it, and he had no problems recovering from the surgery.

It is an absolutely incredible thing to be able to walk in, introduce yourself as a surgeon, and then recognize that you're going to operate on someone that you went to school with. While it wasn't an everyday occurrence for me, it must have happened at least a half dozen times. Some people I remembered well, and others I barely knew, but I knew they went to my school.

Sometimes people would ask me, while I was in the emergency room as an admitting surgical resident, "Are you Edgar from Phoenix Union High School?" I would reply, "Yes, it's me." They would say, "You went to school with my mother [or uncle, father, aunt, etc.]."

Lonny Ramirez was the only person whom I operated on— whose life I saved—who had previously assaulted me to the point where I'd feared for my own life. For a brief second after putting all that together I felt deeply unsettled, but I quickly recovered, for I'd taken an oath and saving lives was my calling.

*   *   *

Margaret always told me that no matter what, I should study hard because hard work would bring success—and that was my guiding philosophy in my years at ASU. In four years there, I earned a bachelor's in biology and a master's in embryology and histology simply because I took huge amounts of credit hours each semester and I took classes all year long, including the summer semesters.

Additionally, I worked almost full-time in the jewelry store over those four years. I delivered jewelry and worked with Miguel and Pedro manufacturing jewelry. Although I was very, very busy, I was rarely tired. I stayed enthusiastic about my classes, my work, my family, and my classmates.

Another important thing I did was help my two younger half-brothers, Jose Angel and Salvador, become legal residents in the USA. They had come to the US illegally, crossing into California. It was my task to take them to Nogales and lead them through the immigration process, so they could become legal residents. It was the easiest immigration process ever because I knew everything that they needed to do.

Towards the end of my fourth year at ASU, which was towards the end of my master's program, I applied to and was accepted at numerous medical schools. I elected to go to the University of Utah College of Medicine. The dean there impressed me when he said, "We have only one goal—to create doctors of the highest caliber. Our professors will do everything in their power to make sure this happens. We want you to be a part of our program."

I'd been in touch with Elvira and Javier through letters over the years, and before going to Utah to start medical school, I returned to Nogales to visit them. Both of them were doing poorly in terms of their health. It was disheartening for me to see. Elvira had developed an eye condition and had to have surgery. Javier had had a stroke and was in recovery. He could walk with a cane. While they had caring acquaintances through the Catholic Church, they had no family members nearby. I was the closest thing they had to a family member, it seemed. It was hard seeing these two lovely people suffering as they aged.

I also visited the immigration department. I looked among the immigration officers working the entry-exit border to see if I could find Larry Murphy. I didn't see him though. I attempted to greet the caring, flat-topped Consul gentleman who'd helped me and my family so many years before, but the agency had reorganized and changed, and I didn't see him. So, all in all, this visit to Nogales was short, yet sad.

On a happier note, before starting medical school, I married a wonderful woman, Lupe Gomez. I met Lupe because her brother, Salvador, married my sister, who is also named Lupe. My wife came from a family of ten children. Her parents were

Mexican immigrants to the United States, and all the children were born in Arizona. Mr. and Mrs. Gomez brought them up very well. Most all of them became college graduates. Lupe ended up earning a bachelor's in psychology and also a master's in Latin American history while I was pursuing my degrees.

Lupe and I rented a tiny apartment that was quite close to the medical school, and we only really saw each other on Saturdays. That was our day for spending quality time together. We'd go out to dinner or to a movie. The other days I had to study and go to classes. Lupe was always patient and supportive of me and my pursuit of my life dream. She never chastised me for the amount of study I was putting in. Instead, she did everything in her power to support me to succeed.

Another constraint on our relationship at this time was finances. We simply didn't have much money. The Arizona Medical Association had given me a generous scholarship to defray some of the costs of medical school, and the University of Utah had also awarded me a scholarship, both of which helped. However, there wasn't money to spare.

The first two years of medical school were tough, a real act of endurance. The amount of work and the amount of material we covered were immense. It was a gruesome two years for all of us in the program. My fellow medical students and I hardly talked to each other because we spent all our time studying. We'd say hello in the halls, and that was it. The classroom was intense because the professors wanted us to learn as much as we possibly could to be ready for the clinical practice that started in the third year. I couldn't wait. I just could not wait to wear the white coat and stethoscope.

Prior to starting school we were given an opportunity to test out of classes based on our experience. Since I had earned a master's in the field of embryology and histology, I was considered already very strong in these areas, so I did not have to take these classes. When a classmate of mine noticed I wasn't taking these classes, he asked if I was doing a "special program," meaning a slower program for someone needing more time to master the heavy and rigorous study load. After momentarily calling on the generous, loving spirit that Miguel consistently modeled to me, I let the classmate know that no, that wasn't the case, I'd actually tested out of the classes. I explained this to him in a kind manner in spite of the prejudice or insult embedded in his inquiry.

There were periods in the summers for fun and relaxation—that's when I went fishing. The fishing and charity clinics I participated in were both amazing. Some of my fellow medical students and I worked with seasonal migrant workers in the charity medical clinics. It was an engaging, busy two years.

Years three and four of medical school were clinicals. That's when we applied the science of the first two years into patient care. For the clinics, a group of us traveled the hospital together—the attending chief resident, junior residents, interns, and, of course, the medical students, who were the lowest on the totem pole. My medical student colleagues and I were each assigned specific patients, and it was our responsibility to give our superiors accurate information on the patient's status, condition, plan for disposition, and any surgical tests, blood studies, and such. We had to report all of this to the attending physician and to the chief resident who ultimately were responsible for the patients.

I remember a chief resident telling me that I was the only student he remembered coming in so early each day and that I was impressively prepared and knowledgeable about the patients when we made our reports in the surgical rounds. Needless to say, I was delighted by this observation.

César, my grandfather, Mrs. Cane, and my mother wouldn't be surprised to learn that many of the residents, interns, and surgeons who guided us during the clinicals informed me that I asked more questions than any other medical student that they'd yet encountered.

One afternoon my chief resident informed me, "The attending surgeon called me because one of his patients, a thirteen-year-old boy, is in the emergency room with abdominal pain. The surgeon asked that you go and see the child. Report whether you think he has appendicitis."

I was fully aware that it was an honor for the chief resident to make such a request of a medical student.

I went to the emergency room to examine the patient. The boy had classic symptoms of appendicitis, which I promptly reported to the chief resident.

"Edgar, I want you to perform the appendectomy on the

patient. I'll supervise you, assuming the attending surgeon is in agreement," the chief resident informed me.

And so the chief resident awarded me the greatest prize that a medical student, particularly one aiming to specialize in surgery, could ever be given—being allowed to perform an appendectomy as a junior. It was not an everyday event. My chief resident told me, "This is something that I'm not giving you, this is something you have earned for your very hard work, and you should be proud of that."

A more common award for high-performing medical students was being allowed to talk to patients about their tests and plans for their future care—so you can imagine how special it was for me to be allowed to perform a surgery as a medical student.

In this way, my career as a surgeon began.

After four very demanding years, the time for graduating from this wonderful medical school was upon me.

I sat with my classmates in a large auditorium. As I waited for my name to be called, I felt like I was going to faint. I was sweating profusely. My heart was palpitating. My physical state reminded me of the panic attacks I'd had at some key, stressful moments in my childhood—like when I thought Miguel had abandoned me in the hotel in Nogales or when I was about to ask the nice immigration officer if I could cross the border to "run an errand" . . . except the event I was so panicked about at the moment was not scary or threatening—it was a major accomplishment. I was graduating from medical school. It was one of the greatest achievements of my life—yet I was panicking.

I looked at the student sitting next to me. He was smiling and sometimes he would wave at his family. He was overjoyed yet collected.

It occurred to me that I should follow his lead. So I looked out in the audience and found Miguel, Lupe, Pedro, and my mother, and I smiled in their direction. I allowed myself to feel their joy and pride—until I could feel it for myself, from myself.

"Edgar Hernandez Hernandez," the dean announced.

I calmly and proudly stood, walked to the dean, and shook his hand. He looked me in the eye and winked. I heard cheering from the crowd, and I knew it was coming from my family. It was a joyous applause for me.

The dean told each of us graduating from medical school that day, "This diploma is vested upon you for a privileged accomplishment and for an opportunity to teach, treat, and save lives wherever your destiny may take you."

The dean continued, "A doctor is a teacher, and you should teach good health and happiness to all of your patients and, at the same time, honor and respect those whom you treat, for they too will be your individual teachers."

The following day, I returned to Phoenix with my family where I would continue my medical training. Although the chairman of the University of Utah College of Medicine had offered me a position as an intern in the department of surgery, an offer that the chief resident told me had never been made to any medical student previously, I elected to do my five-year surgical residency in Phoenix, Arizona, at the Maricopa County General Hospital under the direction of Dr. Harry Hale, Jr., chief of surgery.

Training in Phoenix meant that my wife and I could be near our families, which was important to both of us, particularly because my first child, a son whom we named Miguel, was born at this time.

Before beginning residency at the Maricopa County General Hospital, Miguel and I drove to Nogales to visit Elvira and Javier. At the border we didn't see any chain-link fences. Instead, we saw high-quality gates and a sophisticated security system. Everything had changed in Nogales.

The stroke Javier had suffered a few years earlier had really crippled him. He'd developed extreme hypertension and asthma from smoking. Apparently he'd been a closet smoker for years and had been hiding it very well, for I was never aware of it. Elvira was also ailing from diabetes and severe neuropathy. It was difficult for me and Miguel to see our wonderful, generous friends so debilitated.

Several weeks after our visit Javier ended up getting severe pneumonia and passed away. He was in his late sixties. Elvira, also in her late sixties, ended up moving to another city in Mexico and lived her remaining years there, cared for by a group of dedicated nuns. She passed away a few years later in 1983.

Elvira and Javier meant so much to me. They were my

caretakers when I was a child. They nurtured me in my time of need. They exemplified the goodness of humanity—that yes, we can trust in total strangers. I will never forget them.

Dr. Hale was a walking surgical textbook and the most talented surgeon I've ever met. He could diagnose appendicitis, gallbladder problems, or anything you could think of in the abdomen. Furthermore, he could diagnose anything in the head and neck area. In fact—he could diagnose anything in the entire human body. He had judgment that was incomparable.

In the first meeting between Dr. Hale and us six interns his manner was soft-spoken, but his message rang loud and clear. He told us, "Here at County Hospital, we surgeons take care of poor and unfortunate people. The patients that come here have serious surgical problems. More often than not, these patients come with neglected issues. They have not sought medical care before because they're poor or they didn't know where to go or they are mentally challenged or they were basically in denial. These patients deserve your kindness, for they'll teach you much. Trust me. However, if you are not interested in taking care of poor people and you prefer to be in a private hospital, now is your chance to leave. The door is there. You can step out. I will hold no grudge towards you. Don't ever forget what I've said."

We, interns, looked at each other with a keen awareness that we were in the right place. We let Dr. Hale know that there was no better place than in his surgical department and that his reputation as an exemplary surgeon was well known even before we'd met him. We communicated the privilege we felt to have been selected to train at the hospital under him.

Surgical trainings were the toughest of all trainings in this hospital, and nobody worked harder than the interns. I started at Maricopa County Hospital with the most difficult of all the surgical rotations—I was an intern in the burn unit where the sickest and most delicate of all the patients resided.

The burn patients were all on respirators and required multiple antibiotics and constant monitoring. At the blink of an eye a patient could die. They could easily get infections in their burns. We had to check their burns every day, the skin, head and neck area, and scalp, and then turn them over to make sure they didn't have any dark spots on their backs. Spots indicated a problem, like skin infections deep in the burns—hidden in the fatty tissue below the burned surface—so we would have to remove chunks of the skin right there on the bedside and send them to the lab to be cultured to check if there were any threatening bacteria brewing. All of these patients were immunosuppressed, so any bacteria could quickly get out of hand and kill them.

We treated their wounds with a warm saline solution. Right when the saline hit the wound area, any damaged skin rapidly shrunk and shriveled away. We made sure to scrape away all such dead skin. Then, to protect these exposed wound areas from infection, to decrease the patient's pain, and to allow new skin time to grow and heal, we wrapped these areas in pigskin. The pigskin came in long rolls, almost like gauze, to make it convenient to wrap around areas of the body. Oftentimes when family members visited and saw their loved one covered in pigskin they would mistake it for real skin—and we'd have to explain what it was and why it was there.

In this three-month rotation we learned everything about nutrition, infectious disease, respiratory medicine, musculoskeletal medicine, and the most important thing—burn surgery—which entailed how to handle burns, how to debrid (clean) them, and how to graft them. Shortly after a patient with burns arrived, we took them into surgery to perform a removal of dead tissue, and then we took skin from unharmed parts of the body to perform immediate skin grafts. The goal was to replace dead, burned skin with new skin, to avoid crippling infections and death.

Burn surgeries were quite difficult technically, very exhausting, and very lengthy, lasting three to five hours. Because burn patients lost tremendous amounts of fluids from their open wounds, they would get very cold. To keep them from getting too cold, we worked under very hot lamps. So, while these lamps were perfect for our patients, they made our working conditions extremely uncomfortable.

The tremendous reward from working on these lengthy and difficult cases was that we saved scores of lives. For a trauma surgeon, saving a life is glorious. Really, nothing can compare with it.

While the rotations were grueling, the amount of medicine and surgery we learned was tremendous. Every fourth night one of us would be on call, which meant we were responsible not only for burn patients but for all the patients in the intensive care unit and in trauma as well. The trauma center included patients that suffered from major catastrophic accidents, like auto accidents, falls from buildings, stab wounds, and gunshot wounds. Any trauma you could think of, we took care of. The responsibilities of an intern on call were immense.

Normally, we, interns, would arrive at the hospital at 6 in the morning and leave between 5 and 6 pm in the evening. However, if we were on call, we would continue working overnight and then start another day of work the next morning, almost as if we'd arrived fresh from home, yet we could have been up the entire night working. Essentially, it was a 36-hour shift every fourth night for each of us during our five years of surgical training. Sometimes we'd spend more than 85 hours a week in the hospital.

Regularly I would not see my family for several days. It seemed the only way that I knew that my first child, Miguel, was growing was when I would find out that his first and second and third birthday parties were coming up.

The second and third years at my surgical training were like the first year—very demanding. However, during the second and third years I developed more knowledge, expanded my comfort level, and became more in-tune with what was going on. In these years, I refined and practiced specific procedures— appendectomies, gallbladder operations, perforated intestines, stab and gunshot wounds to the abdomen, and a variety of other types of surgical procedures, including some breast procedures.

Dr. Hale usually met with each resident after every year to let us know about our individual performances. It was after the third year that it was decided whether or not the particular resident was progressing as required and prepared to finish the five-year program—or not. Dr. Hale would cut off residents in the third year if they were not, according to him, "cutting the mustard," which means he didn't think the person was equipped to become a surgeon. Dr. Hale gave me a thumbs up to proceed onto my second, third, fourth, and then fifth years.

In the second and third years we, surgical residents, became responsible for any interns (first-years) under us; plus, we became the admitting surgeons in the emergency room. This meant that we had to evaluate every patient that arrived with a surgical problem and with the help of the senior resident make a decision about that patient's care. Either the patient was discharged, was admitted, or went directly to surgery. In this way problem solving, decision-making, and refining our diagnoses composed a critical part of the second and third years.

During my fourth year, I did some rotations in pediatric surgery at a downtown hospital. I worked with three pediatric surgeons. I loved it so much that I contemplated for a while becoming an open-heart pediatric surgeon. However, when it came to seeing small babies with congenital heart disorders die, I didn't have the spirit for it. That poignant first memory from my childhood—when I witnessed Santos Ortiz making the violin cry at the little boy's funeral—continued to haunt me. My ears seemed to ring with the wailing of Santos Ortiz's violin, and my heart ached terribly when any baby didn't make it through a surgery or died of a complication later on. I'd go so far as to say that it seemed like a sort of PTSD got activated in me. I knew I couldn't emotionally and psychologically live and work with the potential for such intense grief hanging over me, always ready to drop, so I decided not to specialize in pediatric surgery. I would practice general surgery and, at times, do some pediatric surgery.

In my last year at the county hospital all of us fifth-year residents were in positions of great responsibility because we acted as "chief residents." We would talk to the attending surgeons. They gave us advice, and we made the major decisions. I like to think that all the decisions that we, chief residents, made were honorable and that we had the best interests of the patients at heart. Also we had to guide and teach interns and any junior residents.

The salary during residency was quite small. It was difficult for my wife and son to live off of it. Both to augment our salaries and to allow us more opportunities to practice procedures, Dr. Hale allowed many fifth-year chief residents—but not all, depending on how the resident was progressing—to moonlight at other emergency rooms, both at the county hospitals and in private emergency rooms with private surgeons.

When working in emergency rooms, fifth-years given the go-ahead to moonlight had the opportunity to meet numerous surgeons with their own private practices. From there they sometimes asked fifth-years to assist them in their private surgeries. While the private surgeons were very generous with their patients, the surgeries tended not to be as complex or demanding as those in public ERs.

The surgeons with private practices often admitted to us, Maricopa County Hospital-trained surgeons, "We love county residents because you all know your stuff and you take really good care of our patients. You make excellent assistants, and we don't have to tell you much. You can pretty much take over the procedure and do it all yourself." I was told this on many occasions by many private surgeons.

The majority of patients at the Maricopa County Hospital were Hispanic, so my Spanish came in very handy. Many were victims of gang violence. In fact, I typically knew all the areas where the assaults occurred. I would be told that a patient was attacked at such-and-such bar, restaurant, street, or neighborhood, and I knew the location because that was around where I grew up.

Throughout my years in surgical training, it remained a privilege to work with patients. It was the most wonderful thing to have people trust us with their lives and bodies. No other profession in this world is given that privilege. It is something that I took to heart. Patients' lives are sacred, and they deserve that we, surgeons, do the best we possibly can to care for them. That was something that I felt I did throughout my entire five years as a resident in surgical training—and beyond.

After completing the five years of surgical training at the Maricopa County Hospital, each resident had to compile, document, and submit a record of all the surgical cases they'd worked during the training. In those years, because we'd been so busy, I had never kept track of my numbers. It wasn't important to me. My interest was in learning, improving, and caring for patients.

Due to this internship requirement, I needed to go through the records and document my work. So, I went down to medical records and pulled out all the cases that were under my name. I counted over 1,400 cases, a number four times as great as is typical of fifth year surgical residents today. My cases included pediatric surgery, orthopedic surgery, urological surgery, neurosurgery, and general surgery cases.

Dr. Harry Hale, Jr., Chief of Surgery, Department of Surgery, and all the staff at the Maricopa County Hospital, had only one thing in mind with the program—to make us into top-quality general surgeons, and that's what they did. I was very fortunate to have received my certificate from such a fantastic institution. Let me add too that both the dean of the University of Utah College of Medicine and Dr. Hale were correct—our patients were great teachers. I owe my learning to every one of them.

Miguel and I saw each other frequently during my years of residency. We would have dinner together at least once or twice a week, and, of course, he loved being with my son, Miguel. He wanted to see Miguel almost every day. He would pick him up from preschool and then from kindergarten.

Miguel got married too. He married a lovely lady, Victoria, who also had immigrated to Phoenix from Mexico. We were very happy for him.

Even still, Miguel maintained that I was the biggest prize in his life and that Miguel, my son, was the second prize.

Miguel, my son, would ask for Miguel all the time. They became very close, to the point that it became almost a guaranteed visit from Miguel to take little Miguel to get ice cream or some type of goody that he liked at least a few times each week. They absolutely, thoroughly enjoyed each other.

After finishing my training at the Maricopa County Medical Center, I opened a private practice for cases of trauma, general, and pediatric surgery. Around this time, our second child, Marisa, was born, and I hoped that I would get to spend more time with her in her initial years than I had with my son, Miguel, but it didn't prove to be so.

Starting a practice was very demanding. First, I had to borrow a lot of money, and paying back those loans, plus having money to care for my family, proved difficult. Secondly, I had to establish myself in the medical community as a surgeon whom primary care doctors would send referrals to—I learned that it was a tight and political community that didn't welcome newcomers. "We have good surgeons here already, and we don't need anyone else," primary care doctors told me time and again, to the point it seemed they'd already formed a coalition against any newcomers.

To prove myself and get referrals I worked about four

different emergency rooms, picking up trauma and general surgery calls—really any type of surgery that was available. Because of the rigorous training I'd had at Maricopa County Hospital, I found these ER cases straightforward and enjoyable. In this way, I started getting to know emergency room and primary care doctors as well as patients themselves so that six months into the start of my private practice I was starting to see patients trickle in, of their own accord, to make appointments to see me.

When I'd been contemplating specializing in pediatric surgery, I became quite experienced in the area. Because there were no pediatric surgeons in the area, I ended up doing a lot of pediatric surgeries. I operated on many babies as young as three weeks, doing procedures, like hernias and intussusception, all small enough cases that I could perform independently of any neonatal, high-intensity, or critical units.

I experienced real enjoyment in taking care of all these young babies and young children. I found nothing more comforting and enjoyable than taking care of a young child that needed surgical intervention. I found the babies and young children so strong with wonderful, vibrant tissues. Their ability to rebound after a surgery was incredible. They were soothing to care for with their tiny voices and tiny smiles melting my heart. I also found special satisfaction in seeing the parents relieved. It was a very pleasant, rewarding experience.

By the end of the first year, I was taking fewer and fewer emergency room calls because I was receiving more and more patients into my private practice. I noticed at that time that I was getting many patients with thyroid and breast disorders, either cancerous or noncancerous. Though it wasn't planned, my practice came to focus predominantly on these types of endocrine surgeries. I suppose once I started doing cases like these, I got more and more referrals from primary doctors and gynecologists in the same areas. I also did a number of abdominal and hernia surgeries.

After a few years, we had our third child, Carlos. I felt guilty that I didn't see my beautiful children, Miguel, Marisa, and Carlos, as much as I wanted to. When I wondered if it would have been better if I worked another profession so that I could see my children more, I concluded that no, it wouldn't have been better. Being a surgeon was worth it because of all the lives I saved and bettered. Even my children admitted to me that they had no regrets.

I saw it as an exchange of quantity of time for quality of time. I didn't see my family as much as I liked, but when I did, we tried to make it count. On this point, my children embraced and supported me, assuring me that the time we did get to spend together was high in quality and worthwhile.

A few years into my private practice, Miguel called me because he wanted us to have lunch together. I told my secretary to block off 11 to 1 pm, so I could spend a lengthy, relaxed, unrushed lunch with my wonderful brother.

Miguel was 66 years old and no different than when I'd first met him when I was a young child. He was neatly shaved. He had striking brown eyes and long eyelashes and a wide, wonderful smile.

Miguel and I headed out to lunch for one of his favorite meals, meatloaf and iced tea.

Miguel confessed, "When a day passes and I haven't seen Miguel, I really miss him. Something else, Edgar, is I look at Miguel like he is my son . . . And I want to know if this is alright with you—if you mind."

Without missing a beat, I responded, "It's way beyond that Miguel. Not only is he your son, he's also your grandson because you're the only one he has known and to have a grandfather is one of the greatest gifts in life."

I added, "Nothing pleases me more than for him to do all the things that fathers and sons do together with you. I haven't been available since I've been trying to grow my practice. I am forever grateful for everything that you do and all the attention you give my children."

Then we talked about how he was doing. Miguel told me that he'd gone to his doctor and they'd changed his medication. He had been experiencing elevated blood pressure and one of the medications was not working very well for him, so he switched to a different medication. Miguel had a very fine primary care doctor that I knew was taking really good care of him. I never worried about anything.

Then Miguel and I shared some memories. We talked about the ride we'd taken so many decades ago in the back of the open truck under the yellow and green tarp and how we'd watched the thick dust clouds behind us as the truck crawled along the bumpy dirt road.

Miguel told me, "I remember every minute of that wonderful ride, which was the first ride you and I took together. It was a long and tough part of the trip. But how about when we got onto the smooth, paved roads? I remember you wanted to get out of the truck and run because you'd never seen such smooth streets. You even talked about getting roller skates!"

"Do you remember what the driver looked like?" he asked me.

"Yes, he had smears of food on his shirt, a real sloppy dresser. He didn't even button his shirt correctly. He had that bushy mustache . . . You know that I hated him? The first time that you came to visit us, then you left, I hated him with a passion because he was taking you away."

Miguel admitted, "Yes, I do recall the way you'd look at him. You were very angry, but I knew why ... I remember when I first arrived, you were hiding from me, you didn't want to see me. Yet, you wanted to see me. I saw you looking in between people, taking quick peeks at me. I wanted to smile at you, but you were trying to hide away from me."

Then he asked, "Do you miss your grandfather?"

"Immensely. I think of him every day," I admitted.

"What's the most fantastic time you had with your grandfather?"

"Impossible. I can't say," I answered.

"What do you mean?"

I explained, "There wasn't a single time that I didn't enjoy being with him. Every moment I was with him was a gift that I waited for every day—when I would see him after school, when we'd go get popsicles, when we walked around town, when he held my hand. I remember everything about him. I remember when he took me to watch the turtles lay eggs. Everything that I remember about him was wonderful. There was not one time with him that was better than another."

Miguel asked, "But what stands out above all else?"

"I would have to say . . . when I thought I was dead, but I wasn't."

Miguel, looking puzzled, said, "Run that by me again."

Putting his hand on my forearm, he urged again, "Tell me what you're talking about."

"When I was quite young, a real little kid, I was at the beach with Abuelito, and I got bitten by a scorpion. When he realized what was happening, he rushed to help me. I knew something bad was happening to me. It felt like I was getting stung from a thousand ants, and then I dropped into an epileptic seizure. He brought me to the ocean to cool me. When I came to, I awoke in the water, gripping the sand, with my grandfather holding me, calling my name. It was very scary. He was so scared—I could see it on his face. I'd already seen the funerals of kids in the town, kids younger and smaller than me, who'd died from scorpion bites, so it was a close call. He knew it, and I knew it too," I quietly told Miguel.

Miguel regarded me with tears streaming down his face. In a hushed voice, he uttered, "I never knew this before. How come you never shared this with me? With all the days and nights we traveled together from truck to bus to train, through all the years you and I have known each other, you never told me this."

"It's something that I never wanted to talk about. It was terribly frightening. There was only one other time that I talked about it—that's when I shared it with a frightened mother, who arrived at the ER after her young son was bitten by a scorpion. I saw this child thrashing in a seizure and though we'd helped him and he was going to come out of it and be fine, it brought back that memory from my own childhood. I re-experienced that childhood fear and pain so acutely that I broke down in tears in front of the mom and ended up scaring her badly. So, to assure her that her son was fine, I told her the reason I was crying—I shared with her that childhood experience. She was the first person I ever told. Now, you are the second."

Then I added, "There's one more thing about it—that I didn't share with that mother, but I want to tell you."

"What's that, Edgar?"

"Do you remember Santos Ortiz, the hermit guy from La Mira?"

"Yes. He never talked, and he always wore the same clothes. He played the violin but only at the funerals of children," Miguel replied.

"Miguel, the first memory I have is when I was 4.5 years old and my father and I came upon the funeral of a child that had died of a scorpion bite. I distinctly recall being frightened sense-less when I heard Santos Ortiz producing those heart-breaking lamentations with his violin at that child's funeral. And that day at the beach with my grandfather when I got bitten by a scorpion—I could hear that wailing violin. No, it wasn't really there, but still—I heard it. Like it was there."

"Oh my heavens, Edgar. That's so frightening. You were such a young boy— "

I interrupted, "But, Miguel, that's not all. Over the course of my whole life, anytime I've been confronted with the death or near death of a child—I hear the mournful sobs of that violin. It makes me feel crazy—like I'm re-experiencing a nightmare. It's a big reason why I didn't end up specializing in neonatal pediatric surgery."

When I finished, Miguel regarded me with wide eyes and took my hand in his. Finally, he stated, "Thank you for telling me this, Edgar. I hate it that you've had to suffer alone with this for so long. You can always talk to me."

"I know, Miguel," I responded.

We returned to talking about the rest of that long trip to the United States of America so many years earlier.

"Miguel, I am forever grateful for everything you've done for me and for the family. It was a sacrifice that very few people in this world would make. You know, there's a lot of wonderful people in the world, but there's very few who'd make the sacri-fices that you made for me and the family. I know no man alive who is greater than you," I told my brother.

Miguel never could handle this kind of praise, so he changed the subject, asking, "Do you remember how you fell on the shiny marble floors at JCPenney's the first time you tried walking in a pair of shoes? And how you were mesmerized by the escalators—up and down and up and down, over and over again? That was something."

Before heading back to the office, I asked, "What type of beautiful jewelry are you making this week?"

"We have an order for some jade stone pendants, a hundred of them for a Canadian jewelry store. I should be done with my part of it today."

With that we stood and exited the restaurant. I gave him a hug and told him I loved him very much and I was as crazy about him now as I was when I'd first met him.

Before leaving, Miguel said to me, "I'm really sorry that I had to bring you across the border illegally. It's been one of the worst mistakes I've made in my life, but the seven and a half months that you were here illegally, I think, served you well and allowed you to survive in Nogales."

I returned to the office and had a busy afternoon in surgery. I got home at about 7 pm. Later that night I got a call from the emergency room that my brother had been admitted with chest pain.

I talked to the emergency room doctor who said that Miguel was having a fever and felt hot, especially in the chest. He was experiencing a shearing pain in the left chest, and he was short of breath.

I arrived at the hospital to find Miguel on a respirator. I could tell he wasn't doing well. He didn't recognize me at all.

I spent a few hours with him, there at his side. Then I went back home.

At 2 am, I received a call that Miguel had passed away. The diagnosis of death was a ruptured ventricular aneurysm, which means that a chamber in his heart had burst. At that time, the chance of fatality from such a rupture was virtually a hundred percent.

The following day I had many surgical cases to work on. I was going to cancel my cases, but my wife urged that I go ahead and do them.

"It's exactly what Miguel would want you to do," Lupe reminded me. "Do what you were trained to do and go and help those patients that need you."

A few days later, Miguel was buried in Phoenix. We had a great celebration for him. His fellow silversmiths were there. Many people whom he'd helped in the immigration process were there. So many people were there, honoring this generous, kind, and caring man. He'd touched so many lives.

I had such mixed feelings—sadness, of course. But I also felt a muted happiness because I remembered how Miguel often told me, "Each of us is here for a reason, and a long life is not always one of those reasons. It is what you accomplish in the time you are here."

And I thought of all that Miguel had accomplished—accomplishments that few people could ever pull off.

Just as Miguel had stood above our father's grave, so many decades before, to speak to him, I stood at Miguel's grave and told him, "Miguel, you are remembered by the many accomplishments and sacrifices you made over the course of your life. I am a product of your sacrifice and accomplishment. I love you, and I am forever grateful to you. You are remembered and loved."

ACKNOWLEDGMENTS

I wish to express my gratitude to these wonderful members of my family for helping me in recalling longtime events of my childhood—my sisters Lupe, Asuncion, Reyna, and Surama and my brother Jorge. You helped me to shape and write this memoir.

Also, I thank my granddaughters who inspired me to write this memoir as a gift for them—a reminder of the power of a child's dream.

Thank you also to my wife, Lupe, my sons, Miguel and Carlos, and my daughter, Marisa. And to Rebecca Ferente and Nancy Pile.

ABOUT THE AUTHOR

Edgar H. Hernandez, MD, MS, FACS, lives in Tempe, Arizona. In addition to being a proud husband and father, he is now a happy grandfather of six granddaughters from the ages of six months to 16 years.

For over thirty years he has been a surgeon in private practice. Additionally he has served as chief of surgery, chief of staff, and member of the board at Chandler Regional Medical Center in Chandler, Arizona.

For over 20 years Dr. Hernandez has practiced general surgery. In the last ten years, Doctor Hernandez has dedicated himself to the field of breast surgery. He cares for women with minimal to devastating breast cancers. Recently Dr. Hernandez joined the Ironwood Cancer and Research Center, a renowned oncology center in Arizona. He is a diplomat of the American Board of Surgery, a fellow of the American College of Surgeons, and a practicing oncoplastic breast surgeon.

Over the course of his career, Dr. Hernandez has worked with charitable groups and various foundations. He has led and participated in many mission trips to Mexico to perform surgeries, teach and train Mexican surgeons, and bring medical equipment and supplies to underfunded Mexican hospitals. In 2000, the Phoenix Hispanic community awarded him its "Humanitarian Award" for his mission work in Mexico. In 2011, Dr. Hernandez was named "Man of the Year," a humanitarian distinction, by Fresh Start Women's Foundation of Arizona for his treatment of uninsured women in need of surgeries for breast disorders, including breast cancers. The Desert Cancer Foundation of Arizona also honored Dr. Hernandez with a humanitarian award. South Mountain Community College of Arizona has selected Dr. Hernandez to speak at their 2017 commencement ceremony.

On The Border of a Dream is a book about a community of people; "family" my family to be exact. Our family touched a young man's life and guided him to become a surgeon which was his dream come true. Personally reading this book is like watching a home movie for the second time. From our meager beginnings to the ups and downs of immigration and finally moving to the United States to pursue a dream. Edgar's descriptive recollection makes this a hard book to put down. My brother Edgar has touched thousands of lives as well as saved many lives with his skills in the medical field and I am so proud of him for sharing his story of triumph.

-Jorge Hernandez
Honored Brother of the Author

Miguel Hernandez
Photo taken 1959

CPSIA information can be obtained
at www.ICGtesting.com
Printed in the USA
BVOW03*2025120617
486266BV00006BA/56/P